FRIDAY NIGHT THUNDERBOLTS

Why High School Football Matters to America's Future

JOHN GILLOOLY

ISBN: 979-8-218-02100-9

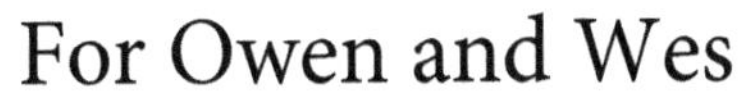

For Owen and Wes

Contents

My last column in a fifty-year career writing sports for the *Providence (RI) Journal* newspaper ran in the August 12, 2018 edition of the *Sunday Journal.* The next day, I was at the first practice of the season for the Cranston High School East football team.

My retirement as a sportswriter didn't last long.

For several years, I had felt there was an untold story about Cranston East football. I felt it was a story that went well beyond the wins and losses of a public high school football team in the smallest state in the nation. A story that, because of a national domestic turmoil the likes of which had not been seen in decades, may have taken on more meaning in the fall of 2018 than in several preceding decades.

It's important to understand this is Rhode Island, where high school football is far from being in the daily consciousness of the average Rhode Islander. Cranston, R.I. may have been listed as one of the "100 Best Places to Live" in the United States by a national magazine a decade earlier, but when it comes to football, Cranston isn't Odessa, Texas, home of the Permian Panthers—the high school football team H. G Bissinger immortalized in *Friday Night Lights.* Nor is Cranston a Florida or

Ohio high school football hotbed, with a long list of local high school alumni who went on to play in the NFL.

The Cranston East football team did win the Rhode Island Division I High School Super Bowl championship in the fall of 2017. But the reality is in 2018, when average Cranston residents thought about football, they were thinking of the New England Patriots—the team of Tom Brady and Bill Belichick, whose home field of Gillette Stadium is only thirty miles north of Cranston Stadium, home of the Cranston East Thunderbolts.

But, in my view, in the fall of 2018, the Cranston East football team had become a standard bearer for the things that had made high school football so important in the development of American character over generations. High school football is based on the idea of developing trust and camaraderie among a group of primarily male teenagers in a quest to achieve an overall team goal. It's the concept of eleven players each having an individual assignment on every play of every game. Meshing those assignments together is what makes football unique from any other sport.

It's those life-development lessons at a critical period in young lives that, for generations, has made high school football about more than final scores or even the few high-profile players who went on to play at big-time college programs, or even in the NFL.

I knew there had been changes at Cranston East since I was a student there in the mid-1960s. I didn't play high school football, but a lot of my friends did. Somewhere I still have a high school yearbook photo of the smiling faces of the forty-three varsity members of the 1963 Cranston East Met Division co-championship football team.

Every one of those forty-three faces was white.

I didn't take an exact count, but as I looked at the faces of the 2018 Cranston East football team members on that first day of practice, about two-thirds of them were faces of color.

If I didn't know better, it would have been easy to surmise it was just another case of a northern urban-ring city whose population demographics had changed dramatically over a half century because of the flight from the city to the suburbs. That definitely had been the case with some northeastern cities and towns that bordered an urban area, and Cranston shares its northern city-border with Providence, the urban center of Rhode Island.

But while I knew the city of Cranston had changed over the previous half century, I knew the demographics of the city hadn't changed in proportion to the change of the composite face of the 2018 Cranston East football team.

In 2018, according to the latest U.S. census (2010), of the 80,300 residents in Cranston, 81.8 percent were white. Even according to more recent unofficial data compiled in 2016, 74 percent of the city's population was white. So why was the football team at one of the city's two public high schools composed of about 66 percent faces of color?

Cranston has two public high schools—Cranston East and Cranston West. The schools' names describe from what part of the city the school's student body is derived. If you draw a line across Cranston separating East from West, Cranston East students come from the eastern side of the city while Cranston West students come from the western side.

Looking at the East football team, some social scientist might be quick to surmise it was another case of political gerrymandering that created a situation where one side of a city is primarily low-cost housing.

But I knew that didn't adequately explain Cranston in the fall of 2018.

The extreme eastern side of Cranston, a section known as Edgewood, borders on the Providence River, an eight-mile-long, half-mile-wide tributary that feeds into picturesque Narragansett Bay. Throughout the warmer months of the year, the river is filled with sailboats and power watercraft making their way south to Narragansett Bay for ventures to world famous Rhode Island seaside locations like Newport and Block Island. Eastern Cranston is home to a pair of well-known Rhode Island yacht clubs—the Rhode Island and the Edgewood Yacht clubs. On some Edgewood streets that run along the water, there are several dozen homes with an assessed value of over a million dollars. In addition, there are several dozen streets that run perpendicular to the river, which are filled with large, picturesque Victorian homes, whose owners made a substantial payment to the Cranston tax base. Olivia Culpo, the 2012 Miss Universe, grew-up in one of those homes.

If the high school age children living in those homes elect to attend public school, they will be Cranston East students.

In 2018, the Cranston East football team also had been bucking a national trend for a few years. Since the release of the movie *Concussion* in 2015, there had been increased national discussion about the safety of football. There were still over one million teenagers playing high school football in America in 2018, but between 2015 and 2017, participation dropped 5 percent. On the first day of practice for the 2018 season, however, there were over 100 young men being issued football equipment at Cranston East.

East is a co-ed school, with approximately 1,400 students in grades 9–12, about 700 of which are boys. That means about 15 percent of the entire male student population at a metropolitan,

New England high school was playing football. That's a high percentage of a public school's male enrollment participating in an unrequired activity.

Did Cranston East have the answer to the question of why high school football still is important to America?

Here was a public high school football team that was bucking a national trend about football participation. It was also a team of about 66 percent faces of color in a city where approximately 75 percent of the city's residents are white, proving diversity works—on and off the field.

Did a group of teenage football players at a public high school in the smallest state in the county have a game plan that might help America through the most turbulent social times this country has seen in five decades?

I decided to spend the 2018 season with the players and coaches at team practices and on the sideline at Friday night games finding out what made the Cranston East football team important to America's future.

The next 90,000 or so words tell that story. It is a tale of my experiences from the first day of practice for the 2018 season until the minute I walked away from the field following the final game of the season. It became a story that—even after fifty years as a sports writer—gave me a better appreciation of the uniqueness and importance of high school football as we headed into the third decade of the 21st century. It also gave me a better understanding of how a high school football coach—if that coach is a person of character—can play a significant, positive role in a young man's future.

Knowing my tendency for procrastination and how, for decades, I aggravated my editors by missing deadlines during my days as a newspaper sportswriter, I planned to give myself a year after the last game of the 2018 season to finish the project.

My plan was to have an unedited manuscript completed shortly after the conclusion of the 2019 high school football season. I surprised myself by actually adhering to that schedule.

Around Christmas 2019, I shared a copy of a completed manuscript with Cranston East coach Tom Centore. But within a few months, the world changed for Cranston East football players—as well as every other American high school student—with the onset of Covid-19. How the pandemic has affected the Cranston East football program is discussed in an epilogue following the final chapter of the story of the 2018 season. Ironically, going into the 2022–23 school year, the senior members of that 2018 Cranston East football team would be the last class of Cranston East football players who didn't have some portion of their school year adversely affected by Covid.

The story of the Cranston East football team and its 2018 season became a character-driven tale. It's a narrative of revelation on how a uniquely diverse group of teenage boys responded to the triumphs, heartbreaks and life-lessons high school football always has - and hopefully always will - offer.

CHAPTER I

TRUST IS THE CORNERSTONE OF HIGH SCHOOL FOOTBALL

"The first thing is I have to trust you are going to do the right thing every time." These were coach Tom Centore's first words to the 100 or so Cranston East football players sitting in the stands in the East gym, anxiously awaiting the start of the first day of practice for the 2018 season.

Trust is the cornerstone of a high school football team. The linebacker has to trust that the defensive end is going to cover the edge on the run, so the LB doesn't need to worry about leaving his coverage of the opposition tight end cutting across the middle on a pass route. The left offensive guard has to trust the left tackle is going to fill the gap in the offensive line, so the guard can pull out to lead the blocking for a running back.

But this mid-August afternoon, Centore was talking about more than simply trusting that the players would execute the correct blocking scheme on a quarterback-sweep or pick up the proper defensive responsibilities on a zone blitz.

"If you come into the locker room and somebody has left his phone or wallet on the bench and not in his locker, you don't even think about taking it. You automatically give it to one of the coaches," Centore said. "Your teammates have to trust you—not just on the field but everywhere. I have to trust you to do the right thing every day on the field and in school. You need to be responsible for everything you do."

He had been talking for several minutes, and Centore had yet to mention touchdowns, tackles, or even say the word football. When you are the coach of a public high school football team in a city of 80,000, where about 75 percent of the city's residents are white, but about two-thirds of your team's players have faces of color, community perception may be as important as 50-yard touchdown runs.

Centore is a fifty-year-old white man, a father, a high school guidance counselor, and a coach who played college football at the University of Rhode Island. So, he has had the experience of playing with a diverse group of players on a New England university football team. But Centore also knows not everybody in Cranston has had the experience of living and playing in a diverse environment.

"A lot of people around this city don't know these kids," Centore had said to me about his players earlier, on the first day of practice in mid-August. "They see the success, but they don't know what some of these kids go through every day. But they think they know them because of the way these kids look. I don't want a 'that's what I thought you were' moment."

The tale of the 2018 Cranston East football team, one of two public high school football teams in Cranston, may be the sports version of how the multiplicity of today's "American Story" can be told. East is not a stereotypical American high school football team. It isn't a team of underdogs. It isn't a team where virtually all the players come from lower-income, racial minority homes—although there certainly are a significant number of players on the team who fit that description. Nor is East a team from a suburban community, where most of the players on the roster are young white men—although some key members of the 2018 Thunderbolts are white kids who live in nice homes and whose parents make a solid financial living. Some teams thrive on a defined team identity. Cranston East's strength is that its identity is diversification rather than definition.

The Thunderbolts, the team's nickname, isn't a team of superstars "cuddled" together by some private school coach whose roster isn't facing the geographic limitations most public high school coaches face. The East football team is the ultimate melting pot of a group of different segments of a defined geographic community coming together to work for a common goal. Getting to a state title game is the ultimate goal, but a lot of life lessons are learned every autumn afternoon on that journey—even if it doesn't end at a state championship game or even in the playoffs.

At the start of the 2018–19 school year, the city of Cranston, which is 29.9 square miles and shares a city line with Providence, the capital city of Rhode Island, was officially listed as the third largest city—population-wise—in Rhode Island. Cranston has the commercial trappings of a 21st century suburban city with the upscale shopping center of Garden City housing stores like Anthropologie, Crate & Barrell, and L.L. Bean, along with a host of upscale restaurants. Yet in many other ways, Cranston has retained the charm of a 1950s New England town.

In the fall of 2018, if the mayor of Cranston had been so inclined, he could have left his office in city hall, walked a few hundred yards down the street, and bought a gallon of paint or have a window screen fixed at the family-owned Durfee Hardware store on Rolfe St.—just like the Cranston mayor could have done in 1958. In a sense, Cranston is still a city of villages.

On the streets of the Knightsville section, which is about a half-mile west from city hall and the Cranston High East school building, generations of Italian families still hold an annual festival and parade honoring their ancestors' migration to Rhode Island from a little town in Italy. Today, historical Pawtuxet Village, located in Edgewood on the eastern side of the city, is an eclectic mix of restaurants, coffee shops, boutique clothing, and antique shops. They all run along a street where a ninety-year-old stone bridge passes over the Pawtuxet River, which was a boundary cited in the original deed for the state of Rhode Island that was given to Roger Williams—the state's founder—by Native Americans.

But like most northeastern cities of more than 50,000, there have also been changes in Cranston over the past half century. Spurted by extensive development of spacious, upscale housing in the western side of the city, on what once was farmland, the overall Cranston population has increased by 18 percent since 1970. In the fall of 2018, it was virtually certain, after seven decades of being the third largest city in Rhode Island, that when the 2020 census was calculated, Cranston would officially move up to being the second largest city in Rhode Island, with a population of slightly over 80,000.

But while there has been extensive housing growth in the western side of the city, there hasn't been much new housing constructed, nor a substantial population increase in eastern Cranston, over the past three or four decades. The majority of the homes in eastern Cranston—from the stately Victorians and Colonials in the Edgewood section, to the bungalows and small capes of the Auburn and Friendly communities, to the two- and three-family tenements of the Arlington section, and the small capes and ranches in the stadium district—still look like they did in the 1960s and '70s. Even the small, two-family duplexes that make up the former workers' village of the Cranston Printworks textile complex near the Providence city line still look the same as they did sixty or seventy years ago. Most of them are still in solid physical condition.

What has changed, a lot, in the past decade is the nationalities and facial complexions of the families living in some of these homes, especially the homes in the areas near the Providence/Cranston city lines.

The gateway to the American Dream has had different points of demarcation in the 21st century. For some, it has been walking across the American/Mexican border; for others, it was arriving at some American airport on a plane from a poverty-stricken Caribbean or South American country, or maybe from a war-torn African or Eastern European nation. But for generations of American immigrants, there has been a common denominator to the gateway to the American Dream. It was the day a family moved into a home in a city with a safe environment and a good public education system for its children.

Home ownership is the fundamental pillar of the American Dream. For nearly a century, the eastern section of Cranston has been that gateway for early generations of American immigrant or first- and second-generation immigrant families moving up in their quest for the American Dream.

In the 1930s and '40s, it was the Irish, whose parents or grandparents had immigrated to America following the Irish Potato Famine in the mid-19th and early 20th century. They moved from tenements in Providence to the Edgewood section of Cranston and started raising big families in the big houses. There were also the blue-collar, first and second generations of various European immigrants who moved into the capes, bungalows, and the two- and three-family tenements in the Auburn and Arlington sections of the city in the early 20th century; as well as the Italian immigrants, who moved into the capes and tenements of the Knightsville section in the late 19th and early 20th century.

For generations, the eastern section of Cranston has been a haven for young Americans whose parent's dream was to see their children reach a higher station in life than they have.

U.S. Senator Jack Reed, who in the fall of 2018 was serving his third term as a senator from Rhode Island, grew up in eastern Cranston, in a home only a few hundred yards down the road from Cranston East High. In fact, Reed's father, the late Joseph Reed, was a long-time employee of the Cranston School department. Jack Reed was a high school football player in the late 1960s, but not at Cranston East. Like his older brother, Reed played at La Salle Academy, the Catholic parochial high school in Providence where sons of Rhode Island Roman Catholics had been attending school and playing sports since around the turn of the 20th century. (An all-boys school when Reed attended in the 1960s, La Salle became a co-ed school in 1983.)

While Reed is the only kid who grew up in eastern Cranston to eventually become a U.S. Senator, there have been multitudes of eastern Cranston kids who went on to illustrious careers in public service, medicine, law, business, and education.

"We are Americans. We are about our families and want to see them get ahead," Michele Obama offered one day in the fall of 2018 while promoting her book *Becoming*.

That has been the mantra of American parents for centuries, especially first- and second-generation immigrant parents. For generations, those parents have used eastern Cranston as the launching pad for their voyage to the American Dream. It was that way in the 1950s, when Jack Reed's parents were raising their family in eastern Cranston; and in the fall of 2018, it was the hope of several Cranston East football parents.

Over the past few decades, many of those small, former Cranston Print Works workers' village duplexes; two- and three-family tenements in the Arlington section; and the two- and three-bedroom little capes in the stadium section—all near the Providence city line—had provided a source of comparatively affordable housing for a large community of first- and second-generation Latino/Hispanic immigrant families. They were families who moved into Cranston from the nearby West End section of Providence. The big draw for a move to Cranston was a good public school system.

Much of American urban public education was in a state of turmoil in the 21st century, and the Providence education system was no exception. In the fall of 2018, the Providence public school system had a reputation of a system in crisis. Low student test scores, deteriorating infrastructure, low learning expectations for many students, and a system where bad teachers were nearly impossible to fire were all part of the reputation of the Providence school system.

On the other hand, right next to Providence, the Cranston public school system was regarded as a good public school system, especially for an urban-ring city.

Over the past decade, it hadn't even cost that much more money to move from the western edge of Providence to some parts of eastern Cranston. The Providence public school system may have become a disaster, but for a variety of reasons—one of which is its relatively close proximity to Boston—Providence had become a hot housing market in the second decade of the 21st century. The result was that home and rental prices in many sections of Providence sky-rocketed.

So, buying one of those capes or ranches or even a tenement in sections of Cranston near the Providence city line didn't cost much more than buying a home in the West End or South Side areas of Providence, which include large Hispanic/Latino communities. Plus, there were an abundance of methods for how people could finance such a purchase.

"FHA and R.I. Housing Corp. offer low down payment loans. Some only need 5 percent down payment. For a $200,000 mortgage, that's only $10,000," said Jim Hackett, a 1977 Cranston East graduate who in 2018 was a regional mortgage broker for a southeastern New England bank. "In certain income categories, R.I. Housing will finance 100 percent of a home for a first-time buyer," Hackett added.

That ability to finance a home purchase—and the fact it's no secret there is an underground economy in Rhode Island where hard-working people, with skills in professions like house painting, landscaping, various aspects of home construction, as well as child care—has made it possible for some immigrant and first-generation immigrant families to save the money for a house down payment fairly quickly.

By the start of the second decade of the 21st century, the ethnic composite of a large swath of residents around the area near the Providence city line in central Cranston started changing dramatically.

In the fall of 2017, in addition to being the home of the R.I. Division I state football championship team, Cranston East high school—in its entirety—was a champion of proportional diversity. According to East principal Sean Kelly at the start of the 2018 school year, 38 percent of East's students claimed Hispanic/Latino heritage; 36 percent defined themselves as white; 18 percent were identified as African American; and 8 percent, Asian or other.

The demographic composition of the 2018 Cranston East football team roster may not have followed those numbers exactly, but there was no doubt the composite face of the

Thunderbolts gridiron forces was different than any other public high school football team in Rhode Island.

You would like to think in the fifty-five years since the passage of the Civil Rights Act that America had progressed to the point where nobody would look at a high school football team and come to a quick conclusion about what type of team it is by the color of the players' faces.

But the reality is, even in 2018, a lot of people were still leery of what they don't know. In a city of 80,000, where about 75 percent of its resident are white, a high school football team that has about 66 percent faces of color is an unknown to many of the city's residents.

So, Tom Centore feels it's important for his players to develop a high quality of personal character that will impress Cranston residents, help win some football games, and most importantly, serve the players well for the rest of their lives.

For Centore knows, even without racial differences, for a lot of people there's a natural human tendency to think negatively about people, to look for the worst in somebody. So Centore lets his teenager players know some of life's realities on the first day of practice.

"I hate to say it, but the reality is, you can do things the right way nine straight times and I will never hear about it. But if you do something wrong, just once, I will hear about it," Centore told the players sitting in the stands that first day of practice. "So, you have to do the right thing every time."

Centore will match the quality of his players' character against the players on any high school football team in Rhode Island—public or private, suburban or inner city. Character has been the foundation of Centore's coaching philosophy for decades.

People said character-building is one of the intangibles of high school sports, which is true. But in football, it isn't just an intangible—it's the core of the sport. There's no question sometimes character can get lost at the next two levels of football—at big-time college football or the NFL—when big money becomes involved. But while you don't see it on the scoreboard, the core of high school football is about character as much as touchdowns and tackles.

Character can be a multi-faceted word. But for Tom Centore, it simply means possessing virtues such as fortitude, integrity, honesty, loyalty, and courage in your daily actions. Character doesn't have any financial, racial, or intellectual prerequisites, but it does have a common by-product. If you have strong character, you're always going to do your best.

Forget all the victory celebrations, college scholarships, and even the paths that have been laid out for future professional fame and fortune. Helping the development of a strong character among teenage males is—or should be—the primary goal of an American high school football coach in the 21st century.

All high school athletic coaches do that to some degree, but it's the nature of football that makes the interaction between coach and players more intense than in other sports.

Centore and I had talked about that a few days before that first day of practice when I approached him about, in essence, becoming a "Cranston East assistant coach." I would be a coach who didn't run any drills or flash any signals. I would just watch and listen in an effort to understand what made his program special.

"I don't need you to promise me you are going to win another state championship," I told Centore. "I just need this season to be interesting."

Centore looked at me with a sly smile, which could have been indicating even before practice started that he felt this was going to be a season that would have more than the normal number of challenges.

"We actually should be pretty good, and I guarantee you, we will be interesting," Centore said, with a slight smirk.

CHAPTER II

THIS PLACE IS DIFFERENT

The rain, which had fallen the previous day, had basically subsided by August 13, but 24 hours of a constant downpour had turned the Cranston East practice field into a virtual mudhole by the time the Thunderbolts were scheduled to hold their first official practice of the season on Monday afternoon. So, the East football team was being forced to hold its first practice of the season in the hot and humid Cranston East gym, with the players running drills in helmets, games shirts, and gym shorts on the wooden basketball court.

For high school football players throughout the country, the issuing of equipment on that first day of practice, followed by stepping onto the field with the feel of grass under your feet for the first time, is one of the highlights of the season. The last place any high school football player wants to spend the first day of practice is in a non-air-conditioned, 90x60-foot gym where the temperature is hovering around 90 degrees and the humidity is soaring near 100 now that the rain had subsided.

There was only one entrance in the gym that opened directly to the outside, and assistant coach Ken Simone was holding the two four-foot-wide doors opened with two large, circular floor fans. The fans weren't really helping moderate the humility, but Simone still had a smile on his face as he sat in a metal chair that was also helping keep the doors open.

"What is it that's special about these kids?" I asked Simone.

Simone didn't take more than a few seconds before answering—as if he had been asked the question a few times over the past few years.

"Once you have them—once they trust that you are in this for them, and they believe you are about them, not just about winning games—you have them forever," Simone said.

Simone has been one of Tom Centore's assistant coaches since Centore became the Cranston East head coach sixteen years earlier. For the past ten years, he has been the Thunderbolts' defensive coordinator, and the past eight years, he has also been a member of the East faculty teaching "literacy." Before teaching at East, he had been a teacher at a few other suburban high schools. He thinks there's something unique about East as a high school in this day and age, well beyond just having a successful football team.

"That's the thing about this place," Simone offered about Cranston East, as the sweat dripped off his forehead. "People accept you for who you are here. My post before school is in the cafeteria. The kids like to meet at the café before they head to homeroom. A kid can walk through that café in the morning with purple hair or some different type of clothing, and nobody even looks up at them. I have been at other places where that's not the case. Other places, kids are judged by the way they look or the clothes they wear."

A Man Born to Be a High School Football Coach

Tom Centore wasn't just born to coach. He was born to coach high school football.

Centore is a former high school and college football star and son of a legendary Rhode Island high school football coach, Tony Centore. Like his father, who started coaching high school football in the early 1950s, Tom had become a teacher and coach almost immediately after he graduated from college in the late 1980s. For more than a decade, he was a history teacher in Cranston but also served as his father's assistant football coach at Johnston High, the only public high school in the town that shares a northwest town/city line with Cranston. Sixteen years ago, however, some people in the Cranston school administration asked Tom to consider becoming the Cranston East head coach. They wanted him to revive a once proud Cranston East football program that had fallen on hard times in recent decades.

The city of Cranston has a long history of high school football excellence. During the decades of the 1930s, '40s, and '50s—when Cranston only had one public high school—Cranston High had one of the best football teams in Rhode Island. In the first ten years of the Rhode Island Interscholastic League's existence, from 1932 to 1941, Cranston High won or shared four Class A (major division) titles. Also, in both the decades of the '40s and '50s, Cranston won at least two Class A titles in each decade.

Cranston opened its second public high school in 1959, and the building that had housed Cranston High since 1925 became Cranston High School East. The new high school building in the western section of the city became Cranston High School West. People in the city quickly began just referring to the two schools as Cranston East and Cranston West, or more succinctly, East and West.

There may have been a new name at the front entrance of the school building located next to city hall on Park Ave. that had housed Cranston High School for decades, but throughout the early part of the 1960s, that building was still home to some of the best high school team football teams in Rhode Island. At a time before an official post-season playoff system determined the Rhode Island state high school football champion, Cranston East won outright or shared the Class A title for four straight years, from 1962–64. When the Interscholastic League (the Rhode Island high school athletic conference that includes virtually all of the state's public high schools and the larger private schools) adopted a football playoff system in 1972, Cranston East won the first Division I (major division) state championship. Cranston East won another Division I state title in 1987. It was the 14th major state football championship won by the Cranston/Cranston East football teams in the fifty-five-year history of the R.I. Interscholastic League. At the time, it was at least four more titles than any other school in the state had won in the state's major football division.

But East football began a downward spiral almost immediately after that 1987 state title. The following year, the Thunderbolts were 1–8 and didn't post a winning season over the next five seasons. Because of its poor combined record, by 1993, Cranston East football had been moved down to Division III (then called Class C), only the third-ranked level of Rhode Island's four levels of high school football at the time. The Thunderbolts didn't even win there. East's combined Division III record during the 1994 and '95 seasons was 1–15. Over a four-year period in the late 1990s, East had a combined record of 3–31 playing in Division II & III.

There can be a lot of reasons why a high school football program falls on hard times. Certainly, the fact that private schools—especially Hendricken, located in the nearby city of Warwick—were draining football talent from East played a big role. Several of the star players on Hendricken's state championship teams in 1994, '95, and '96 lived in eastern Cranston. But at virtually any level of high school football, when a team is having problems winning, one place some people place blame is the coach.

So, it's not surprising by the early turn of the 21st century, some people in Cranston were saying Cranston East needed a new coach, and they knew exactly who it should be. Tom Centore had been teaching in Cranston for a decade by then, but he had always coached with his father at Johnston High. People in Cranston knew Tom and respected him, both as a football coach and as a man of character. They certainly knew his family. His father had been an assistant Cranston East coach during the East football glory days of the mid-1960s and had also been a Cranston East guidance counselor for twenty-five years. Some people in Cranston tried to convince Tom Centore to apply for the East head coaching job when the position opened in the mid-90s, but while Tom was intrigued by the idea of coaching his own team, he was dedicated to helping his father coach the high school football team in Johnston, the Centore family's hometown.

Tom had become one of his father's assistant coaches the season after he graduated from URI in the late 1980s. He knew how much his father loved coaching a football team, and with Tony Centore then in his seventies, gradually Tom gladly took on more and more responsibility so his father could continue coaching. But by the start of the 21st century, Tony Centore knew it was time for his son to be a head coach. So, in 2003, after twenty-nine years as the Johnston High head football coach, Tony resigned at Johnston so his son could become the Cranston East head coach. Basically, in addition to changing teams, father and son simply changed coaching responsibilities, with Tony immediately becoming one of Tom's assistant coaches at East.

When Tom was named head coach in 2002, Cranston East was still playing in the Division II, only the second highest level of Rhode Island high school football. But after eight years under Centore's tutelage, East earned a promotion back to Division I. Despite a domination by private schools in Division I football since the turn of the 21st century, Cranston East, under Centore's stewardship, has been relatively successful since its returned to Rhode Island's top level of high school football. In the eight seasons since its return to Division I, going into the 2018 season, Cranston East had enjoyed five winning seasons and won two regular season divisional championships.

There's always a combined mix of why a high school football coach is successful. But the undeniable reality is that Tom Centore has been successful at Cranston East because East players over the past sixteen years have come to understand he is a man who cares more about them as young men than as football players.

There are people who say high school football coaches don't make better men—they just make better football players. That certainly could be the case for some high school football coaches for whom—to steal a line from the legendary Vince Lombardi—"winning isn't everything, it's the only thing."

I'm sure, even in 2018, there were guys with that mentality still coaching high school football in America. But I like to think it's a minority of the nation's high school football coaches these days.

It's easy to romanticize football coaches and their inspirational pep talks and halftime speeches. The entertainment industry certainly has done its part through the decades. From Pat O'Brien's portrayal of Knute Rockne's "Win One for the Gipper" speech in a 1940 movie to Denzel Washington's depiction of Coach Boone in *Remember the Titans* in 2000, Hollywood has had a love affair with football coaches and how they inspired their teams to great success. But today, probably even more than a few decades ago, in the real world's grand scheme of life, building a young man's character should be a high school football coach's primary aspiration.

There's no doubt for some high school football teams around the country, building a "better man" doesn't need to be a head coach's major concern for a majority of his players. The player's direct family unit, with two involved parents, takes on much—maybe most—of that responsibility. But, regardless of where a high school team plays under Friday Night Lights, in today's American society, there are some teams where—for one reason or another—there is a lack of family involvement in some of the players' day-to-day activities. That's where, "building the better man" becomes a big part of a high school football coach's mission.

Today, across America, there are a substantial number of families constantly struggling financially to stay on course to the American dream. So, nobody should be surprised that in the largest participation American high school sport, "building the better man" and "just keeping kids in the program" has become a big part of a high school football coach's game plan.

It definitely has altered Tom Centore's coaching strategy over the past decade.

In the state of Rhode Island, where, in 2018, the average medium income of a white family is anywhere from 20–25 percent higher than that of an African/American or Hispanic/Latino family, it shouldn't have been surprising that as the composite face of the Cranston East football team began to change for more and more of Centore's players, economic issues were part of the challenge of being a high school football player.

"From 2003 to 2008 or so, I still needed to do some things for them beyond what people outside the program would think a coach had to do," Centore offered about some of his players.

"But it wasn't as demanding as it is today. In 2011, 2012, and 2013, those types of cases started becoming more challenging. Some of the players needed more. They needed to get stuff to just get on the field. I would have to buy an occasional pair of cleats for some kids," Centore continued.

It wasn't always the star player. In fact, it usually wasn't the star players who needed "some stuff" from Centore just to get on the field. Often, it was kids who just wanted to be part of the program who "needed things."

"Those kids are very important to our program," Centore offered about the kids who would never be football stars but were at practice every day.

All good high school football coaches are teachers. Every day, football players are receiving constant feedback from coaches that encourages resilience in the face of failure. Failure is the reality of a daily high school football practice, as players attempt to learn a new game plan for the upcoming opponent. But the reality of football—a lot like life in general—is you often only succeed because you once failed. That's what high school football teaches every day.

A lot of the nation's high school football coaches, probably a majority, are actually classroom teachers. But it doesn't matter if they made their full-time living in a classroom or have some other full-time occupation before coming to football practice. All good high school football coaches are teachers. They communicate that they care about a player's goals—on and off the field.

That's certainly Tom Centore.

Norman Rockwell Poster Boy

Tom Centore is a 21st century Norman Rockwell portrait. A fifty-year-old high school football coach who idealistically cares about the things that are important in a young man's everyday life, along with wanting to win football games. He is about the things that are right, the things that should mean something in people's lives, even if it doesn't make him famous.

There wasn't much racial diversity on his own team when Centore was playing high school football at Johnston High School in the 1980s, or the decade or so he was his father's assistant at Johnston. Or even in his first six years as the East head coach.

But as the composite face of the Cranston High East student body, especially the East football team, began to dramatically change about eight years ago, rather than give up coaching because of a change in his team's make-up that wasn't part of his personal history, Centore relished a new coaching challenge. He cherished the idea of working with some players who needed his help in many ways beyond the Xs and Os of a football game plan.

By the time the demographics started dramatically changing at East, Centore had already been a high school football coach for twenty years. In this day and age, when more and more family commitments and/or financial needs makes coaching high school sports more demanding than ever, twenty years makes a person a veteran high school coach. Yet, here was a veteran coach with a proven record of on-field success who needed to learn a new way to coach. Some veteran coaches might have thought it wasn't worth it. Centore feels it is.

Centore leads a life of deep commitment to human values—on and off the football field. On the field, winning brings excitement and pleasure to Centore like it does for any coach. But it's the improving of his players' lives beyond football—but through the winning in football—that seems to bring Centore a special joy. It's what Tom Centore saw his father doing throughout his life.

Tony Centore, Tom's father, loved to win games when he coaching high school football players. But he loved it so much more when he saw that winning helped build a better young person. That was Tom Centore's role model.

The first few years Tom was the East head coach, he didn't feel his team looked much different from most of the other teams the Thunderbolts were playing. However, around 2006 and 2007, the composite face of the team started changing a little bit. Then, around 2010, there started to be a significant change in the racial make-up of the team, with more faces of color. Centore also started noticing that the players on those teams didn't seem to have that family type of team bonding on the practice field that he had seen on previous teams. That natural sense of team bonding had always been a hallmark of Centore's coaching philosophy.

"It wasn't that they were mean to each other; they just seemed to have their own groups that they gravitated toward during breaks in practice. You can't have that on a football team, at any time," Centore said.

Centore knew sometimes family economics might determine whether some teammates hang out together away from the field. But there can be no social stigmas, no tribalization on a football practice field. It might be a challenge at first, but it's a challenge a football team has to solve. Society has years, decades—maybe even generations—to solve that type of challenge. A football team, however, only has a season. It wasn't something Centore would write into the pre-season list of team rules he distributed to every player. It was something that needed to be natural, something that needed to happen without the players even thinking about it. Fortunately, the game of football readily provides for that type of harmony without any special consideration.

Considering the tenor of the nation, a stranger walking onto the Cranston East practice field in August of 2018 might have considered it unique that the Thunderbolts were a team of about two-thirds faces of color in a city that was about 75 percent white. Cranston East football players never even think about it.

A Major Decision Before the Season Started

Tom Centore had thought about not coaching for the 2018 season. His ninety-year-old father—the man who molded his son's character and had been the paragon for Tom Centore's belief that a man must be willing to accept change if he was going to help people—was seriously ill. Tom Centore was worried his father, who lived with Tom, could die during the season.

But Tom Centore couldn't leave his team. For Centore hadn't just built a successful high school football program at Cranston East; he had created a high school football family. It was a 21st century American football family, whose appearance and challenges had changed dramatically over the past decade, just like America has changed. It wasn't a change Centore had sought or had recruited in an effort to win more games. It was a change that had been handed to him, and he had nurtured it into this special corps of young men. It was a family with all its hardships and rewards. So, Centore couldn't leave his football family, even though he knew it could be the most challenging season of his life.

One afternoon, a few days after practice for the season had started, I stood on the side of the practice field watching Centore helping a player with his helmet. It wasn't unusual to see Centore or one of the assistant coaches help a player fix a busted chin strap or some other more serious helmet malfunction. After all, there's no official equipment manager at Cranston East football practices. Helping a player fix a helmet problem or even a somewhat more complex equipment malfunction falls on the shoulders of the coaches. But this didn't seem like a serious equipment repair. Basically, Centore seemed to be just helping the player snap up his chin-strap. Plus, Centore seemed to be making a concerted effort to keep his body between this player and the other team members, who were standing about ten or fifteen yards away on the field. It seemed he was trying to hide the fact that he was helping a player perform what seemed like a basic football player's ritual.

Centore finished working with the player, said a few words to the young man, and the player trotted out on to the field to join the other players in drill. But Centore's interaction with this player intrigued me. In nearly fifty years of watching high school coaches interacting with student athletes, I could usually sense when something was a little different.

So, after the practice ended and Centore had delivered his usual practice-ending discourse to the players, I asked Tom,

"What's the story with that kid you were helping with the helmet?"

At first, Centore was a little surprised I had even noticed anything and seemed a little hesitant to talk about it. But then, a smile came to his face, and he quietly offered, "Oh, he's a great kid. I don't know the whole story; I think he's on some level of the autism spectrum. He's a senior, and he has been with us for four years now. He has come so far in these four years. The coaches keep an eye on him to make sure he's okay, but nobody makes a big deal of it. He's just one of the guys on the team. He goes through the drills in practice, like the other players. He hasn't played in any games yet, but he's on the sidelines, dressed in his uniform with his teammates every game. I'm hoping this year, there might be a chance to get him in a game for a play or two. We'll see."

Just then, another player came walking up to Centore, sheepishly asking whether the coach might be able to help him make a change in his class schedule. Centore turned and started walking with the kid toward the parking lot, probably asking why the player felt he needed to change his schedule.

As I watched Centore walk with the young man, I realized I had just witnessed the execution of what Ken Simone meant that first day of practice when I asked what made this team special.

"Once these kids know you care about them as a person and not just a football player, you have them for life," Simone had said that day.

Now I understood.

In the game of football—where orchestrating a practice so that every minute is purposely used is the hallmark of a good coach—there was Tom Centore taking time in the middle of a practice to help a kid who would never be involved in a meaningful play in his high school career.

The perfect balance of guidance, encouragement, and—love.

CHAPTER III

TWO SCHOOLS IN THE SAME CITY, EXISTING IN DIFFERENT WORLDS

Cranston High School East and Cranston High School West are two high schools in the same city, with about the same enrollment and run by the same school system whose school buildings are only three miles apart.

But while Cranston East ranked No. 1 in diversity among Rhode Island's thirty-nine major high schools in 2018 according to the educational rating company Niche, Cranston West is more typical of a northeastern suburban high school, with its limited diversity. In the fall of 2018, the Cranston West student profile was 79.5 percent Caucasian; 10.8 percent Hispanic/Latino; 5.9 percent Asian; and 3.0 percent African American. Because of economical and racial differences between the student bodies at the two schools, East and West students tend to exist in socially different worlds in the same city—except when it comes to football.

"We don't worry about the Cranston West kids," said East senior captain Hector Duran. "We know they think they are better than us because they have bigger houses and more money. But we don't think about them except for football. That's why football is so important to us."

Going into the 2018 season, the football teams from Cranston East and Cranston West had met in an annual Thanksgiving Day game for forty-five consecutive years. And while there was only a three-win differential in the overall holiday series, with East holding a 24–21 advantage coming into the 2018 season, in recent years, East had dominated the intra-city series. The Thunderbolts won nine of the twelve games since 2006 and six of the past seven holiday meetings.

"We spotted them 40 points last year," Duran offered with a broad smile about the Thunderbolts recent domination of the rivalry.

Actually, it was in 2016, Duran's sophomore year, that East rolled to a 39-point victory in the rivalry game. In 2017, East "only" won the game by 14 points, 51–37. But regardless of the final score the previous year, it was evident that at the start of the 2018 season, East has been the city's high school football power for several years.

No Good Guys-Bad Guys

The Cranston East–Cranston West rivalry isn't a good guy-bad guy scenario. There are good people, both students and parents, in both school communities. A lot of Cranston West parents over the past few decades were Cranston East graduates. Like their parents and grandparents, who moved to Cranston in the 1930s, '40s, and '50s as part of their step up in the quest of the American Dream, the East grads of the '60s, '70s, and '80s liked the city where they had grown up. A higher level of advanced education than their parents had put these "Baby

Boomers" in position to take another step up in the "American Dream's" ladder of home ownership. So, they bought a bigger house than their own childhood home, with more land in one of the numerous upscale housing developments that were being built on former farmland in western Cranston.

They had the same type of aspiration for their children that their parents had for them in the 1960s, '70s, and '80s. But their teenager children of the 1990s and early 21st century were Cranston West Falcons rather than Cranston East Thunderbolts. The modern-day Falcons are good kids, many of them growing up in the same city that their parents had. But Cranston high school students of the 21st century have lived in a metaphoric—as well as a real financially—different world than Cranston students of the 1960s, '70s, and '80s did. Like a lot of America these days, the city of Cranston seems to be experiencing a larger financial gap between the top 20 percent or so of what sociologist would call the upper middle class and the rest of the city's so-called middle class.

There are a host of studies that claim across America those gaps are growing on a wide range of dimensions, including family structure, education, and lifestyle. In Cranston, the most evident gap between Cranston East and Cranston West students over the past ten to fifteen years would seem to be the material goods lifestyles of the two groups of students. That difference—or at least the perceived difference in some people's eyes—was thrust into the public awareness about eight years ago, and it was a high school football issue that fueled the media spotlight on the topic.

For decades after its opening in 1959, Cranston West had played the majority of its home football games on a field next to the high school building. The field was a nice, natural turf gridiron, with a grandstand section on one side that seated about 1,000 fans. But the West field, unlike Cranston Stadium where East played its games, didn't have lights. So, West football players played the majority of their home games on Saturday afternoons, with maybe one or two "home road games" per season at the stadium so they could play under the lights. But by the 21st century, as more and more Rhode Island high schools added lights to their athletic facilities, the idea of playing games on Friday night under the lights became a Rhode Island phenomenon like it had been in other parts of the country for decades.

It wasn't surprising that Cranston West football players wanted to be part of the statewide excitement of playing under "Friday Night Lights." So, around 2012, even though it meant putting the team on a couple of busses and driving a few miles for a home game, Cranston West also started using Cranston Stadium as the site for virtually all of its home football games, sharing the facility with Cranston East. For years prior, there had been a vinyl banner hanging across the front wall of the stadium declaring—"Home of the Thunderbolts." Which, of course, meant home of Cranston East. Now, with Cranston West also using the field, somebody in the Cranston school department decided to change the sign to read, "Home of the Falcons and Thunderbolts."

Some Cranston East fans were not happy about the new, re-worded signage. Cranston Stadium had been the home field of the football team from the high school on Park Ave, regardless of the school's name, since the day the stadium was built in the 1930s. Allowing Cranston West to schedule games at the stadium on Friday nights when East wasn't scheduled to play at the stadium was one thing, but calling the stadium, "Home of the Falcons," was just too much for some Cranston East fans to take. To them, the stadium would always be, "Home of the Thunderbolts."

It was Rhode Island parochialism in full bloom. But for some East supporters, it was another case of the "rich people" from the Western side of the city—who always seemed to get the new school facilities—trying to take one of the few special things in the city that belonged to eastern Cranston residents.

Social media hadn't reached the level of influence that it is today, but for better than a half-century, there had been a vibrant weekly newspaper in Cranston and also the statewide daily *Providence Journal* published a regular West Bay regional section that focused on news from Cranston and the neighboring city of Warwick. It was the type of local journalism that thrived on a provocative "war of words" between two factions within a city or town.

Unfortunately, when a young Cranston West student was asked by a newspaper reporter about her take on the "feud" between the East and West sides of the city, the student replied something to the effect that the east side of the city is "the slums." It was just a case of a teenager commenting on a situation she really didn't understand. Obviously, the young lady had never even traveled the six or seven miles from Cranston West high to the stately, large waterfront homes on Narraganset Blvd. in Edgewood. The officials at Cranston West apologized to the students of Cranston East, and eventually the sign was removed and replaced by permanent lettering across the wall that simply spelled out Cranston Stadium.

Over the years since the sign episode, Cranston city officials have gone to extensive measures to organize functions that would bring the students from both schools together in a show of city-wide harmony. But despite all the efforts of city officials to promote intra-city harmony, there was probably an even greater social disconnect between East and West students in 2018 than there was a decade ago.

In the fall of 2018, it's a safe bet most Cranston West students wouldn't see any substantial similarities between themselves and Hector Duran. Duran is a teenager of color, the son of first-generation American Latino immigrants. In 2018, the vast majority of Cranston West students were white kids whose parents and grandparents, maybe even great-grandparents, were born in America. Immigrant is not a word they equate with their social status.

By all standards of 21st century society, most West students are "quality kids." They are teenagers who strive to have a moral compass and a principled code of respect for other people. It's just that on a daily basis, they don't encounter many people whose social status is much different from their own. Yet, even without delving back into more than a century of historical ancestry, it would be easy to find a similarity between Duran and some cross-city neighboring students at Cranston West. Given that a significant number of Cranston West students in 2018 were of Italian heritage, there's a good chance some of their ancestors emigrated to Cranston from a little town in Italy around the turn of the 20th century.

These days, many high-school level educators lament that, despite an easier access to information than any previous generation, today's teenagers don't have a true understanding of history, nor a desire to learn how it has affected their lives. In the case of Cranston West students, only three—maybe four— generations ago their ancestors living in Cranston were battling the stigmas of being immigrants. But it's a safe bet in 2018 most of the current Cranston West students walking the sidewalks of the upscale Garden City shopping, about a mile from their school, didn't equate themselves with the term immigrant.

For them, that's what some of the kids over at East are.

A Different Kind of Dividing Line

The dividing line between today's Cranston East and Cranston West high school communities isn't marked by railroad tracks or an interstate highway—it's Pottery Barn, Anthropologie, J. Crew, and L.L. Bean.

The Garden City section of Cranston, which is located about an equal distance from the Cranston East and Cranston West school buildings, was developed shortly after World War II as a blend of a shopping center and suburban residences. Almost eight decades later, it is still trying to maintain that balance. The 200 acres of primary single-family capes, ranches, and some colonials that were built in the late 1940s and '50s, are still attractive, well-maintained homes populating a winding network of side streets with a public elementary school and a Roman Catholic church in the midst of the community. But for several decades now, the characteristic that has best defined Garden City to most Rhode Islanders is its cornucopia shopping center.

When the Garden City shopping center was first constructed in the 1950s and '60s, the development consisted of a centerpiece shopping village with a multitude of small, separate-entrance specialty stores along the sidewalks that circled both sides of a 250-car parking lot. That original classic New England shopping center still existed in 2018, but through the decades, a large track of land south of the original shopping center has been developed, adding more retail stores and eateries. What Garden City has never added, however, is a Walmart, Costco, or any other big chain national retail outlet or warehouse-club type facility. Instead, what now can be found in Garden City are street-level individual stores of almost every national chain of middle to upper class retail brands.

Walk along the sidewalks of the shopping village with soft music floating out of the hidden speakers, and you pass by the front doors of Pottery Barn; J. Crew; Crate & Barrel; Gap and Baby Gap; L.L. Bean; Williams-Sonoma; Victoria Secret; and a host of smaller, regional and local boutique brands. It's a dreamscape of suburban upper-middle class commercialism. Garden City is not the place you come looking for deals or factory-outlet close-outs.

Even the eateries in Garden City are not the type of places teenagers who need to work part-time jobs to help support their family go looking for an inexpensive cheeseburger. There's no McDonald's, Burger King, or Wendy's restaurants on the side-walks of the Garden City shopping center. While it's certainly far from gourmet dining in 2018, a "Big Beef" cheeseburger at the Rhode Island chain Newport Creamery restaurant in Garden City costs a little over $8.00, and the "Classic Burger" at the national chain Applebee's in the middle of the Garden City shopping center is around $10.00. That's compared to $2.50 for a double cheeseburger at the McDonald's a few hundred yards up the road from the entrance to Garden City, or $1.50 for a cheeseburger at the Burger King across the street from Cranston East High, about a mile from the Garden City entrance.

In a city where almost 75 percent of the city's population is white and, in a state where the average medium income of a white family is anywhere from 20–25 percent higher than that of an African American or Hispanic/Latino family, it's not surprising you don't see a lot of faces of color strolling the sidewalks of Garden City on a regular basis.

Even when some Cranston East football players do occasionally venture into Garden City, they can feel like they are the visiting team in their own city.

"I went to Applebee's one night with a few of my friends," said Robinson Antoine, an East senior wide receiver and young man of color. "It wasn't that anybody said anything negative to us. The waitress was very nice. But it seemed like the whole Hendricken football team was there," Antoine offered about the private, parochial all-boys high school located in the adjacent city of Warwick, which draws a significant number of students from Cranston.

"They didn't say anything to us, but they looked at us like we didn't belong there. This is our city. This is where we live.

"Things like that don't bother me, but some of the guys on our team don't feel comfortable in Garden City," Antoine concluded.

The irony is that the parking lot of that Garden City Newport Creamery restaurant was once where members of Cranston East football teams, like the players on that 1963 Met A championship team, went to celebrate their victories. That was when many Cranston East football players lived in those capes and ranches on the residential streets of Garden City. For two decades after Cranston West was built in 1958, creating two public high schools in the city, public high school students who lived in Garden City attended Cranston East. But in the 1970s, the city started changing the geographical residency lines for the two high schools, so by the 1980s, all high school students who lived in Garden City were Cranston West students.

Now, some Cranston East football players don't feel comfortable in Garden City.

CHAPTER IV

THE THUNDERBOLTS' HEART AND SOUL

Almost every football team has one player who coaches and teammates call the "heart and soul" of their team. He's the guy who possesses all the necessary elements that help make a team whole. Sometimes he is a team's offensive star. In 2018, for a decade, some sportswriters and broadcasters have been proclaiming Tom Brady the "heart and soul" of the New England Patriots. Yet through the years, several times Brady himself has described various other teammates as the Patriots "heart and soul." It's a title that often can't be quantified by looking at the stat sheets. But if you're on the team, you know who is the team's "heart and soul."

In high school football, often a team's "heart and soul" isn't the guy who spends a lot of time in the spotlight. A team's star quarterback will always be an instrumental part of a football team, but if a coach is lucky, he also has that special type of kid who contributes to a team's success through an assortment of his actions. He may be a lineman, a running back, a defensive back, sometimes even a special team's player. Usually he's a veteran starter; somebody who has earned the respect of his teammates with his consistent play over more than one season. No matter where he plays, he's often the kid who, regardless of his own personal challenges, always puts the team's concerns ahead of his own. At Cranston East in 2018, that kid was Hector Duran.

On the roster, Duran is listed as a 5-9, 205-pound running back and outside linebacker. He's not the biggest, fastest, or overall, most athletically-talented kid on the team. But throughout his high school career, his philosophy has been, "Wherever you need me, coach." That's part of why he has been a starter since his sophomore year, playing at a host of positions. He's also a kid who doesn't let his own extensive family responsibilities stop him from finding time to help others.

"He's the type of kid who, if you tell these guys you need somebody to volunteer to help some organization, would be the first one there," Tom Centore offered about Duran.

Duran is a first-generation American of Hispanic heritage. He knows who his father is; but the man hasn't played much of a role in Duran's life. "I would talk to him, but he's not really in my life," Duran told me one afternoon about his father.

Hector lives with his mother, grandmother, and younger brother and sister in a home in the South Elmwood section of Cranston, about a mile from the Providence city line.

South Elmwood is an area where there are still some remnants of the type of industrial manufacturing that started leaving much of the northeast in the middle of the 20th century. Along Elmwood Ave., a four-lane state highway that runs north to south through Cranston from the Providence city line to the Warwick city line, there's a quarter-mile stretch of large, brick buildings that once were used by light-industry manufacturing companies. Over the past half-century or so, those manufacturing operations left, but the buildings had been repurposed to house a variety of small businesses.

Duran lives on one of the streets off Elmwood Ave., adjacent to those old manufacturing complexes. From his bedroom, Duran can see the changing face of American industry and hear the rumble of the trains speeding along the mainline tracks of Amtrak's northeast corridor, which is a couple of hundred yards from his home. Cars and trucks traveling along Interstate Route 95 are also only a few hundred yards from his house.

Duran was born in Manhattan and spent some time in Hartford, CT when he was younger. But about seven years ago, his grandmother wanted her family to have more opportunities, so she moved to Rhode Island and settled in Cranston. Duran has been a Cranston resident for a decade, which means he has had the advantage of receiving most of his formal education in the Cranston school system. He's always been the type of kid who wanted his family to be proud of him, so he has always been a better-than-average student. Years ago, he vowed he would become the first person in his family to go to college and now, at least academically, he has created a path for that to happen. With a solid "B" average, his grades alone should get him admitted to some state colleges or universities, and he has begun to think about where his next stop will be after Cranston East. He's only seventeen years old, but for a few years now, he has been worrying about more than just his self-preservation.

"I'm the big guy in my home. I have responsibilities," Duran said, in a matter-of-fact tone after one of the early season practices.

He started playing football when he was about ten years old, and he has always loved being part of a football team. Now, he has come to think of football as his personal allegory—the kid who gets back up when he gets knocked down; the kid who is willing and excited about working for team success without being the star; the kid who understands being a leader doesn't mean being in the spotlight all the time.

"Football is me," said Duran. "Football is my home. I feel at home on the football field.

"This is me. I don't know where I would be if it wasn't for football. My marks are good. They probably still would be good even if I didn't play football because my mother would kill me if I came home with a bad mark," said Duran, using "kill" as a metaphor rather than a reality.

"My mother likes football because she knows how much it means to me, but she doesn't care about football. My mother wouldn't let me play football if my marks weren't good," Duran said. "For her, football is just something I like to do. For me, it's why I am who I am."

He's not in the spotlight scoring the touchdown; he's the one willing to absorb the aches and pains of being the blocking back and loving every minute of it because he knows he's helping the team. So, when Tom Centore and the assistant coaches started thinking about who should be the captains of this year's team, they started with Duran.

"My being captain this season is similar to my role in my own house," Duran said, with wide smile that reveals the braces on his teeth.

"I'm the man of my family. I'm not only a big brother. I'm a father figure to my brother and sister. I have to make sure they are on the right track," Duran said. "I have to show them the right way to do things. It's the same thing with this team. I feel like I have to be the big brother to some of the young guys."

Football has become another modus to fulfil his commitment of holding himself accountable for his own actions. Now he wants to bring that credo to *his* team.

"My biggest thing is, I always wanted a father figure, and I never had it," Duran said with conviction. "So, I want to be the father figure I never had to this team. That's my mindset. I want to be better than him," Duran said. "A hundred times better," he added, flashing another soft smile.

Ask Not What Your Football Team Can Do for You...

When the senior members of that 1963 Cranston East championship football team were starting their season in the fall of 1963, the U.S. President was declaring, "Ask not what your country can do for you; ask what you can do for your country."

When Robenson Antoine, Quinn Lanigan, Mack Hanley, and Hector Duran were starting their senior season in the fall of 2018, the U.S. President was proclaiming, "Nobody is as successful as me."

The American psyche has changed in five-plus decades.

"This has become a selfish country," Tom Centore said. with an angry tone as he stood in front of his team a few days after the start of practice for the 2018 season.

Centore wasn't making a political statement. He was talking as a high school football coach.

"I get it. America has changed a lot since I started coaching here," Centore said, as he stood in front of his players following a practice session.

But in Centore's mind, high school football can't change when it comes to the concept of every player putting the team above his personal goals.

"We have become a selfish team," Centore declared.

Now the coach is on a roll, and anybody wearing a helmet can be in his line of verbal firing denouncing self-centered playing habits.

"We have only been practicing for a few days, but I come here and all I hear is, 'I'm not getting enough reps,'" Centore proclaimed. "I come here and see some people sitting on the hill waiting. Some people say, 'I will do my work in the drills' rather than going out before practice starts and seeing if you can help with snaps. Seeing if you can become the person who helps us. I can put anybody at guard, but I need a snapper."

Centore knows the society in which these players are becoming young men; the time at which they are adopting their first adult convictions is sending a different message than what he was hearing from his father/coach when he was their age. But a football team can't change.

"This has become a selfish world—me, me, me," Centore said, as his head moved around the circle of players kneeling in front of him with their helmets off and resting by their knees. He looked into their eyes as he panned the circle, wanting each player to think the coach was talking to him.

"Don't think about you. Think about this team," Centore implored. "Think about what this team needs. You may be what this team needs. But it may not be the way you think the coach should be using you."

How could American teenagers who have grown up in a world dominated by omnipresent social media not think about life in the first-person? Facebook, Twitter, Instagram, YouTube, they were all created as a way for people to tell their own narrative in some fashion. An ego-obsessed American culture is nothing new, of course. Some people say it has been that way since "The Sixties," that decade of counterculture and revolt to existing social norms, which paved the way for greater individual freedom. That may be the case, and it seems the American ego has just continued to grow over the decades. Today's social media has made it so much easier for teenagers to become ego obsessed. It's a byproduct of a generation that has lived its entire life in an Internet world that encourages people to choose their own gathering of information and cultivate their own reality. It's a system that plays a huge role in creating a national epidemic of selfishness. It's the omnipresent challenge every high school sports coach deals with in the 21st century, but especially in football, where a coach is dealing with so many egos.

How do you get eleven teenage males to buy into the concept of collectiveness, on every play, over a two- to three-hour game in a world that idolizes individualism?

It's the challenge that has brought Tom Centore out to a football field almost every autumn afternoon since he graduated from college. It's why he is a high school football coach. It's the challenge that has always been there. But now, in this ego-obsessed era, it may be tougher than ever.

It's only a few weeks into this season, and already he is detecting some players are looking for someone else to blame other than themselves for why they are not getting enough snaps; why he isn't playing the position he's thinks he should be playing.

"You're looking for someone else to blame," Centore proclaimed to the sixty or seventy varsity players kneeling in front of him.

"The coach doesn't like me. He's always getting on me," Centore continued, mimicking a hypothetical player. Suddenly, Centore stops talking and just stands there without saying a word, as his head moves along the faces of contrite teenagers. A good coach knows how to hold his audience.

Finally, Centore resumes his discourse.

"I have been coaching for thirty years, and let me tell you. You don't need to worry when me or any of the coaches are getting on you about your mistakes. It's when we stop talking to you that you need to start worrying."

A Football Lifer

Leroy Shaw is a football guy.

Shaw came to Rhode Island in the mid-1970s to play football at the University of Rhode Island and never left the state of Rhode Island. A man of color, Shaw is recognized as one of the best running backs in the history of URI football. He was one of the three running backs on the 1978 ECAC Division I-AA first team All-Star squad. After his playing days, he became a well-respected assistant high school football coach for some of the top Rhode Island high school programs, including a tenure at Hendricken High, when future NFL star Will Blackman was playing for the Hawks.

For the past two years, he has been a member of Tom Centore's staff, although the 2018 season will probably be his last on Rhode Island high school sidelines because he is in the process of building a home in South Carolina, after having recently retired from a career in construction. He's now a man in his sixties, but he still enjoys being on a practice field bestowing football wisdom and exchanging good-natured, verbal jabs with a bunch of teenage high school football players.

He had been away from practice for a few days while checking on his new home construction in South Carolina. When he came back—as a football guy—something upset him.

"I came back after being away for a few days, and I think this has become a selfish team," Shaw declared to a few players at practice. "I hear people talking about not running with the ball enough, not playing offense. That's not football."

The Unwritten Playbook

It's nothing the Cranston East players saw on the playlists posted in their "huddle" account that every player was supposed to review by the first day of practice. But it's a mindset Tom Centore knows he needs to ingrain in seventy-some varsity players quickly. A successful football team cannot be a collection of self-narratives.

"For us to be successful, we cannot be selfish," Centore declared. "You are going to go out into the working world someday soon. If you are a firefighter, and they tell you to get water at the fire, you can't say I don't want to do that. I want to be the one who saves the person in the burning building. You are going to get married someday and have children. Do you want your kids to grow up like that?"

CHAPTER V

HE KNOWS TOO MUCH NOT TO BE OUT THERE

In the sixty-year history of Cranston East football, there have been great players, but nobody's football talent progressed more during his high school career than former East player Alex Corvese's.

Corvese was born and raised in Cranston on a street in the middle of the city, a neighborhood of two- and three-bedroom Capes and Colonials with well-manicured lawns on 8,000 or so square-foot house lots about a half-mile from Cranston East High. The vast majority of Corvese's neighborhood friends when he was growing up in the early part of the 21st century were kids who looked like him—young white boys. He was always an outstanding student, and education was his parents' priority. So, when it was time for him to decide what high school he would attend, if he had decided he wanted to go to one of the private parochial schools where a lot of Cranston kids—especially good student-athletes—were going in those days, it was a choice his parents would have gladly funded. But for Corvese, the only place he wanted to attend high school was Cranston East.

His sister, who is a few years older, had attended East and had gone on to Brown University. Alex had the same type of academic aptitude as his sister, so his academic course load at East was filled with Advance Placement and Honors courses. He had played youth football growing up, but never played quarterback. Tom Centore, however, felt he was the type of athletic, intelligent kid who could be a good quarterback—if he could just learn how to throw a football.

"He couldn't throw the ball more than ten yards when he was freshman," Centore offered about Corvese. "But he was willing to work."

Corvese became both a good passer and a gifted student of the game of football.

By the start of his senior season in 2015, Corvese was on this way to becoming the all-time Cranston East career passing leader. That year, he led Cranston East to a berth in the state's major football Super Bowl against Hendricken, the private school that had won four straight titles coming into the 2015 season. East lost in that Super Bowl game, but going into the 2018 season, that 2015 game marked the only time in a seven-year span that a public school team had played in Rhode Island's major high school state title football game. What always impressed Centore about Corvese was the way he never let his emotions control his game, regardless of the numbers on the scoreboard.

"Alex's demeanor never changed, even if things were going bad," related Centore.

Corvese finished his high school career as the Cranston East career passing leader, and with his academic credentials, he probably could have been admitted to a host of highly regarded academic colleges whose athletic teams play in the NCAA Division I rank. But no Division I football coaches had made an effort to recruit him, and Corvese wanted to play college football. So, Corvese went to Curry College, a Division III school in Milton, Mass, just outside of Boston.

He became a Dean's List student and quarterback of the school's football team. He finished his college football career as one of Curry's all-time career passing leaders, and in the spring of his senior year, the college's president selected Corvese to address a gathering of high school seniors who had been accepted to the college on why they should attend Curry.

Corvese treasured his time at East when he was one of only two white players on the starting offensive unit. He knew he had developed a passion for football under Tom Centore's mentorship, and being a member of the Thunderbolts had opened his eyes to a social world he barely knew existed before he entered East.

The high school building was less than a mile from his neighborhood, but East exposed him to the type of global diversity 21st century colleges were trying to achieve on their campuses. He was the smart white kid who had other options, but this was his school, and his team, in his city. He loved working with such a diverse group of people to give Cranston something it hadn't experienced in over a decade—having one of its two public high school football teams playing in Rhode Island's major high school football title game.

"When I was in college, I told the guys on my team that I had been one of only two white kids on the starting offense on my high school team. They didn't believe me," said Corvese. "I will always be grateful to my parents for giving me a good home in a neighborhood that enabled me to attend Cranston East."

Corvese's willingness to spend long hours perfecting his passing ability certainly played a big role in his development as an outstanding quarterback. But it was more than just an improved throwing arm that made Corvese a great quarterback. He was the type of person who wanted to get involved with everybody on the team. He understood at East, he may have only been a few miles from his home, but he had moved into a world he didn't know much about when he was growing up. Many of his new teammates were kids who came from different backgrounds than he did, and Corvese wanted to know about them. Part of it was a natural intellectual curiosity, but he also felt it would help him become a better quarterback. A quarterback who understands his teammates can understand a football offense much better. Corvese not only wanted to understand where everybody on the team was supposed to be, but also why they should be there. That's why he loved his time at East with Centore and the other coaches. He always felt it made him a better football player—and in the grand scheme of life, a better person.

He graduated from Curry in the spring of 2018 and had already secured a position as an accountant with Rhode Island's largest foreign car dealership. But even though he knew his football playing career was finished, he didn't want to leave the field completely. So, he asked Tom Centore if he could be a volunteer assistant coach and help with the quarterbacks. Centore was thrilled to have Converse on his staff, a shining example of what football and Cranston East could do for a young man.

So now, every weekday afternoon after he leaves his office at his paying job, Corvese heads to Cranston, where he walks onto the East practice field still wearing his business casual dress slacks and a collared shirt, making him the best-dressed coach on the field—by far.

"Now I know too much *not* to be out here," said Corvese. "I have to pass on the stuff I have learned."

A Classic Home

Cranston Stadium, the home of the Cranston East football team, is a classic New England high school football stadium. It is located on Park Ave. about a quarter-mile west from the Cranston East school building. "The Stadium "was built as a "New Deal" WPA project in 1935. The reinforced concrete walls on the front and west side help form a horseshoe-type football complex—somewhat like a small version of Harvard Stadium, without stands behind one end zone. During the heydays of Cranston High football in the 1950s and early '60s, before the city had two high schools, it wasn't unusual for all of the 8,000 or so spots on the wood bleachers in the stadium—that ran along three sides of the complex—to be filled for a big game. But by the 1980s, with the increase of televised professional and college sports, along with other changes in American society, interest in local high school sports, especially in New England, had diminished.

So, when "The Stadium" was renovated in the 1990s, the stands behind the south end zone were removed, and the curved ten-foot-high area around the end zone was turned into a grass berm. That cut a few thousand seats off the stadium's seating capacity, but even then, "The Stadium" was still the largest high school football venue in Rhode Island.

When the playing surface was changed from natural grass to artificial turf, around 2007 or 2008, it became an even better place to play a high school football game. Obviously, the R.I. Interscholastic League thinks so because in 2018, all four of the League's divisional State championship football games were scheduled to be played at Cranston Stadium over a two-day period in November.

The problem for the Cranston East football team is that, in addition to the Cranston West football team, "The Stadium" is also where the Cranston East and Cranston West boys' and girls' soccer teams and the Cranston East girls field hockey teams play their home games. With five other non-football teams besides the East football team playing games on autumn afternoons and nights at "The Stadium," it doesn't leave much open time for practice on the stadium's "turf" field during the week. So, the Cranston East football team usually can't use its home facility for practice until late October, when the other sports teams have finished their seasons.

The First Challenge Is Getting to Practice

Most American high school football players go out a door of their school building each afternoon and walk to a nearby practice field. But because their school is fronted directly on Park Ave. and abuts Cranston City Hall on one side, a strip-shopping mall on the other side, and three to four blocks of residential homes behind the school, there are no practice fields near the school for any outdoor Cranston East athletic teams.

Cranston Stadium may only be about a quarter-mile from the Cranston East school building, but Thunderbolts' fall outdoor athletic teams have to find other places around the city to practice. For the Cranston East football team, that's a 100 by 80-yard field about a half-mile from the school. During the spring and summer, the field is used for softball and youth baseball. The half-mile trip from the Cranston East locker room to the practice field may not be all that far, but it includes crossing Reservoir Ave., a four-lane state highway that is the most heavily traveled road in Cranston.

For student safety, school officials will not allow student athletes to walk across Reservoir Ave. to get to practice. Students are allowed to drive to practice fields on the other side of Reservoir Ave., but only a few East football players regularly have the use of a car after school. So, while the players at cross-city neighbor Cranston West just walk out their locker room door to the practice field a few yards away, the vast majority of Cranston East football players have to be bused to the practice field every afternoon.

The school department only funds one bus for the trip, so it takes two, sometimes three, round trips to get the whole team to practice. That means it can take a half-hour—or more—to get the entire team to the practice field every afternoon. If a football player has to stay after school for any reason—like see a teacher about a make-up a test, attend a tutoring session, or has after-school detention—and misses one of the bus trips, he can't just walk out to practice a little late. He needs to get a ride from somebody, and that's not easy at East.

"For us, it would be a luxury to be able to just walk to practice," said Alex Corvese. "But this is the way it is. You learn not to worry about it."

The Days a Kid Can Make His Mark

Unlike the private schools, which are loaded with kids who have grown up playing in high-powered youth football programs, for a variety of reasons a lot of the East players never played organized football before entering high school.

"At least half of these kids didn't play football before they got here, and now a lot of them can't afford to go to the camps and clinics run during the summer on college campuses," said

Tom Centore. "That's why we just get together a couple of nights a week for conditioning drills during the summer."

For some East players, there's another of life's realities that affects their football careers.

"Once they get old enough, most of our kids work because they need to," said Centore. "That's the only way they have spending money. Some of these kids also help support their families. That's why the pre-season practice is in the evening, rather than in the morning, like most schools."

It all means these early days of pre-season practice are very important for some kids. They are the days a kid who doesn't have much of a football resume can impress a coach by showing how he has improved his foot work and his strength by working out by himself or going to the gym with a few friends during the summer. But even in the first few days of practice, Centore was already worried about this season. The Thunderbolts may be the defending Division I state champion—and there are a couple returning All-State players on the team—but Centore knows this year's team, overall, is inexperienced, especially at linebackers. Every football coach worries about what will cause his team to lose focus and make mistakes. Will it be a lack of conditioning? Will the team be able to come back with a good play after one bad play? Or will that one bad play initiate a cascade of poor plays?

"I worry about how they'll react when things go bad," Centore offered about the Thunderbolts. "And there will be times this year when things go bad."

CHAPTER VI

A DIFFERENT KIND OF CRANSTON EAST FOOTBALL PLAYER

Maclaan "Mack" Hanley is a unique Cranston East football player—he lives in Edgewood.

"There aren't many guys on the team from Edgewood. I think there are only two of us this year," Hanley offered about the team members who come from the far eastern section of the city, the area with the streets running parallel and perpendicular to a picturesque waterfront.

Hanley lives on one of those streets that runs perpendicular to the water in a home with his mother, father, and three brothers. He's a 6'1", 210-pound white kid and is the poster boy for the proverbial "All-American Boy." His father attended Hendricken, the private school athletic power that's located only twelve miles from the Hanley home. But Mack always wanted to attend Cranston East.

"There was never any question, I would go to East," said Hanley. "I always wanted to go to East. My older brother went here, and I wanted to go here. Everybody on my mother's side of the family attended East."

For a teenager in the 21st century, he had an astute appreciation of an actual geographic sense of community—not just some type of digital community that so many of today's teenagers call home.

"There's something about representing the city where you actually live," said Hanley. "If you go to a private school and accomplish something special like a championship, it just another championship in another year. But if you do it at your public school, you will be remembered by the people in the city where you grew up."

Hanley participates in three high school sports: football, basketball, and outdoor track. He is also an outstanding student. His academic course load for the 2018 fall semester includes Advance Placement classes in English, physics, and history. He didn't play football growing up, and basketball, which his older brother currently plays at Hartwick College in New York, would have to be considered his best sport. But Mack always wanted to play football. So, he convinced his parents to let him play in his freshman year at East, and he has loved being a member of the Thunderbolts football team.

"I don't know if it's just being part of this team. I love the diversity of this team, the different guys," said Hanley.

He's only seventeen years old, but already Hanley understands you learn by being engaged with people who are different from you.

"Diversity is part of life. It's not everywhere, but we're lucky to have it here," Hanley added. "Just learning from other people about their different backgrounds. It's just the overall communication between all the players. Football is fun, but it is even nicer to be part of that experience; living through it with your friends."

His football talents have progressed to the point that, even though Tom Centore hadn't yet discussed college plans with him, Centore felt that with his academic credentials and his improved level of play, Hanley had the potential to be admitted and play football in the NESCAC Conference, the group of nine academically-elite Division III northeastern colleges like Williams, Amherst, Wesleyan, and Trinity. But what Centore didn't know as practice was beginning for the 2018 season was that this would be Hanley's last football campaign. Hanley hadn't developed a passion for football in the three years since he'd first put on his helmet and shoulder pads—he just loves playing for the Thunderbolts.

"This is the last year for me," Hanley offered in early September. "I'm not playing football in college. People who know me will tell you I don't have a passion for football. I just love playing for this team. Being part of this team is special."

People who have known Hanley for years are probably not surprised that football has always been about more than just the excitement of playing under Friday Night Lights for Mack. Hanley has the actual biological brotherhood of three male siblings who have all grown up as part of a loving, middle-class family. But he has come to realize this football brotherhood that has been a part of his life for four years now has also become an important part of his life.

"Football teaches you a lot," Hanley told me one day, as we talked prior to practice. "You learn how to respond to adversity, how to react to pressure situations. It teaches you accountability—like making sure you are doing things for your friends. In a word, basically, in football you need to do your job."

Hanley also realizes he's in a unique situation being on the practice field every afternoon with his Thunderbolts teammates.

"The diversity on this team. Just being around other people, you are learning things. These kids have taught me a lot," said Hanley, a National Honor Society member.

Hanley knows there are other kids on the team who aren't lucky enough to have the solid family structure role-models in their lives that he has in his. He thinks football has helped give those teammates some of that structure.

"Football has given some kids a goal. It gave them directions," said Hanley. "Everybody is different. You have to find a way to put it all together. That's what makes football so special."

In his junior year, last season, Hanley had learned enough football technique that he finally started seeing some playing time in games. But he knows, as a newcomer to the game when he came to East, in reality, for the first three years of his football career he was learning "how to play" the game. But this season, for the first time in his career, Hanley really felt like he was part of the team because he could make an actual contribution to the team's success with his play at tight end. Unfortunately, in a drill during the first week of practice, he suffered a hand injury that now had him standing on the sidelines with his hand in a cast.

Some people might have said, with football not being his best sport, that he should turn-in his football gear and focus on rehabbing his hand so he would be ready for the basketball season. After all, the word was East could be one of the best basketball teams in the state during the 2018–19 winter season, and the team's success would depend heavily on Hanley's rebounding ability. But Hanley never gave a thought to not being on the football team this fall. Even if he wouldn't be physically able to practice on the field for close to a month, this was his team, so he vowed he would be there every afternoon. He would stand on the sideline with his hand in a cast, offering verbal encouragement to his teammates as they run through drills;

even offering some suggestions from what he had learned in his three years as a football player.

"It was the first time I felt that special connection to the team," Hanley said about the 2018 season. "If I had that chance to be part of a high school football team. I wanted to do it."

A Feeder System That Doesn't Feed the Thunderbolts

One of the most successful youth football programs in Rhode Island over the past half-century has been the Edgewood Eagles. A Pop Warner program, which involves players from ages 6–14, the Eagles was first organized in the early 1960s by a small group of people who lived in the Edgewood section of Cranston. To this day, the Eagles still use a large athletic field on Park Ave. in Edgewood for their practice sessions. So, there's a degree of irony in Mack Hanley's words that, "There aren't many guys on the team from Edgewood."

For generations, the Edgewood section of Cranston has been populated by an economic cross-section of the American middle class. When I was growing up in Edgewood in the 1950s and '60s, I had friends who were the sons and daughters of doctors and businessmen as well as kids, like myself, the son of a blue-collar skilled craftsman. The result was for decades, Edgewood kids were involved in a wide cross section of sports activities. A few Edgewood guys played significant roles in the success of that 1963 Cranston East Met A championship football team.

Also, in the 1960s and '70s, Edgewood was known as a breeding ground for ice hockey players. Two of my teammates, and fellow Edgewood residents, on the 1964 Cranston East state championship hockey team went on to become first-team collegiate hockey All-Americans, Joe Cavanagh at Harvard and Curt Bennett at Brown University.

The Edgewood neighborhood and the Edgewood Eagles football program continued to be a decent source of players for Cranston East football players through the 1980s. An All-State running back on that 1987 Cranston East state championship football team was Tom Pelderian, a kid who grew up in the Pawtuxet Village section of Edgewood and who had played for the Edgewood Eagles.

"We had several guys from Edgewood," Pelderian offered about the '87 Thunderbolts' roster.

But within a couple of years after that '87 championship season, for a variety of reasons, the private school lure—some people will say recruiting—started to draw football players away from Cranston East, especially Edgewood kids. When Tom Pelderian's young brother Jayson reached high school age, in the early 1990s, he attended Hendricken. In his senior season in 1994, Jason and a few other graduates of the Edgewood Eagles program played big major runs in Hendricken's ride to the state title, which began a three-year state title run for the private school. Also, the reputation of the Edgewood Eagles success began to expand beyond the Cranston city line. So, it's probably not surprising with the Eagles' practice facility less than a mile from the South Side of Providence that a significant number of young faces of color joined the Eagles association in their quest for a quality youth football experience close to their homes.

Through the past few decades, the Eagles program has produced a host of outstanding high school football players, but because many of those players live in Providence, they have attended one of the private schools that don't have any geographic restrictions for their student bodies.

In the fall of 2018, the Edgewood community was still a wonderful mix of people who make their living in a variety of professions. Although with Rhode Island's largest medical complex, which consists of three hospitals and the Brown University Medical School, only a few miles down the road in Providence, these days there is probably a preponderance of Edgewood residents who make their living in medical related fields. And while Edgewood residents are still predominately white, in 2018, Edgewood was a much more racially diverse community then it was when I was growing up there in the 1950s and '60s. But Edgewood is still not a great training ground for future Cranston East football players.

"We don't get many kids who played for the Eagles," Tom Centore offered about one of the most successful youth football programs in Rhode Island, whose practice facility is located only a little over a mile away from Cranston East High.

I'm Right Where I Want to Be

Assistant coach Isaiah McDaniel knows the modern-day Cranston East football back-story as well as anybody. After all, he has played a major role in its formation.

McDaniel grew up as one of the few faces of color in Edgewood in the 1990s. Both of his parents were in the military, so he certainly didn't grow up in one of those big houses along the waterfront. But he lived in a comfortable house about a half-mile from the water, and even while some of his childhood friends, including future NFL player Will Blackmon, went to the private Hendricken High, Cranston East was the only place McDaniel wanted to spend his high school days.

He had played youth football growing up, so he naturally joined the football team when he enrolled at East in 1999. But his early days as an East football player were not the best of times. Not surprising, as the Thunderbolts' win-loss record diminished in the 1990s, so, too, did the number of players wanting to wear a Cranston East football uniform. Trying to recruit classmates to join the team became as much a responsibility for McDaniel as trying to score touchdowns. But in McDaniel's senior year in the fall of 2002, Tom Centore became the new East head coach. It literally changed McDaniel's life.

McDaniel, an outstanding running back, played a big role in helping Centore turn around the perception of East football. He was one of the few upperclassmen who talked to other boys in the school who were not playing football, trying to convince them that this new coach was different.

"That first year Tom was coach, you could tell it was different," said McDaniel. "You could just tell how much Tom cared about you as a person. I kept working on getting more and more guys to come out for the team. We only won five games, but you could tell it was different. It was the start, and we have kept building on it every year."

Even after he graduated from East, McDaniel still thought of himself as a Thunderbolt. He came back to be one of Centore's volunteer assistant coaches when he was still a college student. Now he is a Cranston East teacher's assistant, an assistant Thunderbolts football coach, and the East boys' head basketball coach—all of which make him a role model for a lot of the football team members. He is a thirty-year-old coach who is physically fit enough to still walk onto the practice field and challenge seventy-plus high school varsity football players to "match my juice" at the start of practice.

"I'm right where I want to be," McDaniel, the married father of three little girls, offered about his current station in life.

McDaniel knows that unlike when he was growing up with the stability of a two-parent family, these days some of the kids who have moved into the affordable housing in the Cranston areas near the Providence city line don't have that solid family structure. As the football team's offensive co-coordinator, he is trying to devise a plan for this season that will produce another autumn of the high-scoring offense the Thunderbolts had demonstrated over the previous few years. But he knows, too, for many of his players, the most important game plan he can teach is the path to a strong moral character.

"We have to teach these kids not to quit when things go wrong here on the field," McDaniel offered. "For a lot of these kids, it is the same thing in the classroom. When things get difficult, when there's problems, they give up. That's why football is so important for them in high school. They learn not to quit. They finish school, and they open up chances for themselves in life."

CHAPTER VII

THE KID NEEDS THE TEAM AS MUCH AS THE TEAM NEEDS HIM

About a week after the start of practice, Tom Centore, with input from the assistant coaches, named five seniors—Hector Duran, Robenson Antoine, Rayven Deoliviera, Jamari Mason, and Quinn Lanigan—the 2018 team captains. The next day, the mother of another senior, who wasn't named a captain, walked onto the practice field and handed Centore her son's uniform.

"He's quitting. He's depressed because he wasn't named a captain," the mother told Centore.

The news upset Centore like an opponent converting a game-winning field goal on the final play of the game.

"I was heartsick because I think that kid needs this team," Centore said. "He has been with us for four years. He would have been a starter this season."

In high school sports these days—especially in football where so many players are involved—there's often a backstory that goes beyond the actual playing field.

"His mother is a single mom," Centore added about the player. "Last year he had to help take care of his little sister some afternoons, so he couldn't make some practices. I got it. We made sure he could get home whenever he was needed."

Centore understood when a woman needed his help in her role as a mother. But now he doesn't feel he is getting reciprocal support in his role as a football coach.

"The problem is, I don't think his mother is encouraging him to stay. She's enabling him," Centore said, with a look of disappointment. "She said she can't understand why he is not a captain. She said he's a good kid, and he's in all the honor classes. That's true. But look at Mack Hanley. He's a great kid who is in all honor classes, and he's not complaining that he wasn't named a captain."

The player's mother told Centore her son couldn't bring the uniform back himself because he was sitting in his room depressed. That worried Centore. So, in the midst of dealing with his own father's serious illness and trying to get an inexperienced team ready for the start of the season, Centore will try to discover more about the young man's mental-health situation.

Another Page Added to The Playbook

By the fall of 2018, mental health had become a major area of concern for American teenagers. The previous spring, the Rhode Island Dept. of Health had released the results of a bi-annual survey titled "Youth Risk Behavior Survey." It was an anonymous survey of 3,700 Rhode Island middle and high school students. While there were some positive trends—like decreased smoking and drinking—there was a disturbing shift involving teenagers' mental health. The survey found that 29 percent of high school students had felt so sad or hopeless for the better part of two weeks that they stopped their typical activities. Like so many other American high school football coaches, Centore is an educator first and a football coach second. As a guidance counselor, he may not be able to cite statistics right off the top of his head, but he reads reports and goes to conferences and meetings where this growing American concern is discussed. Issues like that are not something a high school football coach should have to factor into his drawing-up of a game plan, but for Centore, and probably a lot of other American high school football coaches, it has become a reality.

One more page added to the "How to be a Successful High School Football Coach" playbook.

Sometimes Diversity Isn't Easy, Even When People Are Trying

Robenson Antoine and Quinn Lanigan, two of the senior captains, were not there when practice started one late August afternoon. One look at Tom Centore as the coach stood in the middle of the practice field watching "most" of his players warm up was all an observer needed to tell Centore wasn't happy. Centore's coaching doctrine is based on being accountable for your actions. Two of the team captains showing up late for practice isn't the example of accountability Centore expects. So, when Centore saw Antoine and Lanigan walking across the field together about ten minutes after the start of practice, he didn't hesitate letting the two seniors know he was pissed.

"Why are you two late?" Centore shouted.

Lanigan quickly offered a defense.

"I got pulled over by the cops," Lanigan replied sheepishly.

Having two of his team captains stopped by police only a few weeks after the start of practice was something Centore definitely didn't want to hear.

"What did you do?" Centore countered.

"Nothing," Lanigan quickly offered in defense. "I was just driving to Robenson's house to pick him up for practice."

Robenson Antoine is a 5'7", 140-pound teenager of color, the son of a bi-racial marriage. Quinn Lanigan is a 5'7", 155-pound white kid who could pass as an Abercrombie & Fitch model with his striking good looks and neatly trimmed hair.

They have been inseparable friends since the day when Robenson was in the second grade, and his family moved from Providence to a house in Cranston that put him in the same elementary school as Lanigan. Their natural athletic abilities made for a quick friendship.

"We always were the two fastest kids when they ran races in the school yard," Lanigan offered about he and Antoine. "We always hung out together in everything we did."

Their homes are about a mile apart, with Antoine living on a street of tenement houses off Cranston St. near the Providence city line, and Lanigan living in one of the small, neat capes on a street directly across from the Cranston Stadium football and baseball fields. Lanigan has lived his entire life in this comfortable home.

Both Lanigan and Antoine are good students, with similar outgoing personalities. They were often in the same classes as they progressed through junior high, then into senior high. In addition to being football teammates, they are also teammates on the Cranston East varsity baseball team. At East, when you see Robenson, there's a pretty good chance Quinn isn't far away.

After his first year at East, some people had been talking to Lanigan's father about his son transferring to one of the private high schools in the state. They talked about helping get Lanigan admitted as a transfer student, maybe even get him some scholarship money. But Lanigan didn't want to hear about it. He took pride in being part of a public school team.

"It would be insulting to me," Lanigan said, about playing at one of the private school athletic powerhouses that have the advantage of building a roster of players who live all around the state. "Even if I made it at one of those schools, what do I prove?" Lanigan asked. "How do you have fun at Hendricken winning four straight titles, especially when you are beating teams 50–0 every night? You have all the advantages."

Plus, at a private school, Lanigan wouldn't be going to school with his friends from elementary and middle school—especially Robenson.

While nobody on the football team, or even at the high school, was ever surprised to see Robenson and Quinn together, Tom Centore knew to some people in a city where almost 75 percent of the residents are white, seeing a white kid and a kid with a face of color driving together might be a strange sight.

"Was Robenson in the car with you?" Centore asked, fearing there might be a case of racial profiling with a young man of color riding in a car that was slowly driving through a Cranston neighborhood.

"No, I was by myself. I hadn't picked him up yet," Lanigan offered.

Centore wanted to know more about why the police would stop one of his players on his way to practice.

"What did they say to you?" Centore asked Lanigan.

"They told me to get out of my car and get into the police car," Lanigan said. "About five minutes later, they came back to me and said, 'You're okay. You can go.'"

There was no racial profiling of a young man of color. But there was a good chance the police were following up on a criminal activity profile—a white kid driving slowly around a neighborhood close to a section of Providence that has had its share of suburban residents coming into an urban neighborhood looking to make drug purchases.

"The cops are always driving around my neighborhood," said Robenson.

But heavy law enforcement surveillance in his neighborhood hasn't soured Antoine on the Cranston police department.

"I have never been disrespected by the police in Cranston," said Antoine. "Some kids I know who live in Providence say the police are always hassling them."

"That Man Is Like My Father"

Jonathan Loy's grandmother escaped the horrors of the war being waged in her native Thailand between the Khmer Rouge and Communist-Vietnamese in the late 1970s by walking through rice fields while she was pregnant with Loy's mother.

"My grandparents don't talk about it too much because it was a very sad time," said Loy, a Cranston East senior placekicker.

Both of Loy's parents are first-generation Americans. They are products of an Asian community that developed in the Providence/Cranston area around the 1980s and early '90s heavily populated by refuges from Southeast Asian wars. Jon has lived his entire life in Cranston, with his parents and grandparents, in the same house his mother grew up in. Although both his parents are native-born Americans, like a lot of first-generation Americans, they didn't grow up in families that had extensive knowledge of American youth sports programs. So, while Jon became a football fan by enjoying NFL games on TV while growing up, his parents never got him involved in any of the youth football programs in Cranston. As soon as Loy enrolled at East, however, he joined the freshman football team.

"I'm not that big or fast, so I figured I would try to be a lineman," said the 5'7", 225-pound Loy. "But then one day the freshman coach asked if anybody wanted to try placekicking because they needed somebody to kick extra points. I figured I would give it a shot."

Loy had found a new purpose in life. Shy and reserved, learning the art of placekicking gave Loy a chance to open up his personality. He started feeling like he was part of a team effort without becoming demonstrative. His shy nature meant he had little experience interacting with other people outside his family and the structure of a classroom, so being part of a team improved his ability to interact with his peers.

Football also helped him learn how to maintain daily focus on a task—something that he often had problems with in the classroom because of a diagnosed slight learning disability. By his junior year, in the fall of 2017, he had become one of the most consistent conversion kickers in the state and earned first All-Division I honors after connecting on 42 conversion boots. He may be the person who actually kicks the ball through the uprights, but Loy knows that never would have been possible without Tom Centore. Centore seemed to understand him in a way no one else in his life had ever been able to. Centore gave him a chance to prove himself, and Loy was successful. Centore seemed to know that in order for Loy to have confidence in his kicking, he needed to come out of his shell—to gain confidence in himself as a person as well as a football player.

"That man is like my father," Loy said one afternoon at practice, while looking over at Centore who was standing at the far side of the field. "I would do anything for him."

CHAPTER VIII

PUBLIC SCHOOLS EDUCATE
ALL OF GOD'S CHILDREN

Rayven Deoliveira says he had always wanted to be a Cranston East student.

"When I was growing up, all my family went to the La Salle games," Deoliveira offered about La Salle Academy, the 150-year-old private, parochial high school located in Providence, a few blocks from the Rhode Island State House. "But I always went to Cranston East games. I always wanted to go to East," said Deoliveira.

But some of Deoliveira's cousins had attended La Salle decades ago. So, when it came time for his older brother Leroy—then Rayven, a year later—to attend high school, they both enrolled at La Salle. Leroy began his freshman year at La Salle in the fall of 2014, and Raven entered in the fall of 2015. For years, some people in Cranston were citing the Deoliveira brothers, two young men of color, as prime examples that the Catholic schools recruited players, and there probably was some validity to that contention—at least indirectly recruiting.

It's no secret in Rhode Island, like a lot of Northeast states, for generations parochial schools have had an underground recruiting system of friends, parents, and alumni, touting the benefits of attending a parochial high school. The public school coaches complained that it's recruiting; the private schools call it marketing their education product. Under R.I. Interscholastic League rules, it's basically legal for a private school to "market" its education programs as long as that "marketing" does not overly emphasize a school's athletic program.

La Salle certainly was "marketed" by relatives, friends, and La Salle alumni to the Deoliveira brothers. It also could have been a case of a single mother thinking that a catholic school would give her teenage sons more discipline than a public school.

Both Leroy and Rayven were outstanding football players. They had grown up in Cranston, in the Auburn section, near Cranston East and City Hall. They had started playing youth football as soon as they were old enough to put on a helmet. Both were youth football superstars. Leroy was a bulky running back with good speed. Like his brother, Rayven was also a big, strong runner, but he had also played quarterback in youth football.

Their father, who was a former Rhode Island high school football standout, had died suddenly when Rayven was only six months old, and Leroy was just a little more than two years old. Their father's death had left their mother responsible for two very young boys and an older sister.

When the two brothers enrolled at La Salle, where at the time the tuition was about $14,000 per student, some people questioned how a single mother who struggled financially to maintain a home for her family could afford to send her two sons to La Salle. Under R.I. Interscholastic League rules, it's illegal to award financial aid to a private school as an enhancement to attract a student because of the student's athletic ability. Aid can only be awarded on a financial need basis. It's very probable that the two brothers received some legal financial aid.

La Salle Academy is run by the religious order of the DeLa-Sallle Christian Brothers, and the DeLaSalle brothers have a 100-year history of financially helping minority students from the Providence urban area attend La Salle. Two of the greatest players in La Salle's illustrious football history in the 20th century were John Rollins and Bernie Pena, two Providence African American kids who played in the 1950s. So, it wouldn't have been a break from tradition if the Deoliveira brothers received some financial aid. Of course, that didn't stop some people from protesting that it was just another case of the private schools having all the advantages.

By the time LeRoy was a junior and Rayven was a sophomore, the two brothers were stars of the La Salle football team. Leroy was one of the top running backs in the state, and Rayven was the run/pass portion of the La Salle two-starting quarterbacks rotation. By late November in the fall of 2016, the two brothers had led La Salle to a Division I regular season divisional championship and a berth in the upcoming state title game.

Then, just before the "Super Bowl," Rayven made a big mistake. The school never made an announcement, but just before the Super Bowl, Rayven was expelled from La Salle. Word around the state was that Deoliveira's expulsion was the result of some obscene photos involving him and a female classmate that were posted on social media.

At first, there was talk about Deoliveira transferring to another private school, maybe even out of state. But within a few weeks, it had become obvious his only choice would be to enroll at the public high school in the city where he lived. By Christmas 2016, Deoliveira was a Cranston East student. As a superintendent of a large Rhode Island public school system once said to me—in a direct dig at the way parochial schools can pick and choose their students—"We educate all of God's children."

Being at East was fine with Rayven. Later during the 2018 season, he would tell me that he never felt totally comfortable at La Salle. He claimed kids sat in their own groups when not in classrooms, and the student-athletes of color would always sit together. I'm not sure if that statement was a defensive mechanism on Rayven's part to alibi his being expelled from La Salle or if there was some legitimacy to it. But that's the way Deoliveira felt in the fall of 2018, and he claimed he was very happy being at East because of the school's extensive diversity.

Rayven, at least the football player persona of the young man, was no stranger to Tom Centore. In the fall of 2015, when he was a sophomore at La Salle, Rayven's performance at quarterback had played a big role in a convincing La Salle victory over Cranston East. Even before he played against his team in 2015, Centore knew about Rayven. For years, long before they were in high school, people involved in Cranston youth football had been telling Centore about the Deoliveira brothers. How they were youth football superstars. But Centore had never actually met Rayven until after he enrolled at East. But that didn't stop people, who also didn't really know Rayven, from warning Centore that he was going to have a problem if Deoliveira joined the team for the 2017 season.

"Some people said I was going to have a problem with him because he was wild and out of control," Centore related.

But Centore refused to pre-judge the young man on the opinions of others. He waited until he and Deoliviera had interacted personally, and for almost two years now, their relationship has been exceptional.

"Since the first day Rayven came into my office to introduce himself, that kid has been nothing but respectful and never questioned anything we did," Centore told me one day after practice.

Deoliveira had been a starting quarterback at La Salle, but when he first started playing for East, in the fall of 2017, Justin Neary, who had been the East starting quarterback since 2015, was back for his senior season. Right from the beginning of the pre-season workouts, Centore told Deoliveira that Neary would be the starting quarterback that season. Deoliveira never questioned his new coach's decision.

"He just did what we asked him to do to help the team," Tom Centore offered.

The result was Deoliviera played running back, receiver, and defensive back during the 2017 season. He played a major role in helping East win the 2017 Division I state title as he enjoyed an All-State season in which he was the Division I scoring leader, with 125 points on 21 touchdowns and 4 conversion rushes.

Rayven liked Tom Centore. He knew, because of what had happened at La Salle, that some coaches might have had pre-conceived notions about what type of kid he was. But Centore judged Deoliveira strictly upon what he had done since he had come to East. Basically, he had given Deoliveira a clean slate to make his mark at East, and Rayven was doing a good job.

There's No "I" in Team

Quinn Lanigan had been playing quarterback since he was a ten-year-old pee-wee player. He had been Justin Neary's backup in his sophomore season when Neary was a junior. In Lanigan's mind, that was fine because Lanigan figured by his senior year, Neary would have graduated, and he would be the starting quarterback. It would be the fulfillment of the dream of a little kid who walked by the Cranston Stadium football field every morning on his way to elementary school and thought about the day when he would be the quarterback of the Cranston East football team.

But when Deoliveira joined the team, Lanigan knew his vision of someday quarterbacking the Thunderbolts to victory under the Friday Night Lights of Cranston Stadium could have become a little hazy. Deoliveira had already proven he could excel as a Division I quarterback with his performance as a sophomore at La Salle. Even during summer workouts in the summer of 2018, Lanigan had hoped Centore might feel the Thunderbolts' attack could be more explosive with him as the starting quarterback doing the passing and Rayven at running back, like he was in last year's championship season.

The fact is, Lanigan was probably the better pure passer at the pre-season workouts. So, if the East system was going to be similar to last year's, when Neary's passing was the mainstay of the attack, Lanigan at quarterback might be the best bet. But by the time official pre-season practice started in August, Centore had decided Deoliveira's double threat option of either passing or running could make the Thunderbolts one of the most explosive teams in the state once again this season. So, Centore made Deoliveira the starting quarterback right from the start of pre-season practice. Now it was Deoliveira's chance to be the person in the spotlight every Friday night.

Rayven Deoliveira's life had not always been easy. Without a father on the scene, it had always been Leroy watching out for Rayven, as if his older brother was the only person Rayven could really trust. Sports had been their salvation. Leroy had graduated from La Salle in the spring of 2018, and he had talked about going to Florida to be a walk-on candidate for a Division I football program. But when practice started for the 2018 high school season, Leroy was still in Rhode Island. He had delayed going to Florida, or anyplace else, so he could be at all of Rayven's games that fall. He couldn't leave his younger brother in what would be the most important season of Rayven's life.

Everybody knew Rayven had talent. But would he use that talent to try to do too much by himself at quarterback? He had become a star last fall. Now the question was could he also become a leader?

"He definitely has all the tools. We just have to get him seeing the field the way the coaches want him to see it. We have to have him thinking as a quarterback," Alex Corvese had said to me at practice one day in late August.

Adopting a Football Family

There are few members of this year's team who have dreamed about playing for Cranston East more than Jarrod Clowery.

Clowery parents are divorced, and he had been living with his mother in North Smithfield, a small town in the northern Rhode Island. North Smithfield is one of the whitest communities in Rhode Island. According to a Providence Journal story in the fall of 2018, the North Smithfield population was 96.6 percent white. So Clowery, a 6'2", 225-pound white kid, blended in perfectly with his North Smithfield elementary and junior high classmates as he was growing up. But Clowery's father lives in Cranston, and Jarrod always wanted to play for the Cranston East football team

"My older stepbrother played for East. I would sit on the bank up there with my father watching them practice and would dream about when I would play for East," said Clowery, pointing to the bank on the side of the practice field.

Part of it was East played in Division I, the highest level competitive-wise of Rhode Island high school football, while North Smithfield High plays in Division IV, the lowest level. Clowery liked the idea of the tougher competition. But there was something more about East. Even though he had grown up in a lily-white community in a wooded area of northern Rhode Island, Clowery liked the diversity of the Cranston East football team. He liked the idea that there were so many kids with different backgrounds coming together every morning at school.

It's rare for a sixteen-year-old kid who has grown up in a primarily white suburban community to understand that learning with—and from—these kids can make for a special school. Maybe it was because his stepbrother had told him stories about how much he enjoyed being with all different types of kids at East, or maybe he wanted the challenge of playing Division I football rather than playing in Division IV. The bottom line is Clowery wanted to play at East. So, he went to live with his father so he could be part of the East football team. It was a higher level of football—a better test of his football talent—and now he has come to believe football has also made him a better student.

"I was never a great student growing up. I was okay, but I never cared that much about school," Clowery admitted. "But being part of this team has taught me to focus a lot more. I'm a lot more disciplined student now than I was a few years ago."

He had played youth football growing up in North Smithfield, so even as a child he had heard the old sports cliché about a sports team being a family. But he didn't really understand it. Growing up you went to a game, played a game with your friends (in North Smithfield youth football, his team usually lost), then you went home.

But now, after two years playing for Cranston East, he was starting to understand what being a member of "football family" means. Clowery had injured his shoulder in a scrimmage during the second week of practice, so if he wanted to, he could have gone home after school and played video games every afternoon. Instead, he's standing on the practice field sidelines with his arm in a sling yelling to his teammates on the offensive line to "work it" as they hit the five-man blocking sled.

"I'm probably going to need an operation after the season, but the doctor thinks I can come back for the rest of this season next week," Clowery declared. "I have to be out here with these guys."

Nobody hopes Clowery is able to be back on the field this season more than Tom Centore.

"We really need Jarrod out there. He's got good size, and he really worked hard this summer. When he gets back, I think we will have one of the better lines in the state," Centore said, in an anticipative tone.

A No-No Any Day

"You just earned yourself ten pushups the hard way," Ken Simone yelled in a disgusted voice to a young sophomore player of color when Simone heard the player utter the N-word while standing on the sidelines with a few teammates during a drill.

It wasn't a racial slur aimed at a teammate; it was just a naïve teenager trying to create some humor by repeating a word that was part of some rap song.

"You can say a lot of things on this field, but that is the one word you can never say on this field," Simone said, as he stood watching the player do ten pushups while facing one direction, then jump up and do ten more while facing the other direction.

"They have no historical perspective of what some people went through so that word wouldn't be part of our vocabulary," Simone offered about the teenage players. "I am hearing it more and more from kids in school. They hear it in their music. If I called somebody on it every time I hear it in school, that's all I would be doing all day. But out here on this field, you're not going to hear it in any context."

Rayven Deoliveira was standing on the outer edges of a group of players watching the sophomore do his pushups.

"That word is not even in my vocabulary anymore," Deoliveira declared.

He Needs a Game Plan

Jamari Mason loves football, and since he first put on a helmet and shoulder pads when he was about ten years old, he has dreamed about playing Division I college football. A young man of color of Cape Verde ancestry, Mason moved to Cranston from Providence when he was in junior high school, and football has been his passion. He's now a senior, and by Rhode Island standards, he is very good football player. A linebacker, last season he was named to the *USA Today* Rhode Island All-State team.

"Jamari is a special type of player. He knows the game better than most high school players, and he's always in the gym working out," Ken Simone offered.

But Mason is only 5'9", 175 pounds, and you don't find many 5'9", 175-pound Division I college linebackers. That hasn't lessened Mason's college dreams, however. A mention in *USA Today* last season as a Rhode Island All-Stater got him a perfunctory recruiting letter from the University of Massachusetts during the summer. They offered Mason two free tickets to a UMass home game this fall if Mason drove to the game on his own expense. It's the type of recruiting letter Division I college teams send to any player in their geographical region who has received some media attention. But nobody on the UMass coaching staff had followed up the letter with personal contact. So, despite not having had any direct contact with the UMass coaching staff, in Mason's mind, he is being recruited by the University of Massachusetts.

But while Mason is concerned that a college coach will notice how well he beats defensive ends on the edge en-route to sacking a quarterback, Tom Centore is more concerned about another of Mason's tendencies. Over the past year, more than once Centore has told Mason he needs to improve his "C" academic average if he hopes to academically qualify to play college football. But football is the only thing on Mason's mind as he begins practice for his final season as a high school football player.

"I keep telling him he needs to have a plan for his future, but he loves football so much that's all he wants to think about," Mason's mother told me one day as she sat at Cranston Stadium watching East playing a controlled scrimmage.

CHAPTER IX

SAFE AND SOUND ON THE
CRANSTON EAST PRACTICE FIELD

Chance McKinney is a speedy senior wide receiver who, only a few weeks into his first season at Cranston East, is showing he could be a major contributor to the Thunderbolts' offense this season. Tom Centore isn't surprised McKinney has been a welcome addition to his team. Last year, McKinney was a junior at Central High School in Providence and a member of the Knights football team.

"I remember him when we played Central last year," Centore offered about McKinney. "He was only a junior, but he stood out."

McKinney had been a Providence kid his whole life. But his single mother wanted her children living in a safer environment than she felt the streets of Providence offered. So, even though it meant taking her son away from his friends in Providence, she managed to rent an apartment in Cranston, literally across the street from the three-building municipal complex on Park Ave. that includes Cranston High East, Cranston City Hall, and the Cranston School Department building.

Initially, the move wasn't an easy transition for McKinney. He was playing football just like he had done at Central, but his new team was different. At Central, virtually the entire football team was faces of color, including McKinney. But at East, there was a mixture of facial complexions. At first McKinney didn't feel as comfortable at East as he had been Central. But since official football practice started in late August, McKinney started feeling more comfortable; he was sharing a common purpose with the seventy or so other varsity guys, most of whom he hadn't known just a few months earlier.

On the afternoon of September 6, McKinney was with his new teammates running drills on the East practice field. The practice field is about 50 yards from Cranston Street, a two-lane road that runs from Cranston straight through the West End of Providence, right by the Central High football practice field. At the same time McKinney was getting ready for practice with his Cranston East teammates, about three miles away in Providence, William Parsons, a fifteen-year-old Central High sophomore, was shot and killed on the sidewalk outside Central High. The shooting took place while hundreds of students were being dismissed from school for the day.

Providence police quickly revealed Parsons' death was a case of mistaken identity in a gang-related shooting. The suspected killer was arrested within a few hours. The shooting, which was witnessed by hundreds of Central students, took place only about 50 yards from where McKinney's former Central football teammates were walking out of their locker room on the way to their practice field. McKenny's practice facility at Cranston East may have been only a few miles away from the Central practice facility, but in a sense that afternoon, McKinney was a world apart from his former teammates.

"I knew him," McKinney said of Parsons the day after the young man was murdered. "He wasn't one my real good friends, but I know a lot of his friends. Everybody said he was a real good kid."

He Missed His Family

One day after practice, as most of the players were heading to the parking lot to board the bus back to school, Isaiah McDaniel stood in the middle field talking to the four team captains. Apparently, the young man who'd had his mother turn in his uniform a week earlier because he had not been named a captain, wanted to return to the team. He's no longer concerned about not having a captain's "C" on his game shirt. Now he just wants to be on the team, back with his football family. McDaniel explained that a lot of what happened about the kid quitting had to do with the player having been prescribed an incorrect dosage of some medication he was taking.

"They think everything with his medication has been straightened out, and he should be fine now," McDaniel told the captains. "He wants to come back with the team."

Tom Centore definitely wants the player back on the team. Centore was upset when the player first quit because he felt the kid needed the camaraderie this team offers. To Centore, the problems with the medication were further proof that this is a young man who needs teammates to help him navigating the challenges of young adulthood. But while Centore has the final say on any team decisions, the Thunderbolts are a family, and family decisions should be shared. So Centore asked McDaniel to talk to the team captains for their feelings on allowing the kid back on the team.

Before McDaniel even completed his explanation of the young man's situation, all of the captains had started nodding their heads to signal their approval of the player rejoining the team. But while the captains have empathy for the young man, they want to make sure he understands being a part of the Thunderbolts comes with a price tag for everybody.

"As a senior, of course we want to see him play," said Rayven Deoliveira. "But we all have problems, and we didn't quit," Deoliveira continued. "We want him to have a chance to play, but he shouldn't just move right back into the scheme of things."

McDaniel looked at the four seniors with an expression of gratitude and quickly assured them that regardless of a player's situation off the field, playing time on this team is earned on the practice field.

"Don't worry, he's not moving right back into a starting spot," declared McDaniel. "He's going to have to work to play."

His Mother Finally Said He Could Play Football

Noah Berg is a 6'4", athletic white kid who lives on the fringe area of Edgewood, near the Providence city line. Berg played for the East varsity basketball team in his first two years at East. Now a junior, he also wanted to play football when he first came to East, but his mother didn't want him to play.

Some of Berg's friends, who played football, had been talking to Noah's mom about letting her son join the football team. Apparently, Berg's friends were good salesmen because Berg's mother finally agreed to let her son try football in the fall of 2018.

Nobody was happier to see Berg at one of the midsummer workout sessions than Tom Centore. An athletic, well-coordinated, 6'4" kid walking the halls of a public high school is proverbial catnip to a high school football coach. Not only was Berg a well-coordinated athlete, but he was also a polite, likeable kid. For two years, occasionally Centore would talk to Berg about the possibility of becoming a football player when the coach would see the young man in the East hallways or when Berg visited the Guidance Office for some academic need. But every time Berg would say his mother was worried about her son getting hurt playing football. That's why Centore was shocked when he saw Berg at a workout session.

"I couldn't believe it when I saw him at one of the workouts this summer," said Centore. "I asked him, 'What are you doing here?' He said, 'I'm going to play this year, but you have to talk to my mother.' All of a sudden, I saw his mother walking across the field. I know her. She's a lovely lady. The first thing I said to her was, 'I can't promise you he isn't going to get hurt.'"

It's a Different Game Than Your Father's Football

Despite Tom Centore's informing Berg's mother that "he couldn't promise her that her son wouldn't get hurt," there's no question by the start of the second decade of the 21st century, the question of football safety had become a vital part of the American sports conversation. Some parents, especially mothers, had come to fear they were putting their sons at danger by letting them play football.

The suicide death in 2012 of former NFL All-Pro linebacker Junior Seau, who spent the final four years of his twenty-year NFL career playing for the New England Patriots, initiated much of the conversation around the country. The dialog intensified with the release of the movie *Concussion*, starring Will

Smith in 2015. So, by the fall of 2018, for several years, mothers' fears of injury to their sons, especially head injuries, had been chronicled in the media as one of the major reasons for the decline of American high school football participation over the past decade. All of which makes it difficult for a mother of a teenage boy to make a decision on whether she should allow her son to play football.

These days, unlike in virtually every other sport, mothers are in unknown territory when trying to connect with their son's desire to play football. For decades through the 1950s, '60s, and '70s, unlike American fathers, the vast majority of American mothers had no personal connection with their son's experiences playing for any high school sports team. For the most part, girls growing up in the first seventy years of the 20th century didn't get to play high school sports.

That all changed, of course, with the passage of Title IX in 1973. By 1978, there were about two million females playing high school sports in America. So, by the mid-1980s, thousands, maybe even a million, of the girls who had been part of that early wave of Title IX high school sports participation were mothers of high school athletes. For the first time in American history, mothers had a direct connection with their children's experience of being a high school athlete.

Unlike their mothers, most of whom never had a chance to play high school sports, these women could relate to the feeling of camaraderie of team members joining together in a quest for an athletic achievement. For some, they could even dream of possibly taking their athletic talent to a level beyond high school. Many could also now understand the mental anguish, along with the physical pain, of an athletic injury. While some people may argue that boys' and girls' high school sports are played at the different levels, basically a girl playing high school soccer or high school basketball confronts the same type of skill and coordination training and game strategy that a boy playing those high school sports does. Even through baseball and softball may have different methods on how the ball is delivered to the plate, the concepts of the two games are the same. So, millions of 21st century mothers who played these games during their high school days have, at least, a direct conceptional understanding of what their sons and daughters are experiencing in their high school experiences playing those type of games.

But football is different. There is no direct correlation between any of the well-established girls' high school sports and football. There's no girls' high school sport that has the constant physical contact of football; the concept of eleven players each having a specific assignment on every play in every game; the concept of learning how to get back up after being physically knocked to the ground during a practice drill; or the camaraderie created by sixty to seventy varsity team members coming together every afternoon to work toward a common goal.

And while there may be a few girls who played high school football according to the National High School Federation, even in 2018 there were only 2,400 females among the 1,008,417 American high school football players. That's only about 2 percent, and it's a safe bet the number of female high school football players was even lower in the '90s, when many of the mothers of today's male teenagers were in high school. So, millions of women who have had the experience of being a competitive varsity high school athlete have no personal understanding of football mentality. That can make it a difficult call for those mothers to sign the permission slip to let her son play football.

"Kids Are Lazy Today"

"Why are fewer and fewer kids playing football these days?" I asked Robenson Antoine one day after practice.

Every week, there seemed to be another national media account on how fewer American teenagers were playing high school football. I knew Antoine wouldn't have any problem giving me an answer. Robenson has an answer for everything, and he's never afraid to tell you what he thinks about his own ability, as well as the world around him beyond the football field. That's why it's always interesting talking to him.

A lot of high school football teams have a kid like Antoine. He can be a coach's consternation because he never stops talking—even when the coach is trying to command the attention of the team. But if he has a likeable personality, like Antoine does, and also a great natural talent—like Robenson's passing-catching ability—a coach may take the kid's loquacious personality with a grain of salt.

Antoine is also a very astute young man. He's not a high honors student, although he probably could be if he put a little more time and discipline into his academic assignments and test preparation. But he does okay in the classroom. He has made the honor roll most marking periods during his high school career. Just like his two older sisters have done, Robenson will go to college. With his academic record, he will not need a college football coach to plead his case with the admissions office at most New England state universities or small state colleges. But even if he doesn't need a coach's help with admissions, Antoine thinks he wants to play college football. So, I suspected he probably had been paying attention to the national conversation about the reduction in high school football participation. I wanted to know what he thought was the reason. Was it the head injury issue that has been the catalyst for the national conversion, or was it something else?

Like I expected, Antoine had an incisive answer.

"Kids are lazy now," he said, in a blanket condemnation of his generation.

"Look, kids still want to be part of something. But football taught me if you want to be part of a football team, you have to work for it. Football is hard, physical work. Some kids today want to be part of it—they just don't want to do the work."

"So, is the declining football participation a question of a fear of head injury or a reflection of a generation that wants to spend more time in front of a video game screen than on a football field?" I asked.

"Football can be more aggressive than other sports," Antoine summarized. "You can get in somebody's face in football. But that's why football is a brotherhood. It makes everybody closer."

CHAPTER X

THE MVP OF EVERY HIGH SCHOOL TEAM

"This team is very important to this school," Cranston East principal Sean Kelly offered about the Thunderbolts football forces one day in early September.

Dedicated, inspiring teachers are paramount in a student's quest for a high-quality education. But at the high school level, it's the principal who plays an unmatched role in creating a learning community that touches countless aspects of students' lives. A high school principal needs to be a creative, innovative, and supportive instructional leader for a school's faculty, but the principal also needs to demand accountability from teachers.

A public high school principal these days needs to be well versed in educational philosophy, financial management, as well as governmental rules and regulations. But maybe, as much as anything, a high school principal needs to understand, inspire, and be a cheerleader for his or her school's students. If you had to name the one person who plays the biggest role in American public education at the secondary level in the 21st

century, it's the high school principal. All of which explains why Sean Kelly is an outstanding public high school principal.

In the fall of 2018, Kelly was beginning his 10th year as Cranston East principal. When he was named principal in 2009, he was only thirty-eight years old. At the time, that was extremely young for a high school principal in Rhode Island, especially at a school as large as Cranston East. Similar to Tom Centore's high school days in Johnston, the Cranston East of today is not reflective of Kelly's upbringing. Kelly grew up in Smithfield, a middle-to-upper-middle class suburban town in northwestern Rhode Island. Like most of the towns in the northwest section of Rhode Island, Smithfield is, and always has been, a predominately white community.

According to the latest census estimates, 93 percent of Smithfield's 21,000 residents are white, while only 3 percent are Hispanic or Latino, and only 1.1 percent are African American. So, Kelly, a white kid, fit right into his neighborhood when he was growing up. But like Centore in his role as a football coach, in his role as a principal, Kelly hasn't allowed the limited exposure to a diverse community of his youth prevent him from taking on the challenges of changing student demographics at East over the past decade.

Kelly did not play football in high school. He actually played soccer at Hendricken, the private, parochial high school sports powerhouse in Warwick, RI. But as a sports fan, Kelly understands the excitement and appeal of football. These days, football, far and away, is the country's most popular sport, especially at the high school level. Even though participation in high school football has been dipping over the past decade, the participation in 2017 of 1,006,000 players was above the level of a generation ago. In the 1998 season, there were "only" 983,625 students playing high school football in America. As an education administrator, Kelly knows how valuable a football team can be in uniting a diverse high school like East.

"It's a team with a lot of players on the roster that mirror the make-up of this school in the country's most popular sport," Kelly offered about the East football team. "A lot of kids go to the games. It's a way of bringing all of the students together in a fun environment."

Football Always a Bridge

Football has always been something that bridged a common interest in a conflicting American society. Even in the turbulent 1960s—when "The Generation Gap" between the "Baby Boomer" twenty-year-olds and their parents' and grandparents' generations had produced national social warfare—Americans found a common ground in their love of football. Author George Howe Colt noted in *The Game*, his 2018 book centered around the legendary 1968 Harvard-Yale football game, that, "At a time when an understanding gap has frequently separated alumni from students, football has provided a bridge of common interest. The Hawks and Doves nested side-by-side in the Yale Bowl."

A little over a half a century later, in the fall of 2018, that hadn't changed. Football is probably not the sport of family heritage for most of the 38 percent of Cranston East students who declare themselves Hispanics/Latino, but it's the sport today's high school kids watch on TV every weekend; play with their "Madden" video game; and—if they are in New England—use their smartphones to keep abreast of the Tom Brady phenonium. High school football provides the local common ground. It's where high school students can sit with their friends and watch their classmates on autumn Friday nights. It's All-American.

Today's teenagers going to watch their high school football team play a game can generate the same excitement, the same sense of school pride for the kids whose great-great-grandparents migrated to American from Italy and Ireland 100 years ago as it can for the kid whose grandparents, or maybe their parents, came to America from the Dominican Republic a decade ago.

"Some people who could go to East attend a private school instead because their parents are scared off by the diversity here," said Sean Kelly. "But then, for some people, the diversity is a big reason they choose East."

So, in Kelly's role as the high school principal, football is more than just touchdowns and tackles. At East, it's the blending of cultures in a common experience. But Kelly also knows that the state championship banner, which was hung on the gym wall following the 2017 season, is significant, too.

"The success helps the image, too," Kelly said, with an expansive smile.

Let the Games Begin

The town of Barrington is the most affluent community in Rhode Island. A town of 16,000, it is located along the east side of Narragansett Bay, with a plethora of beautiful million-dollar homes located on large waterfront lots. Located only seven miles from Providence, it's the bedroom community for leaders of the Rhode Island business and medical communities. It has the highest medium household income of any Rhode Island city or town, and in 2018, the average home price in Barrington is $425,000.

In a state where a majority of public school education is funded by cities and towns, rather than the state, it's not surprising Barrington has one of the best public school systems in Rhode Island. In almost every survey of Rhode Island public high schools, Barrington High is ranked either one or two academically. Virtually every year, there are several members of the Barrington High graduating class who head off to Ivy League schools, including several student-athletes.

When Hendricken and La Salle, the two large Catholic schools in the state, began dominating the top level of Rhode Island high school sports around the turn of the 21st century, rather than trying to out-market the private schools by promoting the academic and athletic benefits of public education, most Rhode Island public high schools simply conceded that they couldn't keep pace with the private school athletic powers, but not Barrington. The people at Barrington High aggressively took on the private schools in the battle to keep the best student-athletes living in the town, going to the town's public high school.

With its economic status, it's not surprising Barrington constantly had some of the state's best boys' teams in the so-called "country club" sports, like golf and tennis, and some girls' sports, like field hockey and lacrosse. But in 2005, after playing in the lower-ranked football divisions for decades, Barrington announced it wanted to move up to the state's top football division and play against the top teams in the state, including the private school powers.

Some people were surprised Barrington thought it could play Division I football. After all, most of the Division I schools had much larger male student enrollments than Barrington, and Barrington was certainly not a school with a diverse student enrollment. According to the 2010 census, 94 percent of

Barrington's approximately 16,000 residents were white, with less than 1 percent African American. It was a safe bet those figures would not change substantially when the 2020 census was tabulated. Barrington is basically a white, suburban town.

But, thanks to an outstanding youth football program, which coordinated its playing style with the high school coaching staff, in only its second year of Division I competition, Barrington won the state's major football title. Four years later, in 2009, the Eagles won the state title again. Coming into the 2018 season, that 2009 Barrington title marked the last time a public school had won the major Rhode Island high school state football title.

But Bill McCagney, a former Barrington High football star, who had championed the move to Division I and coached the Eagles to both the 2005 and 2009 state titles, retired as the Eagles head coach after the 2016 season. Also, like a lot of affluent northeastern cities and towns, the intense discussion of the potential head injury issue was having an impact on Barrington football. As Barrington came to Cranston Stadium on Sept. 7 for a Friday night non-league game that would count on the team's overall record, but not count in the tabulation of points for playoff consideration, there was talk about the Pop Warner youth football program being disbanded in Barrington.

"We are hoping even if they don't have a tackle league that they will have a touch football program," Steve Lenz, one of the veteran Barrington assistant coaches, offered about the future of Barrington youth football.

No Respect

There was nothing mellow or composed about Tom Centore's voice as he spoke to the Cranston East football team before the Thunderbolts boarded the bus for the half-mile ride to Cranston Stadium for their non-league game with Barrington. Centore felt his team was being disrespected, and he was upset.

"This team has only lost two regular season games in three years, but nobody gives you any respect," shouted Centore to the seventy-some varsity players standing in full uniform in the parking lot behind the high school ready to board the bus.

"Look at the state football preview in today's paper. You were a regular season co-champion last year, and the DI state champ, but they didn't even mention you as one of the top teams in the state this season. This program deserves respect, but nobody is going to give it to you. You are going to have to earn it, and that starts tonight."

Centore was right that in a preview story in the *Providence Journal,* Rhode Island's only state-wide daily newspaper, the writer had not mentioned Cranston East. That irritated Centore because in a poll of Rhode Island sports media members, which included writers and sportscasters from weekly newspapers as well as TV stations, East had been ranked third, behind only Hendricken and La Salle, the state's two private school powers. But Centore had been looking for something to shake-up what he felt had been a sense of complacency at many early season practices. That lack of recognition in the state's major newspaper gave it to him.

"Three private schools and North Kingstown, a team that hasn't even played in Division I for seven years, were mentioned before you," Centore offered. "You're playing for respect tonight."

It had been a tough week for Centore. He had suffered a slight seizure—or possibly a panic attack—on the sidelines during the previous Friday night's twenty-four-minute exhibition scrimmage against La Salle. Monday was Labor Day, so he couldn't see the doctor until Tuesday, forcing him to miss practice. Fortunately, the tests didn't show any serious heart problems, but his own health condition wasn't Centore's major concern. Earlier in the week the doctors had finally agreed, against their recommendations, to release Tony Centore from the hospital so he could go home. But the doctors told Tom Centore there was nothing more they could do to extend his father's life. In essence, they told Tom Centore they were sending his father home to die.

You could tell Centore was a man whose nerves were frayed at practice Wednesday. Shortly after the start of practice, a player had come up to Ken Simone and asked if the assistant coach had a spare mouthpiece because the player had forgotten his at home when he rushed out to school early that morning. At most schools, retrieving a spare mouthpiece would simply require the player to walk into the equipment room in the nearby school building and grab a mouthpiece from the locker room or equipment room. But there's no nearby equipment room at the East practice facility. The East equipment room is better than a half-mile away back at the school. So, unless one of the assistant coaches had stockpiled some mouthguards in the little concrete building at the far end of the field, which served as the storage room for the hydration cart and a few items used at practice, there was no easy access to a mouthpiece—one of the basic pieces of equipment for a football player. Just one more example of the tribulations the East football team deals with compared to most other teams.

Centore had seen the player asking for the mouthpiece, and from the expression on his face, it was obvious he was upset one of his players might miss some valuable practice time because of a lack of preparation. But Centore wasn't going to let a teachable moment for the whole team be wasted by his knee-jerk reprimanding of one player. So, he waited until later in the day when he called the team together for the usual end-of-practice talk.

"Guys, you have to be ready," Centore calmly said, after calling the team together at the end of practice. "You have to be prepared. Pack your bag with the things you are going to need for practice the next day, the night before. Don't be doing it at 7:30 in the morning at home, when you have to be in homeroom at 7:45. That's what life is going to be about. You are going to have to be prepared."

In an era of "snow-plowing" parents—who are constantly trying to clear obstacles out of the path of their teenager's journey toward future success rather than letting the kid forge their own course—football is the sport where attempts at parental hand-holding are basically fruitless. Every day on the football practice field, there is no parent to offer help or advice when their son is faced with a new or different challenge. No parental hand-holding when a kid has to get ready to play a different opponent on Friday night.

It can all be accomplished, of course, but you have to be prepared.

Another Day, Another Problem

Tom Centore had missed two practices this week because of his own—and his father's—health needs. But now he was here trying to get a young team to understand, despite all the success of the past few years, that nothing comes automatically in football.

Centore was concerned about whether Rayven Deoliveira could execute the game plan as a quarterback. He also worried about how the defense would play with Jamari Mason, Mack Hanley, and Jarrod Clowery all standing on the sidelines with injuries.

On Tuesday afternoon, in one of the final plays of practice, Mason had twisted his ankle in one of the little holes found all around the practice field. He had left the field saying he didn't think it was anything serious. But before he was even off the field, he was on his cell phone calling his father. Wednesday morning in school, he had told Centore he would be late for practice because he was going to have the injury checked. Late Wednesday afternoon, he walked onto the practice field with the ankle in a boot. He said it wasn't anything serious, but he wouldn't be playing Friday night. There were a lot of things weighing on Centore's mind, but most of all he was questioning whether he was making a mistake even being at the game.

"I'm not sure my father will make it through the weekend. I probably shouldn't even be here tonight," Centore said to me, as we headed toward one of the buses for the short ride to the stadium.

The Coach Was Right

Tom Centore knew what he was talking about a few days after the first practice of the season when he had said to me, "I'm worried what some of these kids will do when things go bad—and things will go bad this year." Centore knew missing some seniors from last year's team, especially a couple strong linebackers, would hurt this season. But he probably didn't think things would go bad so quickly. Some strong running by Rayven Deoliveira, combined with nice pass receptions by Robenson Antoine and sophomore Eric Thomas, and the Thunderbolts had started the game with touchdowns on its first two possessions. But just when it looked like the Thunderbolts would put the game away early—like most East fans had expected—the East defense made some mistakes on critical downs. Twice the Thunderbolts allowed the Barrington quarterback to escape from potential sack situations for long gains on third and long situations. At halftime, the game was tied, 20–20.

Centore wasn't happy about the lapses of concentration as he addressed his team at halftime.

"You have given them confidence," Centore said, in a disgusted tone. "A team that didn't think it could play with you—you are giving them confidence that they can play with you."

At times throughout the second half, it seemed East was going to break the game wide-open. Early in the third quarter, Antoine gave the Thunderbolts the lead when he grabbed a long right-sideline pass from Deoliveira and broke into an obviously untouchable sprint to the end zone. Unfortunately, he was so untouchable that even before he crossed the goal line, Antoine broke into a taunting waving of the ball toward the Barrington players following him up the field. The premature celebration caused one of the officials to throw an unsportsmanlike penalty flag before he even signaled the touchdown. The 15-yard penalty would be assessed on the ensuing kickoff.

Centore couldn't believe what he was seeing. Thanks to Robenson's lack of focus, rather than having momentum completely on its side after Jon Loy's conversion gave the Thunderbolts a 7-point lead, Barrington would be taking back the momentum with good field position on the ensuing kickoff.

"This will not happen again," Centore bellowed about the lack of discipline and focus. It didn't help Centore's state of mind when, added by the good field position on the kickoff, Barrington quickly scored a touchdown and tied the game again early in the third quarter.

Finally, midway through the fourth quarter, East regained a 7-point lead. Then the Thunderbolts' defense finally made a big stop, creating a Barrington fourth and nine from the East 20 with two minutes to play in the game. Hold Barrington to less than 9 yards on one more play and this nightmarish game would finally be finished. But this time, the East defense allowed the Barrington quarterback to make a quick cut on an option-right, and the QB breaks between three potential tacklers into the end zone for the touchdown. A few second later, Barrington adds the conversion kick, and the game was going into overtime.

In high school football overtime, each team is given four downs to score from the opponent's 10-yard line. If the first team scores a touchdown within its first four plays, it can either kick or run the conversion, but regardless the other team has four chances to score.

It probably wasn't surprising with the way momentum had shifted in its favor that Barrington won the coin at the start of the overtime, and it only took the Eagles three plays to score the tie-breaking touchdown. Barrington booted the conversion and took a 7-point lead. But East responded immediately when it got the ball and scored a touchdown on only two plays. Giving the option of forcing the game into a second overtime period with a Jon Loy conversation kick or going for the win with a 2-point conversion, Centore didn't hesitate going for the win. The gamble paid off when Deoliveira rolled to the right and kept the secondary honest by looking toward Antoine, who was heading toward the right corner of the end zone. But rather than pass, Deoliveira made a nice cut to the left that opened a clear path for him into the end zone for the 2 points.

Tom Centore had a solemn look on his face as he began to address the seventy or so varsity team members, all of whom were kneeling on one knee in the north end zone a few minutes after East had survived its erratic performance.

"Congratulations," Centore said to his team, after the nail-biting victory in a game most people felt East would win easily.

"Never, don't celebrate a victory; no matter how it was done," Centore proclaimed.

Some coaches who felt their team had delivered an erratic, error-prone performance like East just had, might have dedicated his post-game remarks to the negative aspects of the game rather than applauding a victory. But Centore never underestimates how much a victory can mean to some of his players. He understands for some of them, the football field is the only place they are experiencing success right now. So Centore never wants them *not* to celebrate a victory. It's the reward for a team coming together to accomplish something. But Centore is trying to create a culture of high expectations, so he wants the players to understand more is expected from them.

"This team can play a lot better," Centore declares. "We have a lot of work to do."

Ken Simone suddenly injects a challenge.

"I will give you the things that need to be done, but you have to be willing to work," Simone offered.

This is a team where everybody is expected to share in the glow of victory, but also accept the reasons for a sub-par performance—including the head coach.

"It may be my fault," said Centore. "I wasn't here sometimes this week. I couldn't focus as much on getting you ready with everything going on."

CHAPTER XI

A MAN OF FAITH

Sunday morning, Tom Centore called to tell me his father had passed away late Saturday night.

Antonio "Tony" Centore was a man of great faith. Centore's faith wasn't just a Bible-thumping religious brand of devotion—although he did attend Catholic mass every Sunday morning. The genesis of Centore's faith was his fidelity to the young people he worked to help throughout his life.

Centore, who spent sixty-seven of his ninety years on earth as a high school football coach, had grown up amidst the jewelry factories and manufacturing plants that was Providence, Rhode Island in the late 1930s and early '40s. His father had immigrated from Italy, met his wife in America, and began raising a family in the heavily Italian Broadway section of Providence. Tony played high school football at Central High in Providence in the late 1940s, shortly after the end of World War II. He had loved football since he was a little kid growing up on the neighborhood sandlots. When he was in high school, he was a 5'8", 140-pound defensive end. Maybe that's why Centore loved football so much. He treasured the idea that a little guy could make a meaningful contribution to his team's success if he was willing to work hard and paid attention to the details of the game that the coaches preached.

Centore's parents never attended college, but from an early age they had instilled in young Tony the idea that knowledge derived from education provides the power that can be used to improve yourself—and help others. So, after high school, Centore enrolled at nearby Providence College with the ambition of becoming a teacher.

Providence College, which had fielded a collegiate football team in the 1920s and '30s, had disbanded its varsity football program by the time Centore was a PC student, but that didn't keep Tony away from the football field. Even while he was college student, Centore was going back to Central to serve as a volunteer assistant football coach. After college, he served in the U.S. Army during the Korean War, then returned to Rhode Island where he got married, started raising a family, and began a teaching career in the Cranston public school system. Of course, he also immediately resumed his career as a high school football coach, which he had started when he was in college.

In Centore's mind, the discipline, camaraderie, and life lessons that are so important in the late teenage years of a young man's life couldn't be learned in any sport—maybe in no other facet of life—like they could be on the football field. He served fifteen years as a Cranston High/Cranston East assistant coach from the late 1950s to the early 1970s. And while Centore may not have been the head coach during that period in his career, there was never any question he was a man who exhibited an enlightened dissection of the complexities of football.

Beyond the ability to conceptualize the Xs and Os into a successful game plan, he was a man who cared about others—especially young people. That made him a good teacher—and a good coach. In the midst of teaching teenagers how to play a game—probably without most of his players even realizing it was happening—Centore was teaching young men how to have purpose and how to learn values that could rule the decisions they made throughout their lives. Through his personal example of hard work, every afternoon at practice he also inspired young men to develop a passion for something that could push them toward reaching goals.

Through his players during his tenure at Cranston East, Centore witnessed what some historians feel was the most dramatic changing of American society over the past century. He went from coaching teenagers during the Cold War and the Space Race of the late 1950s; to the first wave of Baby Boomers and their inclination to question authority in the mid-1960s; to coaching in the late '60s and early '70s when he saw some of his players go off to war in Vietnam shortly after they graduated from high school.

He was the type of man who could yell at a player in the middle of practice for poor footwork during a drill or a half-hearted effort pushing the sled, then after practice quietly counsel the same player individually on a personal or academic concern. He never changed his personal core values of faith, responsibility, trustworthiness, loyalty, self-respect, and optimism. Yet, maybe because he was a history teacher, he understood that the mores of a generation could change without changing the basic character of a young person. That ability to understand the societal changes throughout his life became the mantra of his coaching career over seven decades. It was the coaching creed Tony Centore passed on to his son, Tom.

"He changed with the times," Tom Centore had said about his father when we talked a few weeks before the start of the season. "Some people aren't able to do that," Tom continued.

"But my father could. That's why he was able to remain in coaching for so long. He understood times change."

A husband and father who raised four children with his late wife Mildred, Tony Centore was one of those unique individuals who understood that if you want to help young people, you have to understand young people, regardless of how old you are. He was a teacher/high school guidance counselor in Cranston throughout his entire fifty-three-year career as an educator. But in 1973, he left the Cranston East football coaching staff to join the staff at Johnston High, the town where he lived with his family. In 1979, he became the Johnston head coach and held that position for twenty-three years.

Centore loved coaching in Johnston, a middle-class town of just under 30,000, with a heavy Italian population. The Johnston kids were Centore's type of players. They were hard-nose kids, many of whom were the sons of blue-color workers who weren't afraid to adopt the "bring your lunch pail to work every day" playing philosophy that Centore preached. Through the years, Centore's teams won some championships and had some outstanding individual talent, including his son Tom, who was an All-State quarterback and defensive back in the 1980s. But for Tony Centore, nobody was ever bigger than the team, not even his son.

He coached high school football players through the turbulent '60s, the psychedelic '70s, the disco '80s, the digitalized '90s, and into the 21st century. In his mind the times—not the kids—change. He never lost faith in the promise young people offered, even if at times some of his peers in education and sports were declaring America was doomed because of the youth of the times. For decades he used the game of football to show young men that sometimes it's hard to control your actions when you are full of emotion, but that's what you need to do. It's what football teaches. It's a lesson learned for a game, for a season, and hopefully, for a lifetime.

A Life-Long Mentor

Through the decades, there have been numerous pieces of literary composition, movies, and TV productions dealing with the relationship between high school football players and their coach. With the physically demanding nature of football, a sport where the "be a man" mentality has been a creed for some high school coaches over the generations, it's probably not surprising that many of those works were tales of a love/hate relationship. In 2003, author John Grisham diverted from his usual legal thriller genre to write *Bleachers*, a story of former high school players who returned twenty years after they graduated to attend their legendary former coach's funeral. One of the questions the story centered around was this: "Did Eddie Rake's players love him or hate him?"

That was never a question asked about Tony Centore. His players loved him. Even when they were teenagers playing for him; even when he was yelling at them for a missed blocking assignment, they seemed to understand he was a man of conviction and compassion. He was a coach who influenced generations of players, imparting values that became part of their moral DNA.

The answer to the question of how much a high school football coach can mean in a man's life was on full display in a Providence funeral home on Wednesday, Sept. 9. Men now in their forties, fifties, sixties, and even a few in their early seventies, who once had played for Tony Centore, came to pay their final respects at Centore's wake. The former players, along with educators and family friends, stood for close to an hour in the long line that stretched out of the funeral home and onto the sidewalk of the adjacent street. Many of the former players were big men now, well over their high school football playing weight, but they were still one of "Coach's Boys."

Most probably hadn't thought a lot about their high school football days over the decades; life brings other responsibilities and priorities. But as they moved close to the casket, their faces told how much Centore meant in the lives. There were looks of sadness that prompted some grown men to raise a hand to rub an eye that was on the verge of tearing. They all have their own stories of their days playing for Centore. Some were simply tales of carefree teenage years, when nothing was more important than playing a football game on Friday night or Saturday afternoon, then hanging out with their girlfriends and some teammates in the parking lot of the Newport Creamy in Cranston or the Howard Johnson's across the street from the Johnston Town Hall.

But for others, Tony Centore was so much more than "just" a football coach. Centore was a man who imparted lessons of character and trust, at a time when it would have been easy for things to have gone the wrong way in some players' lives. But their lives turned out well, and as they walked toward Centore's body ,they realized "Coach" had played a big role in their successes.

"He changed so many lives, including my own," wrote one of his former Johnston players in the funeral home's online guest book. The former player went on to write about an episode in a game, decades earlier.

"You could have scored, if you ran," Tony Centore had yelled at the player, implying that a little more effort on the player's part would have produced a touchdown.

"I was never good at football, but those words and so many others have stayed with me throughout my adult life, encouraging me to work just a little bit harder," the former player wrote. "He was a great influence and role model."

About an hour after the wake had started, two school buses pulled up in front of the funeral home. About seventy teenage boys, all wearing their white Cranston East football game jerseys, filed out of the buses and joined the line heading into the funeral home. Earlier in the afternoon, those same players had been on the East practice field preparing for their first official league game of the season the upcoming Friday night at Cranston Stadium.

Because most of the players didn't have use of a car, Isaiah McDaniel and Ken Simone had asked principal Sean Kelly whether the school department could provide school buses to take the players to the funeral home for the wake, about fifteen miles away in Providence. Kelly, along with the city athletic director Mike Traficante, made sure it happened.

So, Wednesday, immediately after school, the players boarded the bus for the usual daily commute to the practice field. Then, after about ninety minutes of warm-ups, a few drills, and playbook run-throughs, they rode the bus back to the school, changed from their practice gear into their school clothes, donned their game shirts, and boarded a bus again for the trip to Providence. They walked into the funeral home led by their team captains.

The seniors who had been with the program for four years—guys like Hector Duran, Quinn Lanigan, Robenson Antoine, Mack Hanley, and Jamari Mason—had fond memories of their freshmen and sophomore years when they would talk to "Mr. Centore" at practices, as Tony sat in the used golf cart his son had bought so his father could be "on the field" during practice.

Some of the younger players hadn't actually spent much time with this coaching legend because by the 2017 season, limited mobility had forced Tony to sit in a chair well away from the field, or in Tom's car, during the practice session. So, attendance at the wake was not a mandatory team requirement. But Monday after practice, when Simone and McDaniel asked the team who wanted to go to the wake Wednesday afternoon, every varsity player said they wanted a seat on the bus.

Some people might have thought it was a strange sight, with seventy or so high school football players, about two-thirds of whom were faces of color, standing in a long line for a chance to knell and pay their respects to a little white man. But if you understood Cranston East football, there was nothing strange about it. That little man in the coffin was the father of their coach—the coach of the coach. He was the man who had inspired Tom Centore to be a football coach, to be a coach who cared about every one of his players as a person—not just a football player.

That's the Cranston East football family.

CHAPTER XII

A DIFFERENT JOURNEY

Tony Centore was laid to rest Thursday morning. Several of his former Johnston players were part of the contingent that carried his casket into the large Roman Catholic church. Mourners filled every pew and stood along the side of the church walls as several hundred people came to honor a man who had dedicated his life to helping young people in his role as an educator and football coach.

Tom Centore knew his father had lived a long and fruitful life, and no son ever did more to make his father's later years meaningful than Tom. Over the last year, even after his father could no longer stand along the sidelines during practice making meaningful contributions as a member of the coaching staff, Tom makes sure that somehow his father was brought to the practice field so Tony could feel he was still part of the team.

Later in the season, when it became too cold for Tony to be outside on the sidelines at practice, Tom brought his SUV up near the field and kept the car running with the heater on for the entire two-plus hours of practice so Tony could sit and watch the practice session. Even right up to the final weeks of Tony's life, if there was anyplace Tom was going, any errand he was running where he could take his father along, Tony would be riding "shotgun" in the passenger seat, even if it meant more work for Tom.

For about forty-five years, ever since Tom was a little kid running around at the Johnston practices, Tom and his father shared their love of football. But, over the past three decades, they also shared a tragic memory no father and son should ever have to endure. By the time they were in kindergarten, Tom and his twin brother Tim were going to their father's Johnston High football practices every afternoon. Their mother would pick up the two boys at their elementary school, drop off them off at football practice, then they would spend the entire afternoon being around a football field with a bunch of teenage boys. The two boys would then drive home with their father to their family dinner. It was an idyllic way for two athletically-inclined young boys to spend their autumn afternoons.

"It was a great way to grow up," Tom Centore once told me.

Both the Centore brothers loved sports and played all the typical youth sports together while they were growing up. As they grew older, it was obvious Tom was the better athlete; and by the time the two brothers had reached high school, Tom had become a great football player. But Tim still loved football, and his strong intellect made him a great student of the game. So, when they were in high school, Tom was the star player, and Tim was the Johnston High football team's chief statistician as well as the quasi-team sports information director. Every weekend, Tim would call the Johnston football scores and statistics to newspapers and TV stations throughout Rhode Island.

Some brothers might have been envious of their twin getting all the media attention while he was relegated to reporting the results. But Tim Centore seemed to relish helping bring attention to his brother's achievements, as well as his father's team's victories. Tim had also inherited the family characteristic of wanting to help people. Like his brother, Tim had attended the University of Rhode Island, and like Tom, he became a teacher immediately after he graduated from college. With his family background, it probably wasn't surprising Tim was a born teacher. Intelligent, personable, and with an innate desire to help young people, Tim became a well-respected, public middle school science teacher in North Kingstown, a large suburban town in the South County section of Rhode Island.

But one afternoon in the spring of 1991, as he was driving home from school, a speeding car sideswiped Tim's car on the highway, causing Centore's car to flip over. Tim Centore, age twenty-four, died at the scene of the accident. Tom Centore had started coaching junior varsity baseball in Cranston that spring, and in an era before cell phones, he didn't learn about his brother's death until he reached his parent's home, where he and his wife were also living.

Does a father ever completely recover from the loss of a son? Does a brother ever get over the loss of his brother, especially a twin brother? Tony and Tom Centore were together almost every autumn afternoon for twenty-six years following Tim's death. How often, through all those fall afternoons together with one of his sons at football practices, did Tony Centore look at Tom and think, in a sense, that his son Tim was also still part of his life?

Conversely, spending autumn afternoons at practices and Friday nights or Saturday afternoons with their father was a shared treasure of the Centore brothers' childhood. How many times over the years after Tim's death, when a Johnston or Cranston East team experienced a big moment on the football field, did Tom look at his father and think it was more than just one son celebrating with their father?

Tom Centore knows his father's memory will always be with him—every time he steps on a football field. But Friday night, just over twenty-four hours after he laid his father to rest, Tom Centore would be stepping onto a football field and know—for the first time in his life—he will not share the experience with his father.

The Coach Influenced His Boys

It's said imitation is the sincerest form of flattery. That may explain why several of Tony Centore's former players are now high school football coaches.

Even in a state as small as Rhode Island, it was a little ironic that Tom Centore will begin his journey of coaching without his father playing against a team coached by one of his father's former players.

Dino Campopiano was one of the former Johnston players in the long line at Tony Centore's wake on Wednesday night. In a sense, Campopiano, who played at Johnston in the late 1980s, was a Tony Centore clone. He's a little guy, only about 5'7", who used football to prove it's not the size of your body but the size of your heart that can determine who you are.

Campopiano was a star running back and defensive safety in high school and went on to play Division III college football. Like his high school coach, Campopiano also always liked to help people and—like Tony Centore—Campopiano felt teaching and coaching could be the best way for him to fulfill his mission in life. He got a job teaching in the Pawtucket, R.I. public school system after graduating from college in 1995, and a year later, he also became the head football coach at Shea High.

Shea is one of the two public high schools in Pawtucket. Pawtucket is a city of 71,000 that calls itself the Birthplace of the American Industrial Revolution because Samuel Slater built the country's first fully mechanized cotton-spinning mill there in 1793. Pawtucket was a prosperous "mill city" in the early part of the 20th century, with a host of large textile and manufacturing mills. In many ways, Pawtucket is like a lot of northeastern cities that saw its economic life-blood dry up when the textile industry moved to the South following the Great Depression of the 1930s. But unlike many of those old northeast mill cities and towns, Pawtucket has retained much of its industrial base into the 21st century, with many of those old mills refitted for other manufacturing purposes.

So, Pawtucket, which borders on the north side of Providence, still has a significant manufacturing presence. In fact, Pawtucket is the home of Hasbro, one of the largest toy and game manufactures in the world. But "prosperous" is no longer an adjective associated with Pawtucket. In 2018, downtown Pawtucket, which once was the city's center of social activity with shopping and entertainment, is now a study of needed urban redevelopment with vacant storefronts and once classic architecture having given way to the wrecking ball.

Shea is a classic case of a northeastern urban high school that underwent a tremendous demographic change over the second half of the 20st century. The high school, which was called Pawtucket West High from the early 1940s until the late 1960s, is located in a residential section in the western side of the city, only a couple of hundred yards from the line dividing Pawtucket and the historic—and upscale—East Side section of Providence.

Shea High is only a few miles directly down the street from the Ivy League Brown University campus. The five-block area of Pawtucket that separates the high school building and the Blackstone River, known as Oak Hill, is mainly composed of well-maintained colonials and capes and has long been considered the up-scale residential section of Pawtucket. So, it's not surprising that during the decades of the 1940s, '50s, and '60s, the student body of Pawtucket West was primarily white kids. But in the early 1970s, in an effort to create more racial balance in the school system, the city changed the lines that determined which of the city's two public high schools a resident would attend. The line was moved so that both of the city's two low-income housing developments were in the Shea High district.

Combined with a flight of many white, blue-collar workers from the industrial city to surrounding suburban communities in the 1970s and '80s, the face of the Shea school community of today has changed dramatically from what it was when the school was called Pawtucket West. These days, not a lot of the teenage residents of Oak Hill attend Shea. Today Shea's student body is more than 70 percent minority. In the fall of 2018, African American and Hispanic students alone accounted for 68 percent of the Shea student body.

The transition of Shea to a minority school was mainly completed by the time Campopiano was named head coach in 1996. Coaching a football team at an urban public high school that's more than 70 percent minority, and where 69 percent of its students receive a free federal lunch compared to a state average of 43 percent, is definitely a challenge. But Campopiano has relished the opportunity to be a coach and a mentor to young men. Like Tom Centore, Campopiano certainly didn't grow up receiving first-hand exposure to diversity. Campopiano's teammates on his Johnston High football teams of the late 1980s were virtually all white guys, many of Italian heritage. But a chance to be a teacher and a football coach brought Campopiano to a city school where, these days, about 90 percent of his football players are young men of color. But in two-plus decades at Shea, once again Campopiano has proven it's a person's heart and not his face that makes him a winner.

While Campopiano is certainly working with a different demographic set on his Shea teams in the second decade of the 21st century than Tony Centore was in the 1960s, '70s, '80s, and '90s at Cranston and Johnston, Campopiano is passing on the same core values of hard work and respect for fellow teammates that Campopiano learned from Coach Centore back in the 1980s. By the fall of 2018, Campopiano was so highly respected by the Pawtucket school department directors that, in addition to being the football coach, he had been the Shea Dean of Students for a decade.

Beating the Opposition—And the Odds

During Dino Campopiano's tenure as Shea's football coach, his teams have compiled extremely impressive win-loss records, mainly at the Division II level of Rhode Island high school football.

But it's more than just wins and losses. Like hundreds of other urban high school football coaches around the country, Campopiano has made the Shea football team the family a lot of kids on the team don't actually have. They are teenagers, many of whom come from single parent families, often led by a mother or grandmother. Sometimes the player is also one of the family's top breadwinners with his part-time job at McDonald's or Dunkin Donuts.

"These kids have a lot of obstacles to overcome, and they don't let those obstacles get in their way of being a successful football team," Campopiano once told me.

"These kids have it different than when I was in high school," Campopiano continued. "When I was in high school, I didn't have to work; my parents picked me up from practice and brought me home for a family dinner. Most of the guys on this team have to walk home after practice or even walk directly to work. They teach me things."

By Rhode Island standards, Shea High is a mid-size school enrollment-wise, with about 800 students. But despite only being a mid-size school, Shea football's impressive win-loss record over the previous eight years had earned the Raiders a—not necessarily welcomed—promotion up to Division I, the top level of Rhode Island high school football for the 2018 season. Sure, Shea teams always seem to have had good speed, and they have a reputation for always being a hard-working team. But football is a game of numbers, especially at the public schools. The more students you have in the school, the better chance a coach has of having a decent number of big bodies to fill those offensive and defensive line spots.

In its ninety-year history of high school football going into the 2018 season, Pawtucket West/Shea had never played in Division I. But for scheduling purposes, the Rhode Island Interscholastic League needed a team to fill out a 14-team Division I season schedule. So, using a formula based mainly on past records, Shea was moved up to Division I.

The feeling among many of the state's football coaches, however, was that an urban public school of only about 400 boys would have a tough time competing in a division with three private schools, as well as the larger public schools. It didn't take Shea very long to disprove that assumption Friday night against Cranston East. The Raiders quickly jumped out to a 7–0 lead in the first quarter.

Meanwhile, Cranston East's season fortunes also suffered a serious blow in the opening period when Jarrod Clowery came to the sideline holding the same shoulder he had been standing on the sidelines holding in a sling every afternoon at practice for the past two weeks. Clowery had only be given the medical okay to play a few days earlier. But on the first series of the game, he made a move with the upper part of his body in an effort to get past a Shea blocker. It was the type of move he'd probably made hundreds of times over the past few years, but this time he immediately knew something was wrong. An excruciating pain suddenly cut through his shoulder. It was the same pain Clowery had felt a few weeks earlier, but this time it was definitely more severe. So, he walked to the sideline holding this arm.

Trainer Kate Chaffee met Clowery before he was even across the inbounds line, helped him to the bench, and started checking the shoulder. Clowery sat on the bench, trying not to let his facial expression reveal the pain he was feeling. Finally, the trainer walked off to Tom Centore, uttered a few words, then headed back and put her arm across the back of Clowery's broad shoulder pad.

"Sorry," she said.

This time, there was no need for Clowery to ask any questions about how bad it was or how long he would miss practice. When the doctor had cleared him to play in Friday's game, he had warned Clowery that if he injured the shoulder again, he would be facing season-ending surgery. Now Clowery knew his season was finished—before it really got started.

He moved down toward the end of the bench, behind where the other players were standing along the sideline watching the game action. He buried his head in his hands trying not to let his teammates see the tears escaping from his eyes.

He might be a hard-nose, "in the dirt" defensive lineman, but how could he not be trying to hold back tears? He had dreamed about being a starter on the Cranston East football team since he was that little kid sitting on the hill at the practice field. He had even left his childhood friends in a comfortable, sheltered hometown of North Smithfield, where virtually all the kids were lily-white like him, to enroll at the most ethnically and racially diversified high school in the state, just so he could play for the Thunderbolts football team. He was loving every minute of the experience, both on and off the field. Even though he hadn't been able to practice for two weeks, he had been at practice every day. He saw what was happening, saw that some of the other underclassmen the coach had hoped would step right and fill the void created by the graduation of last year's starter weren't catching on as quickly as the coaches had hoped. He knew with the work he had done over the summer, his game had improved to the point where he could seriously help the team this season. Over the past few weeks, as he stood on the sideline watching some unimpressive line drills during practice, he had even heard some of the coaches quietly say, "It will be better when Jarrod gets back."

Now Clowery's season was finished—a season when the team of his childhood dreams needed him even more than the coaches had expected. Sure, he's a junior, so he would have another season in 2019. But when you are sixteen years old, and your dream has been snapped away from you on a freak play, it's tough not to cry—even if you are a 225-pound defensive lineman.

Hail Mary or Field Goal Attempt

A pair of touchdown pass receptions by Robinson Antoine enabled the Thunderbolts to come into the second half deadlocked at 14–14. East even forged a 23–20 lead in the third quarter. But all night the East defense had been making mistakes in key situations. Shea had overcome its third quarter deficit with an early fourth quarter touchdown. Then the most frustrating East defensive miscue of the night came midway through the fourth quarter. The Thunderbolts had the Raiders in a fourth-and-nine situation near midfield, but on the fourth-down play, the Thunderbolts' defensive unit let a Shea running back break free right up the middle on a 45-yard touchdown run.

"We told him right where to go," Ken Simone screamed about the coaches' instructions to one of the Thunderbolts defensive linemen.

"But he goes the other way leaving the hole wide open," Simone added in a disgusted tone.

The missed assignments, along with what Tom Centore felt were a few bad calls by the officials, and the stress of his father's death, literally brought Centore to his knees early in the fourth quarter. When Isaiah McDaniel looked to his right and saw Centore drop to his knees along the sidelines—Centore's face a ghostly shade of white—McDaniel immediately signaled for a call to be made for the fire department's rescue squad. Two weeks ago, at the Injury Fund 24-minute exhibition game against La Salle when McDaniel had seen Centore suffer a momentary seizure, McDaniel was scared. He had wanted Centore to call for medical attention at that time, but Centore had said no. Now McDaniel was panicking.

Once again, Centore had regained his footing and told everyone he was fine. But this time, McDaniel wasn't taking any chances. He had the officials stop the game while the trainer checked Centore's vital signs. The rescue squad arrived while the trainer was checking Centore, and despite the coach's insistence that he was okay, the paramedics insisted the coach sit on a stool while they performed further tests. Watching this transpire from a few yards away out on the field were a stunned group of East players. Two days earlier, the entire team had marched into a funeral home to view the body of their coach's father. Now they were watching their coach sitting on a bench on the sidelines being treated by several paramedics.

McDaniel and the city's athletic director wanted Centore to leave the field in the rescue squad to be checked out at the hospital, but Centore said, "No." He wanted to stay with his team. Eventually the paramedics consented to letting Centore remain at the field as long as he agreed to stay seated on the stool with a paramedic standing next to him. But Centore had to remain at the far end of the coaches' box while Simone and McDaniel moved up and down the sideline calling the plays.

Another fourth quarter touchdown gave Shea a 10-point lead with less than half of the fourth quarter remaining. But as if the game were being scripted by some Hollywood screenwriter, the Thunderbolts staged a late comeback. With Isaiah Daniel running back and forth along the sideline to check with Centore on almost every play-call, the Thunderbolts methodically marched down the field.

Quinn Lanigan completed the drive when he raced into the end zone after making a great catch of a Deoliveira pass along the left sideline. Jon Loy followed with the conversion boot, but East still trailed by 3 points, and time was running out. Shea had been ripping off big gains on the ground all night, and now all Dino Campopiano's team would need to do following the kickoff would be just pick up one first down. That would give Shea enough downs to run out the clock without East ever getting the ball again.

But an East defense, which couldn't seem to make a big stop all night, made three consecutive key stops after the kickoff, forcing Shea to punt with just over a minute to play. East would have one final minute to at least get close enough to try for a tying field goal and send the game into overtime. After all, they'd won last week's game against Barrington in overtime. That was a game that never should have been that close, but it was, and Cranston East won. Maybe that's going to be the mantra of this year's team—bend, but don't break. They will let underdog teams push them farther than they should be pushed, but in the end, the Thunderbolts will win.

After a good Shea punt, East eventually took over the ball on its own 25-yard. Seventy-five yards for a game-winning touchdown or between 40–45 yards for a legitimate shot at a game-tying field goal, and less than a minute to go.

Centore sat on his stool a few yards back from the field at the white line, which signified the end of the 50-yard coaches' box that runs along the sidelines in the middle of the field. It's where Centore would finish the first official game that would count in East's quest to repeat as a champion; the first game in Tom Centore's coaching career that he wouldn't have his father with him at the game, or least be able to go home and talk to his father about how the game.

Isaiah McDaniel was standing a few yards into the playing field near the 50-yard line relaying the play to quarterback Rayven Deoliveira, but while Centore had put McDaniel in charge of the team, on virtually every play, McDaniel looked at Centore for some type of collaboration. But Deoliveira was doing an excellent job taking the Thunderbolts up the field with some good running yardages before going out of bounds to stop the clock, or quick slant passes to the sideline that also stopped the clock. The Thunderbolts picked up a couple of first downs as they drove the ball into Shea territory.

The Cranston East fans were on their feet, verbally expressing their affection of Thunderbolts football. But when an East pass on a third-and-six from the Shea 30 just slipped out Robenson Antoine's hands, with only a few seconds to play, the game had come down to one play.

Do you hope Deoliveira can produce some type of "Hail Mary" 30-yard touchdown play to win the game? Or do you try to kick what would be about a 44-yard, game-tying field goal and send the game into overtime? East had used all its time-outs. The clock did stop after the incomplete pass, but the officials were about to spot the ball and signal for the clock to start running. That meant the Thunderbolts only had twenty-five seconds to get the play off.

McDaniel quickly moved down to Centore sitting on the stool. Obviously, they both had been thinking the same way. Expecting a 30-yard touchdown play on the final play of the game was a desperation call, especially since East did have two decent place-kickers.

"Go for the field goal?" Centore said, in a tentative tone of voice as McDaniel approached him. McDaniel nodded his head, but immediately the assistant coach had a second question.

"Who?" McDaniel asked Centore.

That was the dilemma. Jon Loy was "Money in the Bank" when it came to conversion kicks. During the 2017 season, Loy had successfully converted 42 of 50 conversion attempts. But Loy had never proven he had the type of "big leg" that could boot a 44-yard field goal.

David DaSilva was a junior who, for the previous two years, had been one of the top players on a very good Cranston East boys' soccer team. But before the start of this season, DaSilva had told Centore he also wanted to kick for the football team, which he could do under a relatively new R.I. Interscholastic League dual sport participation rule that allowed student-athletes to play for two teams in the same season. So, DaSilva had been coming to some football practices, and he had shown he had a powerful leg. The coaches quickly decided the best chance for a 44-yard field goal was with DaSilva doing the kicking.

DaSilva's kick cleared the line-of-scrimmage and floated straight toward the middle of the uprights. The Cranston East fans, still on their feet, held their collective breath. Had their Thunderbolts done it again, delivering on a late-game clutch play? But from his berth on the stool on the sideline, Tom Centore was worried. He knew while the kick was straight, there might be a question of whether it was long enough. It was so close to the crossbar, even the officials standing behind the goal post moved up a little closer to get a better view of whether it passed over the crossbar.

From the stands, the fans couldn't really tell. Even some of the players standing on the sidelines didn't have an accurate view. But then, one of the officials standing behind the goalpost started crisscrossing his arms in front of him, signifying the field goal attempt was no good. Cranston East had lost the first game of the season that counted in the standings.

CHAPTER XIII

"WE WILL WORK IT OUT"

It was about four o'clock Monday afternoon, and Ken Simone was standing in the middle of the practice field making mental notes of which players were walking down the hill from the parking lot after they embarked from the practice shuttle bus. Simone, Isaiah McDaniel, and a few of the other assistant coaches had dissected film of the Shea game with the varsity starters for about an hour after school, but everyone was anxious to get out on the field. That tends to happen when a team loses a game. You want to get right back on the field as if you can make immediate amends for the loss.

Simone knew it was going to be a strange day at practice, maybe even a strange week. Even though Tom Centore had seemed fine by the time he left Cranston Stadium Friday night after the loss to Shea, East principal Sean Kelly had told Centore he couldn't go back on the field for either practice or a game until he had undergone a complete medical work-up—from a cardiologist, not just a trainer.

"He was trying to get an appointment with a cardiologist for this afternoon, but he might not be able to see a doctor for a few days," Simone offered about Centore. "We don't know when he will be back."

Friday night—in a short meeting with the team on the field after the game—Centore had declared, "Maybe this is my fault." Along with dealing with his father's death, now Centore was also placing the blame for the team's disappointing performance on his failure to be there for his players last week. Centore had missed practice every day last week, dealing with his father's funeral arrangement. But despite not having input from Centore, McDaniel and Simone had put together a good game plan for Friday night's game. If the players had focused on their assignments, especially the defense, the Thunderbolts' offense would have controlled the game. But in his post-game speech, Centore had given his players an out—putting the blame for the poor showing on his own shoulders. But Centore left them with a challenge.

"We have a lot of work to do. Now I'll be there to help you, but only you can decide if you're willing to do the work," Centore had declared after the game.

But now it's Monday afternoon, and Centore isn't here— and nobody is sure when he will be back.

Friday night, the Thunderbolts had lost a game nobody thought they would lose. "What happened?" was a common question on social media sites like Facebook and Twitter. Ken Simone thinks he knows the answer.

"They were fatigued," Simone offered about the team's starters. "When they become fatigued, they cannot mentally engage in the game. They lose the ability to focus on executing the game plan."

It had only taken a few games for the glaring weakness of the 2018 Thunderbolts to become evident—lack of depth. Despite having basically the same number of players on the team as last year, there wasn't the same number of "football players" this season. Being a "football player" isn't just about wearing a uniform or even about purely physical talent. It's about being able to carry out assignments; about understanding the concept of a play; about a sense of knowing in which direction the play will go as soon—maybe even before—the ball is snapped. Innate athletic talent certainly helps, but much of what makes a teenager a "football player" is experience, and this year's team doesn't have much experience at some of the key defensive positions.

"Last year we only had three or four guys who needed to be on the field all the time," said Simone. "It's starting to look like this season, we are going to have seven or eight guys who we are going to need all the time. That's why some of these guys are getting tired quickly. Every injury will be magnified this season," Simone added, with a painful expression. "I don't like to rely on one player, but we are going to have to rely on Jamari a lot. If he goes down again, we are in trouble."

Mack Hanley was standing on the sideline, his arm in a cast, but the constant positive attitude of the kid from Edgewood was on full display.

"We will work it out," said Hanley. "That's what we do here."

Thank God for Grandmothers

If you check the biographic profiles of every NFL roster, there's a good chance there will be at least one player on each team who has or had a matriarch like Dayshaun White's grandmother. Each one is a story of a courageous women who, for a variety of reasons, took over directing the life of their grandson.

White is a 6'4", 245-pound senior lineman and one of the four co-captains of the 2018 Thunderbolts. Five years ago—when White was a middle school student—if you had asked anyone who knew him at the time whether they thought one day Dayshaun would be the captain of a high school football team, laughter probably would have been the kindest response you would have received.

"My eighth grade was terrible," White told me one day after practice. "I was suspended so many times. They said they were going to press charges against me unless I went to a different middle school in a different town."

White now realizes he was an angry young man when he was growing up in the nearby town of West Warwick. A young man of color, he always seemed to be living in a home where turbulence was the only constant. His mother and father always seemed to be arguing even before they split up when White was about ten years old. Complicating the situation was that, according to White, both of his parents had been in prison at times. Even White's introduction to organized sports had been perpetrated by one of his parents' run-ins with the law.

"I started playing football in the sixth grade, but that was only because my dad was in jail and he wanted me to play sports," said White. "I had never played sports. I was a big kid, and I couldn't even do a push-up. But I was thinking if my dad gets out, he can come and watch me play. I wasn't that good; it was more to just make him happy. Also, my parents were splitting up, so I figured if I was playing a football game, they would come to the game and be together."

He was living with his mother while he was attending middle school, but then she was arrested, forcing White and his younger sister to live with their father and his girlfriend. It wasn't a good situation.

"We were living with my dad, and my dad was arguing with his girlfriend, so he was leaving the house," White related.

One day, White's father put Dayshaun and his younger sister in a car and took them to their grandmother's house in Cranston near the Providence city line. There were no plans made for his father's return to pick them up.

"Literally we just got dropped off at my grandmother's house. So, the next day she went out and bought us a bed," White said in a matter-of-fact tone, as if that was a common occurrence for all pre-teen children.

"It was the best thing that could have happened to us," White offered about he and his sister being entrusted to his grandmother's care. "She provides us with everything we need."

His grandmother provided both a place to live and the stability in his life that White had never known.

"It was my grandmother who straightened me out. My grandma took me in, and she taught me to be wise, to listen to people who were trying to help me," said White.

People like his football coaches.

White hadn't played football again since that one year when he was in the sixth grade, but when he enrolled at East as a freshman in the fall of 2015, he noticed a lot of guys were playing for the freshman football team. He realized that despite all the turmoil surrounding his life, that one season of youth football were some of the most enjoyable months of his childhood.

"I said to myself, you know football was fun when I played. Let's try it again," White related. "I tried it, and I loved it."

But White was still an angry young man the first year he was wearing a Cranston East uniform.

"Dayshaun was a dickhead in his freshman year," said Jamari Mason. "He screwed up in school. On the field, he just tried to beat up people. Now he's thinking about what he is doing on the field. He's getting good marks in school. Since his freshman year, he has had a good cum."

Through football, Centore and the other coaches showed White a new way to think about his day-to-day life. Being part of a team, especially this team with so many different types of guys, gave White's life purpose in everything he did. It wasn't just on the football field. It was everything, everywhere, because it all centered around being part of the team. If you want to be part of a successful football team, you have to think about the team at the same time you are thinking about yourself. You are the team, and the team is "We, Not Me."

"Football saved me," said White. "The things the coaches were saying were pretty much the same things my grandma was saying, just in a different way. Now football is my life."

In varying degrees—and under a variety of different situations—it's what high school football does for hundreds, probably thousands, of teenage boys around the country every year. It's the concept of showing up for practice every day and taking on the challenges of that day knowing it is going to require a lot of tough physical work. It builds self-esteem because it's something you chose to do while a lot of your fellow male high school classmates are spending their autumn afternoon sitting at home "gaming" with electric devices. Most players probably don't even think much about it, because for them football is fun. But that taking on the responsibility of showing up every afternoon helps build discipline and self-esteem. It develops a sense of structure, something that all teenage boys need, but especially a kid in a problematic family situation like White.

"I had a whole new mindset," White offered about his approach to life after joining the football team. "Coach Centore taught me every day you have to go to practice. Football players have a different mindset because of the discipline you need in a tough physical game."

White then looked out toward the practice field.

"It sucks," White declared, as he flashed a wide smile to let me know he was being sarcastic.

"You are running every day; it's terrible for a big guy like me. My lungs are this big," White said, as he expanded his hands beyond both sides of his broad chest. "To do that every day, it trains your mindset. You have to work toward something. Coach Centore helped me learn that."

It's that daily high that a football practice can give a kid, along with a new sense of self-awareness and purpose. For a kid like Dayshaun, having that sense of purpose is magnified. It doesn't matter what the socio-economic situation is, some kids can be good at finding the wrong people to associate with. In the perfect scenario, it's the parent's job to keep a kid from steering toward those bad influences. But if there are no parents, or even if the parents are there, but having their own problems, finding that positive purpose can be a challenge for a teenager. Who is going to steer them in the right direction? For thousands and thousands of American teenagers, it's a high school football coach, like Tom Centore.

"It's more than just playing football," declared White. "You are going to come out of high school with many skills. But it's also important about the mindset you come out of school with, and that's what football helps you develop."

Generations of former high school football players have claimed that relationships built on the football field are unlike teammate relationships built in any other sport. White definitely believes that, and he also thinks his football relationships are unique because he has experienced them while wearing a Cranston East uniform.

"We are from so many different back grounds, but we are all about discipline," White offered about his East teammates. "Our coaches are all about discipline. You have to do it the right way. You can't let another team distract you from doing it the right way. I think those are important skills to have," White said. "I'm not sure that happens everyplace. Other places you just do what you have to do to win a football game."

For Ken Simone, watching White's personal development over the past four years has been one of the great rewards of coaching. "He was in a shitty situation, but now he's one of the ones who can make it," said Simone. "He's actually a good student, which is a miracle considering the situation he grew up in. It's a lot of credit to him—and his grandmother."

Like most kids with a tough backstory for whom football has helped, White is not headed for the NFL. Maybe, with his size and, if he keeps improving, Centore might be able to get a coach from one of the numerous New England Division III colleges to take notice. But even if he doesn't attract a college coach's attention, his improved academic performance has possibly put White into position to be admitted to University of Rhode Island, under the University's special academic talent development program.

White knows his future prospective has changed, and he thinks he will be ready for college in large part because he has spent the past four years at Cranston East.

"These days, colleges are trying for diversity in its student body. For kids from some of the schools we play—like Portsmouth, Cumberland, and (Cranston) West—when they get to college, diversity is going to be like a whole new world for them. But it's just going to be continuing everyday life for me," White offered.

"East, in general, is all about that diverse culture," White added. "It's about what you are going to learn from different people; what different skills and aspects of life you learn from them. I don't think the people in Cranston have any idea of what it's really like at East."

The Coach Is Back

It rained heavily Tuesday, so there was no practice, just film sessions with the assistant coaches. By Wednesday afternoon, Tom Centore was back at practice. He had cleared the battery of tests; the doctor told him nothing heart-related had caused the light-headedness at Friday night's game, which dropped him to his knees. Centore rationalized that because he had been trying to work out at a local gym a little more the past few weeks, maybe the upper body weight training had tightened up his chest muscles. That was possible, and along with his still thinking about his father's death and his team making a lot of mistakes, he probably wasn't paying attention to staying properly hydrated. Whatever it was, at least now he wasn't worrying about a heart attack so he could get back with his team.

Wednesday was a Jewish holiday, which in Cranston means no school. So Centore was worried there could be some players who would have a problem getting to practice because most of them don't have cars. So, the coach was pleased when he started taking a head count, and there were more than sixty varsity players on the field. There was a lot of work that needed to be done. They needed to get the defensive front-five a lot more aggressive and more disciplined on their option assignments—and there wasn't a lot of time. They had lost a game at home Friday night, and now this Friday they were going on the road to play against the most individually explosive quarterback in the state.

The Best Rhode Island Has to Offer

Portsmouth High's Kyle Bicho was the proverbial naturally athletic kid. On the Portsmouth football roster, he was listed as a 5'10", 190-pound quarterback and linebacker, but he was also one of the best high school baseball players in Rhode Island. On the football field, he could do it all—run and/or pass the ball on offense and make the key tackle or big pass interception on defense.

In the fall of 2017, he had quarterbacked the Portsmouth football team to a berth in the Division I football Super Bowl against Cranston East by passing for 2,500 yards, including 27 touchdown tosses and running for 13 touchdowns in only 11 games.

Cranston East had rolled to a 42–28 victory in that 2017 title game, but it certainly wasn't a lack of effort on Bicho's part that kept the state title plaque out of the Portsmouth trophy case.

"Bicho was great in that Super Bowl last year," said Ken Simone. "We kept scoring, but he kept coming back. Just when you think you have stopped him, he finds a way to run past you or get the ball to a receiver. It is going to be really tough to stop him; our defense will need to play a lot better than they did last Friday night."

But Simone was starting to see reason for optimism. Practice had been going well. Maybe the guys were starting to focus after the turmoil that had been going on the past two weeks, with Tony Centore's death and the loss to Shea.

Unfortunately, it was almost as if Simone had a premonition about this being a cursed season. Practice was drawing to a close. There were just a few more drills to complete when Jamari Mason seemingly just grazed his shoulder against another player's shoulder pad as Jamari ran past him in a drill. It wasn't much of a hit, but when practice finished, Jamari came to the sidelines saying his shoulder hurt. Before he even left the field, Jamari was on his phone calling his father telling him what happened. The next day, Jamari was not at the start of practice.

"He is having his shoulder checked out," Simone offered about Mason's absence.

Midway through Thursday's practice session, Jamari came walking onto the field with his right arm in a sling.

"They said it's a tear in my shoulder. I'm out of tomorrow's game," Mason declared.

Ken Simone stood off on the sideline as Mason stood on the field talking to some of his teammates.

"It's going to be a problem," Simone said about playing Friday night's game against Portsmouth without Mason. "I'm not superstitious, but maybe there is something about this being a jinxed season. What else can go wrong?"

CHAPTER XIV

GRIDIRON AMERICANA

The Portsmouth High School football team has Americana stamped all over it. The Patriots home field is the John F. Kennedy Memorial Field; the school colors are Red, White, and Blue; and in addition to cheering wildly for their football team, Portsmouth fans take immense pride in the school's marching band, which performs at every home football game. The town's youth football program—which also sports red, white, and blue uniforms—practices right next to the high school field. Young Portsmouth football players can see their dreams playing out less than 100 yards away from them at practice every afternoon.

And if that isn't enough to make the Patriots the northeast version of America's high school team, for several decades, some of the players who have helped Portsmouth become a Rhode Island high school football power were the sons of U.S. Military officers who were attending the nearby Newport Naval War College.

A town of 17,000 located on Aquidnick Island along the shores of Narraganset Bay, and only few miles from historical Newport, Portsmouth had become a highly desired East Bay bedroom community by the 1970s. Large plots of early 20th century farmland had been turned into extensive, upper-middle class housing developments, and by the turn of the 21st century, Portsmouth's public school system was considered one of the best in Rhode Island. Every extracurricular school event, from the Friday night football games to the student arts festival, is well staffed by an army of parental volunteers. It wasn't coincidental that as the town became an upscale Newport bedroom community in the 1980s, the town's public high school football program became one of the best in the state.

For decades, Portsmouth played in the lower divisions of Rhode Island high school football because of its smaller enrollment. But the Portsmouth program continued improving throughout the 1980s, so in 1991, the Patriots were moved up to Division I, the top level of Rhode Island high school football. They proceeded to win three straight major state championships from 1991 to 1993 and have stayed competitive ever since.

Several of the Portsmouth players from those championship teams in the '90s went on to play DI college football, including Mike Cloud, who became an All-American at Boston College. He later spent six years playing in the NFL for the Chiefs, Patriots, and Giants. Cloud was a face of color, but he was one of the few faces of color in the Portsmouth football program through the years.

Portsmouth, R.I. is American suburbia at its whitest. In the 2010 federal census, 95 percent of Portsmouth's 17,000 residents were classified as white. The demographics hadn't changed much in 2018, so it was a sharp contrast between the collective faces of the Cranston East and Portsmouth football teams as the Thunderbolts and Patriots warmed up for Friday night's game.

Make Or Break Game

In a state where it's only about sixty miles from the northern-most point in the state to the southern-most point, the thirty-mile ride from Cranston East to Portsmouth, which includes traversing into Massachusetts then back into Rhode Island, is a long school bus ride. Tom Centore sat in the front seat of one of the two team buses not saying much. It was only the second game of the season, but Centore knew this night could make or break the season. The Thunderbolts had already lost a game nobody had expected them to lose, and they still had to play Hendricken, the state's perennial powerhouse. They also still had to play North Kingstown, a veteran team some people were saying might be the second-best team in the state behind Hendricken. Also, this year the regular season schedule, which would determine who makes the playoffs, had been reduced from last season's eight games to only seven games.

Now, East had lost one of those playoff consideration games, and probably the top two ranked teams in the state loomed farther down the road. Lose tonight, and the Cranston East season could be over before the calendar turned to October.

Tom Centore knew Portsmouth would be missing a few starters because the players had been injured in an auto accident the previous week, and also the Patriots still might be getting accustomed to a new coach. But Portsmouth had the best quarterback in the state—a player who had shown he could make things happen. So far this season, nobody wearing a Cranston East uniform had been making many good things happen.

Portsmouth would also be on its home field with a big crowd. Plus, tonight East would be missing Jamari Mason, the kid Ken Simone called a "special player," on defense, and the player who had sacked Becho four times in the 2017 Division I Super Bowl.

Just before the Thunderbolts had boarded the two team buses in the East parking lot, Centore had issued a plea for everybody to stay focused during the bus ride. "Think about what you need to do," Centore had declared. But this was a team that was having problems staying focused on assignments, and for some of the players, a long bus ride that would pass over an expansive bridge was an invitation for distraction.

Centore, however, had been pleased during the ride. It had been virtual silence throughout the bus during the forty-five-minute trip. "There hadn't been much talking. Everyone seemed to be thinking about the challenge facing them," Centore said after departing the bus in the Portsmouth parking lot.

Ten minutes before the scheduled 7 p.m. starting time, the Thunderbolts completed their warm-ups on Portsmouth's new artificial turf field and headed to a small meeting room in a building directly behind one of the end zones. Centore was composed. He wasn't harping on the multitude of mistakes made last Friday night against Shea. This was a new day—a new chance to show what Cranston East football is all about.

"This is a good team," Centore said about Portsmouth when he started talking to the Thunderbolts. "They don't think you can come here and beat them. To do that, you will have to play like men."

"Play like a man" is a favorite rallying cry of high school football coaches from Connecticut to California. There's no exact definition of what it means. Ask a hundred high school football coaches and you probably will get fifty different answers as to what the expression means to them. Some people would think it's simply a reference to physicality, a demonstration of male physical strength. There's certainly some creditability to that interpretation. Football is a physically demanding game. Often those battles on the line of scrimmage are won by the stronger, more aggressive player; those extra few yards needed for a first-down can be the result of the running back over-powering a linebacker or corner-back. That physical strength is often the result of lonely hours working in a weight room.

But for Tom Centore, "playing like a man" in a football game goes well beyond power, strength, or some abstract feeling of machismo. For Centore, "playing like a man" has always been about responsibility. In Centore's world, a man does not quit when he is physically tired; a man looks for the second effort within himself. A man takes responsibility for his assignment; he doesn't look for somebody else to do his job. A man is responsible to his teammates; just like someday he will be responsible to his family. In the Cranston East football family, "playing like a man" is about being accountable to yourself and your teammates—accountable for your responsibilities on every play of a game. It's about your responsibility to stay focused on your assignment so your teammate can trust you will be there when he needs you to help him make a stop or open a hole on the offensive line. It's the culmination of those little football homilies Centore often delivers after a practice session.

The game certainly hadn't started on an encouraging note for Cranston East. Portsmouth, led by Bicho, scored on the game's opening series on only six plays. Tom Centore couldn't help but think it was already starting to look like another night of lack-of-focus and missed assignments. However, then East took the ensuing kickoff and started driving down the field, mainly on the ground, deep into Portsmouth territory. But the Thunderbolts can't convert on a fourth-and-short at the Portsmouth 9-yard line. The season was only three games old, but already East was becoming known as a team that didn't know how to stay focused on the big plays.

Two weeks ago, against Shea, Cranston East had been stopped near the goal line on its first possession, and the team never really recovered from that disappointment of not taking advantage of the early scoring opportunity.

Portsmouth regained possession and immediately began driving down the field again. On the sidelines, Tom Centore didn't need to say anything. The disgusted look on his face told an observer that Centore was harboring that, "Here we go again" type of anxiety. But this time, it would be different. Robenson Antoine intercepted a Bicho pass near the East 20-yard line and returns it past midfield. Rayven Deoliveira then took control of the offense, ripping off a couple of good runs, highlighted by a 5-yard touchdown run. Jon Loy followed with the conversion boot, and East was ahead 7–6.

Even without Mason as linebacker, the East defense did a good job containing Bicho on Portsmouth's next two pos-sessions. Then, with a few minutes remaining in the first half and East driving toward another touchdown, Antoine showed why—if he was only a few inches taller—Division I college coaches would be swooning all over him. Even though he was outnumbered and outsized by a couple of Portsmouth defenders, Antoine leaped over the defenders and pulled down a touchdown pass from Deoliveira. Another Loy conversion boot gave East a 14–6 halftime lead.

As Tom Centore headed off the field for halftime team meeting, he was pleased. He had just watched his team deliver twenty-four minutes of good, solid football. But Centore knows you don't win a game in twenty-four minutes. The Thunder-bolts would need another twenty-four minutes of solid play, and so far this season, they hadn't shown they could do it.

It's More Than a Game of Stats

Statistics can tell a lot about why a football game played-out the way it did. Total team rushing and passing yardage; time of possession; some individual stats, like a quarterback's pass-completion percentage or a linebacker's number of solo tackles. They are all numbers that can tell the story of how a game was won. But stats don't tell how Hector Duran's blocking, while he was in the game as a running back, gave Rayven Deoliveira that extra second he needed to make the cut into the opening his offensive linemen had created. How Duran's efforts gave Deoliveira the opportunity to again and again eat-up yardage in a Cranston East ground drive. Duran's ten tackles from his linebacker berth on defense were listed on the stat sheet. But that stat sheet doesn't show that even when Duran wasn't directly involved in a tackle, he was right there as the pile untangled, patting his teammates on the back, yelling encouragement to guys who are often unrecognized by the fans. Their captain knew what they were doing for the team.

Duran was leading by example, personally committing his body to a physical battering as much—if not more—than any other player on the team. At the same time, Duran understood how important it was to keep his teammates inspired. More than any other player on the field, the kid who never really knew his father understood how important it is for some kids to be told they are making something important happen this night.

Rayven Deoliveira's running keyed an eleven-minute ground attack on the first series of the second half that concluded with Rayven rushing 5 yards for a touchdown. For the first time his season, Deoliveira seemed to be running at people. He was using his size and strength advantage to punish defenders, pushing them back rather than his trying some TV highlights sidestep move. The touchdown—and a 2-point conversion rush by Quinn Lanigan—gave East a 22–6 lead with a minute to play in the third quarter.

Not surprisingly, Bicho didn't stop trying to rally his team. Early in the fourth quarter, he directs a Portsmouth touchdown drive, cutting the East lead to 22–12. But this night, the East defense wasn't going to self-destruct. Portsmouth had a chance to pull closer later in the fourth quarter, but the Cranston East defense held on four plays near midfield, including a big fourth-down stop on a short yardage situation. A team that for two weeks couldn't come up with the big defensive plays when they needed it, suddenly delivered on almost every critical stop.

A few minutes later, Deoliveira started rolling out to the right side. The Portsmouth defense, having seen Rayven rack up big runs all night, committed to the run. But this time, Deoliveira slowed his run; he looked toward Robenson Antoine heading into the right corner of the end and, while still on the run, fired a strike toward Robenson. Once again, Antoine leaped over a defender and pulled down another TD pass. Another Jon Loy conversion boot gives East a 28–12 lead.

A few minutes later, I watched Hector Duran coming off the field after the East defense had made another big stop with less than a minute play, preserving the 28–12 victory. Duran sat on the bench and took off his helmet. The steam rose from his forehead, and he had the look of a totally exhausted, but completely satisfied teenager. It was the type of look few people ever really experience. The teenager who wants to be the "Man of the House" at home had delivered for his football family.

The Reason He Loves Coaching

Tom Centore needed this victory. For almost two decades now, he had made all the personal sacrifices needed to make the Cranston East football program successful, even as those needs in recent years had become more varied and more demanding of his time. He understands there's a value to his vocation that goes well beyond those numbers on the scoreboard at the end of the game. But Centore is a football coach, and for a football coach the immediate reward for all his sacrifice is a game like this. A game like this makes all the sacrifices make sense. It was the proverbial "complete game." A night when his instructions and words of support come together in the actions of a group of teenage boys over a two-to-three-hour period.

That's the reward felt by every high school football coach. But over the previous three weeks, Centore had gone through a personal hell with the death of his father and questions about his own health. Now, at least for one night, a group of teenagers from a varied mix of backgrounds had brought smiles to their coach's face.

"One of the reasons I love coaching is because you can do things like you did tonight," Centore said to his team as the Thunderbolts gathered around him at midfield after they had exchanged postgame handshakes with stunned Portsmouth players.

The look of the Portsmouth fans and some school officials standing on the running track that circled the field told the story better than any sportswriter could put into words. The Portsmouth faithful didn't think it could happen. How could Portsmouth lose on its own field to a team that most Portsmouth fans consider a city team because of the composite face of the Thunderbolts? Portsmouth doesn't lose to a city team on its own field.

"I said it would take men to come here and beat a good team like this on their field," Centore continued in his talk to the players at midfield.

Then Centore concluded with one final reminder that this team—because of its composite team face—often needs to do more than just score the most points to leave the field a winner.

"You played like men. Now leave here walking off this field like gentlemen," Centore preached.

CHAPTER XV

HE NEEDS TO BE A WEATHERMAN AND A COACH

The Rhode Island Interscholastic League mandates a team must have two days of off-field rest between games, but even if the League didn't have that rule, Tom Centore would give his players two days away from the field after a Friday night game. Giving the players' bodies forty-eight hours to recover from the physical punishment in a game is a good idea for any teenage football player, but at East those two days serve more than just a chance for physical rest.

"Most of our kids have to work. This way they can work on Saturday and Sunday without worrying about taking time away from the team," offered Centore.

Plus, a portion of Monday afternoon is devoted to dissecting the film of the Friday night game and looking at film of their upcoming Friday night opponent. That means there really are only three full days of on-field practice between Friday night games. So, Centore was anxious to get on the field Tuesday. He wanted to immediately continue building on the good vibes from the Friday night game against Portsmouth.

He was looking forward to two-and-a-half to three hours on the field Tuesday. Instead, the Thunderbolts were running drills in the gym on a wooden basketball court. Tuesday morning it had been raining heavily, although by noon it had been looking like the rain might subside by later in the afternoon—and it did. By 3 p.m. the skies had cleared. At most schools, waiting out the weather to see if the football team could practice outside wouldn't have presented a problem. The players can wait around in the gym to see if the rain subsided enough to practice outside and if it did, just walk out to the practice field. But at East, there isn't room for uncertainty about the possibility of practice being rained out because of the coaches' need to schedule the bus to take the players to the practice field.

"If it's raining, we have to determine early in the day if we need the bus to go to practice," said Ken Simone. "If we say we want the bus and don't get on it, we are in trouble," Simone added, with a disgusted look. "The forecast in the morning was for heavy rain, so we didn't order the bus. Our inability to just walk out to practice truly hurts us in situations like this. But it's just something that we have come to accept."

It is one of those things Centore and his coaching staff might accept, but they certainly don't like it. No football coach wants to give up a valuable day on the field, especially this early in the season. There are so many important early season drills that can't be executed the way they should be working on a hardwood basketball court.

Cranston East players live in New England, so they understand that later in the season the weather might be too uncomfortable—maybe even dangerous some days—to be out on the field at practice. But it's the third week of September. It's football weather time, and the Thunderbolts are practicing on a wooden basketball court.

After missing outdoor practice on Tuesday, by Wednesday afternoon Centore was itching to get on the field. He was already standing in the middle of the practice field as the players started walking down the hill from the parking lot after debarking from the first trip of the shuttle bus.

"Let's go, let's go," Centore shouted. "We have a lot of work to make up."

For two hours, Centore didn't just walk between the various team units conducting drills—he ran from one end of the field to the other. He was energized. He was a fifty-year-old man who had given an extra measure of his life to his ailing father over the past few months. He had tried to make his father's final days rewarding, and after a few days of questioning whether he had done enough to keep his father alive a little longer, he had come to peace with his father's death. He realized he had done all he could have done.

Now he could devote every autumn afternoon to just being a football coach again.

He Could Hardly Walk, but "It Felt Great"

Just before the start of practice Wednesday, I had spotted Hector Duran kneeling on the sidelines. It was the first time I had a chance to talk to him away from his teammates since Friday night's game. He had played a great game Friday night on both sides of the ball. He would get hit by a much larger Portsmouth offensive lineman, but he would still be involved in the tackle. Then he would pick himself off the ground and be right back directing the defensive huddle. He isn't that big, but he never stopped moving. He had been a big reason East was able to contain Becho's running Friday night. I remember thinking toward the end of the game that he must be sore. So, I asked him, "How did you feel Saturday morning?"

"I could hardly walk, but it felt great," Duran offered, flashing a big smile that exposed the braces on his teeth.

It's that physical soreness and exhaustion that's unique to football. You are exhausted from running a marathon or even a three-mile-high school cross country race, but your body isn't also constantly being hit and physically punished like it is in a football game. Maybe an ice hockey player taking body checks while going full speed for a sixty-second line shift can somewhat match the physicality of a football game. But even in hockey, one of the players is trying to avoid the hit. In football, players on both sides of the ball are purposely hitting somebody or being hit on every play. It can be a block, a tackle, or getting hit trying to run through a gap in the offensive line. That's what makes football unique.

Anybody can be a high school football player if they have what it takes. What it takes is the willingness to get back up after being knocked down. You can get mad, but you can't get angry. Anger causes you to lose focus on your assignment on the next play. One of Vince Lombardi's numerous classic football quotes was, "It's not whether you get knocked down, it's whether you get up."

That's Hector Duran. At 5'9", he gets knocked down a lot on the football field, but he always gets back up, ready to look for the next challenge. The football field is his life's metaphor. Growing up in a home without a father it's plausible he has taken some societal hard hits through the years. But he always got back up—looking for another challenge.

Keeping the Mojo Flowing

In the early going of their game against St. Raphael Academy on September 28 in Pawtucket, it seemed the Thunderbolts were determined to keep the mojo—built up in the victory over Portsmouth—flowing for another Friday night. The word around the state was St. Raphael, a parochial co-ed school in Pawtucket with only about 230 male students, had a serious depth problem this season. The Saints had lost their first two games of the season, and East stopped them cold on the game's first possession. Cranston East then took the ball and drove the length of the field for a touchdown, highlighted by Robenson Antoine's diving TD catch of a Rayven Deoliveira pass. Robenson and Rayven combined on another touchdown pass later in the first quarter. Those TDs, combined with two of Jon Loy's conversion kicks, gave Cranston East a 14–0 lead going into the second quarter.

When East took its third possession and started driving into St. Raphael territory, nobody could blame the small group of Cranston East fans who made the twenty-mile ride to Pawtucket if they started thinking this game would be decided by halftime. But apparently it only took one good game for this Cranston East team to become susceptible to complacency. Rather than continue picking up big yards, the East offense started making mental mistakes, and the drive stalled. Then, on East's next possession, another drive stalled in St. Raphael territory.

To the East coaches standing on the sidelines, the problems were obvious. Although they had started strong, the Cranston East offensive and defensive lines had not continued dominating the play like they had against Portsmouth last Friday night. East still led 14–0 at halftime. But rather than coming out strong and cushioning its lead in the second half, the Thunderbolts allowed St. Raphael to get back into the game. St. Raphael scored on its first possession of the second half. Fortunately, the Saints missed a 2-point conversion, so East still had an 8-point lead.

But, the same East players, who a week earlier had stayed focused for the entire forty-eight minutes of playing time, were constantly losing focus tonight. Early in the third quarter, the Thunderbolts had good field possession, but two penalties stopped the drive. That's the thing about football; it can't be just one or two guys. It has to be the collective will of eleven players, focused until the whistle blows on every play.

Jamari Mason was missing another game. However, Mack Hanley—the kid who doesn't have a passion for football but does have a passion for this team, so he came to practice every day even though his arm was in a cast—was finally getting a chance to help his team. His name hadn't appeared in the scoring summaries, but he was making contributions with his blocking from his tight end berth. Unfortunately, not all of the Thunderbolts were demonstrating Hanley's focus. With East still holding a 14–6 lead midway through the fourth quarter, apparently St. Raphael figured it had to take a chance on a fourth-and-two in its own territory. If the East defense made the stop, they would have good field position for a "put-away" touchdown. But one of the Thunderbolts defensive ends was drawn off-side by a long count, giving St. Raphael a first down without running a play.

The euphoria he had felt last Friday night was turning to frustration for Tom Centore.

"This is embarrassing," Centore yelled at the top of his voice. "Watch the ball."

A few plays later, the St. Raphael quarterback flips a screen pass into the right flat, a couple of East defenders missed what should have been sure tackles, and the receiver ran 35 yards for a touchdown. The Saints also rush the 2-point conversion; suddenly the score was tied 14–14 with a few minutes to play.

For the East coaching staff, it was a nightmarish mental flashback as they stood on the sidelines watching what was transpiring. Once again, the Thunderbolts were letting a team that shouldn't even be in a game against them in the fourth quarter hang around and make it a game. They had done that against Barrington in the season-opening game before finally pulling out a victory in overtime. The following week against Shea, they lost when a field goal attempt on the last play of the game that would have sent the game into overtime, fell short. Now it was happening again: a team that hadn't won a game yet this season was all-even with the Thunderbolts, with only a few minutes to play. Was it going to be another Friday night of overtime?

But this night, the Thunderbolts made sure their fans could head back to Cranston on time.

Rayven Deoliveira began driving the Bolts down the field on the ensuing series and kept the drive going with a couple of big third- and fourth-down runs. With only fifteen seconds to play in the game, St. Raphael looked like it might have stopped the drive and forced the game into overtime, with East facing a fourth-and-five from the St. Raphael 22. The high-percentage course of action would have been to only try for the 5 yards needed for the first down. Instead, Centore went for broke on one play.

Deoliveira rolled to his right, but then fired a pass across the field at Antoine, who was heading into the left corner of the end zone with two defenders around him. As usual, the defenders were taller than Robenson; but once again, Antoine leaped over the defenders and pulled the ball down. This time it produced a game-winning touchdown.

The St. Raphael players were in shock. A few seconds earlier, they thought they were heading into overtime after having staged a great comeback. Now, with only a few seconds remaining to play, it was obvious they were going to lose the game. How could that little kid come down with the ball, right in the middle of two St. Raphael defenders?

The little guy who isn't afraid to let people know he believes he's the best receiver in the state just delivered the type of play that backs up that type of boast.

For generations, there have been kids like Antoine who have excelled in high school football because they play their entire careers with a "chip on their shoulder." At some point in their early life, somebody told them they couldn't be a good football player because they were "too small," or "too slow," or "too something." That's the thing about football. There are so many different opportunities for kids who were once told they are "too something" to be successful on the football field.

A Complicated Relationship

As soon the final buzzer sounded, Tom Centore broke from his spot on the sideline and headed out to the field to join his players in a victory celebration. Standing in the middle of the field, Centore spotted Rayven Deoliveira headed toward him. Within a few seconds, coach and player were knotted in reciprocal bear hugs. It wasn't just a coach patting a player on the back with the type of "good game" acknowledgement that you see after many high school football games. It was a full bear hug that lasted for a full minute or more in the midst of a fifty- to sixty-player celebration. It was an expression of emotion that you might expect to see at some type of championship celebration. But that level of emotion after a regular season victory demonstrated that one of the knottiest associations on this year's Cranston East football team is the relationship between the coach and the star quarterback.

Every high school football coach and his quarterback have a unique relationship. It is a relationship unlike a coach-athlete relationship in any other team sport. The football coach must have confidence that his quarterback can execute his game plan. The quarterback must trust that his coach will put him in position to succeed by devising a game plan that best suits the quarterback's talents. But Centore's and Deoliveira's bond has been taken beyond the boilerplate coach-quarterback relationship. Centore has confidence Deoliveira has the talent to direct the explosive brand of football that has become the trademark of East football over the past six or seven years. The question is, will Rayven be willing to do it the way Centore wants it executed.

"He definitely has all the tools. We just have to get him seeing the field the way the coaches want him to see it," former Thunderbolts All-State quarterback Alex Corvese had said to me before the start of the season.

Since the first day Deoliveira became a Cranston East student in December of 2016, he seems to have understood he was indebted to Centore. His episode at La Salle could have completely derailed his high school athletic career—wiped out his chances of getting any attention from college coaches. But Centore has given Deoliveira a clean slate to restructure his dreams of being a college football player someday. Some people would say, of course, a coach would welcome a talented athlete like Deoliveira onto his team. Centore certainly did welcome adding Deoliveira's talent to the Thunderbolts roster. But Centore's early relationship with Deoliveira could have been jaded if he had listened to the warnings he received from some people that the "kid was trouble." Instead, Centore let Deoliveira's actions as a Cranston East student set the parameters for their relationship. and as Centore had said earlier in the season. "Since he has been here, he has done everything we asked."

In fact, the more Centore has come to know Deoliveira, beyond the football field, the more Centore liked the kid. The fact is a lot of people like Rayven. He is one of those charismatic kids who makes friends easily among his peers—not just because he's an athlete, but because he makes people feel he generally cares about what they are saying.

But that doesn't mean Deoliveira doesn't have some baggage. He is a very preceptive kid with average, maybe even above average, innate intelligence. But at times, Centore can't help but think Deoliveira feels his football talent will allow him to do the bare minimum in the classroom. Last year, Centore constantly needed to remind Deoliveira about missed academic assignments. At the end of last spring, Centore had to convince Deoliveira into taking some summer school courses so he would have the specifically required courses needed to pass the NCAA Cleaning House requirements. However, the biggest challenge now that Deoliveira was the starting quarterback, might be getting Rayven to buy into Centore's "team first" concept of playing football. It's the concept of getting out of yourself and into the team.

His father died when he was an infant, so Rayven's childhood certainly had some challenging days. Like a lot of kids growing up in single parent home, Deoliveira seems to have learned how to be a survivor. He wants to help his teammates enjoy a successful season; he wants to be a good teammate; he wants to be cooperative with the coaches, but he has grown up with a sense of bottom-line self-preservation.

Growing up, the one male Rayven could always trust, the one guy who was always there protecting Rayven's back, was his older brother Leroy. Just how much Leroy feels it's his responsibility to protect his young brother might be playing out this season on the East football team.

Leroy had graduated from LaSalle last spring, after a great high school football career, but rather than immediately pursuing some opportunities to be a "walk-on" candidate at some out-of-state Division I school, he was staying in Rhode Island this fall to help Rayven navigate his senior season as a high school football player. All of which might create some stumbling blocks in the coach and quarterback relationship. Rayven respects Centore and wants the "Coach's" team to be successful. But at the first few games, occasionally, when the East defense was on the field and Rayven was standing on the sidelines, Leroy would come out of the stands and motion for Rayven to come over about 5 or 10 yards behind the bench area for a little chat. An observer can't help but wonder whether the discussion centered on whether the coach's game plan was best way to employ Rayven's skills.

Tonight, however, everything had meshed. Centore, along with input from his assistants, has scripted the perfect series of plays to showcase Deoliveira's talents, and Rayven had delivered under pressure. For the second straight Friday night, Rayven had shown he's one of the best quarterbacks in the state. Also, after that season-opening week of chaos surrounding Tony Centore's death, Tom Centore had directed his team to two straight victories. The fact that tonight's victory transpired on Centore's 50th birthday was all the more reason for the coach and quarterback to be hugging at midfield.

After following his players through the midfield exchanging of handshakes with all the St. Raphael players and talking to the St. Raphael coach for a few minutes, Centore headed for one of the end zones where his players were all on one knee waiting for their coach. Centore still had a wide smile brought on by the thrilling last-minute victory, but he was already thinking about making sure this was both a victory and life lesson learned.

"Congratulations on the victory, but you are a better team than this," Centore declared.

His team had won a game, but Centore knows he needs to prepare these players better as a group. An important component of this team is still missing. It's that quality that can make a program special. All football coaches can sense when their team has it. It's a sense of self-confidence without an arrogant attitude. It can't be just one or two great players; it's a team-wide sense of self-confidence. You feed off your teammates' self-confidence—up and down the offensive and defensive lines, throughout the offensive backfield, and into the defensive secondary. Centore knows right now it's not there like it has been in the past few years. Some players are still look-ing for others to do the job rather than having confidence that their work ethic has put them in position to deliver when their number is called. They knelt there looking up at their coach. Some were satisfied with the victory, but some knew Centore was right. They could be—they should be—better.

"When you have the ball, you have to think you are going to score. You need to have that mentality," Centore said. "Maybe it's my fault with all the things going on I haven't always been there, and we missed two days of practice this week with rain. But I will be there now."

Cranston East is 3–1 overall and 2–1 in the league play, but three of the four games were still undecided in the final few seconds of the game. East is not a team for anybody with a weak heart, nor a coach who already has momentarily blacked-out once this season from anxiety issues.

A Mother's Dream

At the same time East was defeating St. Raphael in Pawtucket, Rhode Island, fifty miles away in Cambridge, Mass., a former Cranston East star was helping the University of Rhode Island's football team register a major ego boost with a 23–16 victory over Harvard.

Marvin Beauvais isn't only the all-time Cranston East pass-receiver; he's also the story of how a high school football coach can make a mother's dream come true—a dream that has nothing to do with touchdowns or tackles.

Nobody was expecting Beauvais would be a football star when he entered Cranston East as freshman in the fall of 2010. He had moved with his family to Rhode Island from Brooklyn, N.Y. when he was seven years old because his mother wanted a quieter place for her children to grow up than the streets of New York. But the family sports background was in soccer.

"My family basically was a soccer family," Beauvais, a young man of color, told me at the start of his senior year at East in the fall of 2013. "But my dad would be watching football on TV when I was a little kid, so I would go out in the backyard and play catch."

He quickly discovered he had a knack for catching a football.

"I always had good hands," Beauvais said in 2013.

He didn't play organized football until his freshman year at East, but those hands, coupled with good speed and a long arm span, quickly separated him from other Rhode Island high school pass receivers. He had the type of hands that allowed him to make catches well away from his body—the type of hands you see making catches in the NFL.

"I had never seen anybody in Rhode Island with hands like that," Tom Centore told me about Beauvais in 2013.

It took the first few years of high school for Beauvais, who was 6'3" in high school, to outgrow a gangly running style. But by the end of his sophomore year at East, Centore knew Beauvais had Division I potential.

"When coach Centore told me after my sophomore year that I might be able to get a college scholarship, that's when the dream really started," Beauvais told me when we talked again in the spring of 2018. "Every little kid dreams about playing in college and maybe the NFL, but it's when you are offered a college scholarship—when college coaches say it with their commitment—that's when you know you really have talent."

So, the journey to become a better football player began in earnest.

"Nobody worked harder or was more dedicated than Marvin," Centore related. "In his four years here, he didn't miss a practice."

Beauvais did more than just show up for practice. His family couldn't afford expensive gym memberships or private training sessions, but he would do anything he felt would make him a better player on his own.

"I would go to the practice field and do parachute-runs up and down the hill by myself," Beauvais once told me.

By his junior season in 2012, Beauvais became a first-team All-State wide receiver as he averaged 16 yards per catch on 35 receptions, including 10 touchdown receptions. He had already developed a reputation as a big play guy. In his senior season, he became the all-time top Cranston East receiver as he made 20 touchdown grabs among his 65 receptions. Beauvais' pass receiving, mainly on tosses from Alex Corvese, led Cranston East to its first berth in the state's major Super Bowl in thirty years. Going into the 2018 season, that Cranston East Super Bowl berth marked the only time in the seven-year span between 2011 and 2017 that a public school team played in the state's major football title game.

The Thunderbolts dropped a 45–34 decision to Hendricken in a thrilling Super Bowl game, but while East didn't win the championship, a public school team proving it was one of the two best teams in the state was important for all of the state's public school football teams.

Beauvais knew the possibility of a college scholarship because of his football talent could also mean the fulfillment of another dream. His mother was a woman who always understood the value of education. She made sure her children were at school every day. But there was no history of college attendance in her family, so having a son with a college degree was her dream.

But Beauvais admits in his early high school days, the classroom was not his priority.

"I never missed school; my mother wouldn't let me miss a day of school," Beauvais told me in the spring of 2018 when we talked on the URI campus. "But in my first few years, I didn't take school seriously. I would be in the classroom, but I was just trying to pass—not trying to do my best."

It's an old story. A kid with athletic talent thinks that's all he will need to live the good life. Fortunately, Beauvais had a football coach who wouldn't allow him to coast through school on his athletic endowment. But Tom Centore did use football as the carrot in Beauvais' academic euphony. Just like in football, where Beauvais had come to understand he needed an extra effort if he hoped to take his game to the next level, Centore convinced him he would need to do more than just "show up" in the classroom if he wanted to pass the NCAA Academic Clearinghouse requirements that would make him immediately eligible to play Division I college football.

It's never too late for a high school student to become serious about studying, but you don't change a high school transcript overnight. So, while Beauvais' grades improved in his junior and senior years, it wasn't until late in his senior year that it was certain he would be immediately eligible to play in college. There's a possibility, with his talent, had his college eligible status been certain in the fall of his senior year at East, Beauvais might have received more Division I scholarship offers. But Beauvais was pleased URI, a DI-FCS school, had stuck with him, so he planned to go to his state university and immediately prove he could be a Division I starter.

But the URI coaching staff felt because he was only seventeen years old, it would be better for him to red-shirt his freshman year. It would give Beauvais' body more time to mature and his physique more time to adjust to college life.

Beauvais wasn't happy about the red-shirt decision at first, but the more he worked against college players, the more he realized his game still needed time to mature.

"I had to rise to the speed of the game," Beauvais said in the spring of 2018. "The talent rises around you, so you have to rise with it. It can expose you or it makes you."

In Beauvais' case, it made him.

In the fall of 2017, as a URI junior, he earned Colonial Athletic Conference All-Conference honors as he compiled 732 yards in pass receptions. But it wasn't just his 46 total receptions that made people take notice. He posted the third highest yards per catch average in the conference (15.9). He had the second longest receptions in the conference when he grabbed a pass and raced 80 yards for a touchdown against Central Michigan.

Just like his high school days at Cranston East, he had become the proverbial "big play" guy.

Now, he had started off the 2018 season in great fashion with a strong showing—four catches against Harvard. (A week later, he would make nine catches in a URI victory over Brown University.)

And while he's now a star, it hadn't been easy during the early years of his college career. There were times in his freshman and sophomore years when he wasn't very happy at URI. URI was a running-team in those days, so Beauvais wasn't seeing much action coming his way. Plus, the academic part of the equation was tougher than Beauvais thought it would be. To make matters worse, the football team was losing. By Beauvais' sophomore season in 2016, URI hadn't had a winning football season in nine years. Beauvais was thinking of transferring, maybe to a Division III school. Maybe he didn't have what it took to be a Division I football player. But fortunately for Beauvais, even after he played his last game in a Cranston East uniform, he was still one of coach Centore's guys. As generations of American high school football players will tell you, once you play for a veteran high school football coach, you're always one of "the coach's boys."

Even after he left East, Centore didn't stop being in constant communication with Beauvais. Sometimes Centore would call to give Beauvais words of encouragement, and occasionally he would go down to the URI campus to watch Marvin in practice. There were even times when the URI coaches, feeling Beauvais wasn't working as much as he should be in a certain academic course, would call Centore and tell him he needed to talk to Marvin about his classwork. Of course, Centore always did. When Beauvais was thinking about transferring, he came back to Cranston East one afternoon to talk to Centore about possibly finding him a new school.

"Marvin was discouraged," said Centore. "He wasn't seeing many passes. I told him I felt he needed to stick it out. I reminded him how far he had come, and how it wasn't always easy."

That's one of Centore's mantras—something Cranston East football players have been hearing at practice now for sixteen years. When things go wrong—and they often do—you need to keep working. You need to stay positive and remember you are learning something every day. So, Beauvais stayed at URI, and Centore remained in constant contact. Now, Beauvais was one of the top collegiate pass catchers in the Northeast.

But for the woman who started the amazing journey by moving her family to Rhode Island when Marvin was only seven years old, her son's most impressive accomplishment doesn't show up on the scoreboard. Using the fortitude and focus he first leaned on the football field, Beauvais was on schedule to receive his undergraduate degree either in December or in the spring of 2019.

"My mother is excited about my football career because she knows how much football means to me. But for her, football as a game doesn't really mean that much. For her, the most important thing is getting my degree. Once I get the degree, I'm basically set with my mom," Beauvais told me with a smile in the spring of 2018. "For her, whatever happens after that is just a bonus."

A mother's dream was about to become reality because of a high school football coach's dedication to one of "his boys."

CHAPTER XVI

THE AMERICAN DREAM
IN SHOULDER PADS

Despite the surprising loss to Shea in the first game of the season, East was in the thick of the fight for one of their sub-division's four playoff berths with their 2–1 record as September turned into October. But Tom Centore knows they are not playing good football. He even knows why. He just doesn't know the answer to the problem.

"This is the toughest group to get to, I have ever had," Centore said, as we walked across the field heading to practice on Tuesday, Oct. 2nd. "They just can't stay focused. They're good kids, but they are immature."

The two-and-a-half-hour practice only confirmed Centore's appraisal of his team. Time after time he would be yelling "on the ball" as he ordered a repeat of a drill. So, when he called the entire team together in the middle of the field after the final drill of the day, Centore was on a tear. Like almost every afternoon, his end of practice team talk is about an immediate football necessity to make the team better. But there's almost always a message about life beyond football.

"All I asked is that you don't tune me out," Centore said, with a pleading look on his face. "I don't tune you out when you come looking for help with a teacher. You need to do the work here that you are being asked to do."

Suddenly, Centore directed his words toward Omar Reyes, the junior offensive and defensive lineman who was kneeling in the middle of the group.

"Look at Omar," Centore said, bringing a shocked expression to Reyes' face that he was being singled out by the coach. "He will practice, go home, eat, then do his homework," Centore said, describing Reyes' nightly routine. "He doesn't go home and see who he can contact to play against in some online game. That's why he is in all the honors classes. That's why he knows every lineman's assignment. He prepares himself," Centore continued.

Then Centore moved a step closer to Reyes. "Your mother would kill you if you weren't prepared for school, wouldn't she?" Centore asked Reyes. Reyes, still with a stunned look on his face that the coach was using him as an example, nodded his head, affirming Centore's metaphoric evaluation of his mother's emphasis on scholastic preparation.

"That's why he has a 4.0," Centore said.

Robenson Antoine couldn't pass up an opportunity to give his longtime friend a good-natured jab.

"He doesn't have a 4.0," Antoine said, with a broad smile. "He has a 3.9."

The Kid Who Once Hated Football

Omar Reyes is the American Dream in shoulder pads.

He is a 6'0", 260-pound lineman and the son of two first generation Dominican Republic-Americans. His mother grew up in

Providence and attended Classical High, the lone Providence public high school where admission is based on test scores. Reyes' father is from New York City. His parents met in college. Omar is their only child, and he has spent his entire life living with his parents in the same well-kept, small cape in the Auburn section of the city, a few blocks from City Hall and Cranston East.

"I was born three streets from Cranston East and have lived in the same house my entire life," Reyes said with smile.

While his Hispanic heritage is unquestionable, Reyes' skin complexion is as white as Mack Hanley's or Quinn Lanigan's. Reyes is one of those kids whose very nature is to please people. They are the type of young people who don't like to disappoint anybody, so they work hard at doing what they understand is the right thing to do. Their parents, their teachers—and their coach—are all beneficiaries of their desire to please.

"I have always been pretty decent about doing what's right; what you should do," Reyes told me one day.

That could be why football has become a fiber of his life. In many ways, football is a complex game. But the game's basic creed is simple: show up every day for practice, do what the coaches tell you to do, and work hard at improving your skills. That basically summarizes Reyes' life since he was a little kid, but there was a time when he didn't expect football to be part of his life's equation.

"I started playing youth football when I was eight years old," Reyes related. "The first day I went to practice, they ran a sprint, and I said, 'That's it. I'm done.' Since I was about five, I had been a big kid, a little overweight. I hated running. I pretty much couldn't run one sprint."

So, Reyes went home looking for an escape from the gridiron.

He didn't find it.

"I wanted to quit right away," Reyes offered. "I went home after that first practice and cried to my mom that I wanted to quit. But my dad made me go back the next day. I think he felt it would be the best sport to get me in shape, and I think he also felt I would eventually like it."

"That first year when my father made me go back after the first day I said, 'Okay, I will give it a month,'" Reyes declared. "Once I got past the running part, I liked it. I was a big kid, so I was good at hitting people. Little kids like to do things they are good at."

But Reyes quickly learned football is a lot more than just big kids hitting people.

"I liked the team bonding," Reyes offered about why he kept playing football. "I played baseball when I was little, but football felt different. You had to be closer as a team in football than you did in baseball."

He realized at an early age that with his size, he was never going to be the star quarterback or the speeding running back who is constantly hearing his name being cheered by the fans.

"Linemen get no glory, but that's okay," said Reyes. "In basketball, if you don't fit the build, you probably are not going to be successful. But in football there is a spot for everybody to make a meaningful contribution to his team. That's what I love about football."

The more he played, the more Reyes developed a passion for the game. He discovered football was a game that was fun to play, and it also mirrored some lessons he had grown up learning at home. His father is, in Reyes words, "A football guy who loves football." But his parents never left any doubt that their son's main priority should be his academic work.

"My parents always told me education will get you places; open doors for you," said Reyes. "My parents were always on me about schoolwork, but they were never like super on me. School and football were what you do. You never miss a football practice, and you never miss a school assignment."

The result is Reyes became an outstanding student and a very good football player. In the eight academic marking periods during his first two years at East, virtually every mark on his report card was an A. "I got a couple of B-pluses," Reyes says, with a coy expression of pride.

On the football field he became a varsity starter in only his sophomore season in 2017, and his line play last season had played a big role in the Thunderbolts drive to the state Division I Super Bowl championship. This season, even though he is an underclassman, he is one of the Thunderbolts' top linemen.

"He's a kid you can always count on," said Tom Centore. "He's smart, he's a hard worker, and he has a real understanding of the game."

The game he once wanted to quit has molded his life.

"I like to know what's happening, in the news and in football," said Reyes. "I like to know why things are done the way they are, and that has made me a better football player. When we go through the plays, some kids just listen. I try to visualize in my head how it will work so I can understand it better. It's the same way in the classroom. It's how my brain works."

A naturally quiet kid, he knows football has also helped him open up his likeable persona to other people.

"I'm quiet, if I am surrounded by people I don't know," admitted Reyes. "Once I get comfortable, I open up. Football has helped me become more sociable, and you have to be sociable to realistically be anything in life."

He already knows he wants to be an engineer, and he wants to play college football.

"I like helping people. I like solving problems," said Reyes. "I want to make other people's lives simpler and better.

"Football builds you as a person; it teaches you how to balance schoolwork and other things in life," Reyes said. "When we have long practices, I go home and all I want to do is sleep, but I have to get my schoolwork done before I can sleep. That's the challenge. Football has become part of life. It has made everything fall into place in my life."

Responsibility Is Part of the Game Plan

Wednesday was a good day of practice. Most of the players seemed to be focusing on the drills. Maybe they are starting to mature. But there always seems to be something that takes Tom Centore's mind off the plan for Friday night's game. During the school day, a junior came into Centore's office to turn in his equipment. It bothered Centore because while the kid wasn't ready to see much playing time this season, by next year, he could become a valuable member of the team. But his mother was having an issue with her health and couldn't work, so the player needed to work more hours to help cover the family living expenses. That's the type of life reality Centore is dealing with more and more these days

"I give him credit. At least he came to me and explained," Centore offered about the young man. "So many kids these days just quit. There was another kid, who I was saving a spot for because he told he wanted to play but had an injury. So, I gave him a uniform. But he hadn't shown up at practice and hadn't stopped in my office to tell me anything. I finally had to go looking for him in school. When I found him, he said, 'Oh, I decided not to play.' I understand if he decided not to play, but at least tell me or one of the coaches. That's what we are trying to teach these kids—responsibility. It's a lot more than football, but football might be where they understand it."

Centore knows kids want to belong to something—especially something as big, something as well known in the school community, as the football team. That has always been one of the big draws of high school football. But Centore wants them to do more than just belong. He wants them to learn to contribute. He knows sometimes players, especially the younger players, stand at the back of the line during practice drills because the fear of failure in front of teammates is humiliating. Other times it's because the kid is lazy; he just doesn't like to work hard. In some sports, these characteristics would get a kid cut off the team. But Centore doesn't cut anybody from the football team, which is a fairly common maxim for high school football coaches.

Every high school football coach wants a player to learn how to contribute so the kid can help the team win games. Tom Centore is no different, but for Centore it has always been about more than the final numbers on the scoreboard. For twenty-five years, Centore has been teaching high school football players you don't hide at the back of the line if you want to improve your chances in life.

A 290-Pound Babysitter

Sometimes there will be obstacles in a teenage football player's quest to be a contributor.

Cote Lietar is a 6'2", 290-pound junior offensive and defensive lineman. A young man of color, he is—in football verbiage—a prospect. With his size and his decent mobility, he's the type of kid who could play college football , and Lietar says he wants to play in college.

Tom Centore knows if Lietar is ever going to get some college coaches to take a serious look at him, he will need to take his game to a higher level. He will need to become more committed. But Centore also knows it's tough to come to practice every afternoon and stay focused on becoming a better football player when you are worrying about your younger brother and sister, who are home alone.

"Cote lives in Cranston with his mother and his young brother and sister," Centore offered. "But his mother works a three-to-eleven shift every night, so there's nobody at home to watch the young children. Sometimes Cote has to leave practice early so he can take care of his little brother and sister. Cote is a good kid. Sometimes he just needs to work harder, but he's in a tough situation."

CHAPTER XVII

LOSING PUBLIC FAITH

East Providence, R.I. is a city with 47,000 residents, yet an appealing, small-town mentality. With the front door of East Providence High School only five miles from the Rhode Island state capital building in Providence, East Providence is unquestionable in the center of what is known as the Providence Metro area. Through the generations, a majority of East Providence residents have been employed in what would be considered blue-collar jobs. Yet located in the city's relatively small sixteen square miles are three private golf courses, including Wammoissette Country Club, often cited by *Golf Digest* as one of the "100 Best Golf Courses" in America.

East Providence is the type of American city that you don't see too often these days—a metropolitan city where a large percentage of its residents still have a sense of local community pride. It has been that way for generations. Some of that is probably related to the continued significant influence of a large number of Portuguese immigrants who moved to East Providence from Providence, Fall River and New Bedford beginning around 1900 until the onset of the Depression in 1930.

Also, like in other cities and towns around the Providence metropolitan area, for generations there had been a significant Irish presence in East Providence. With a heavy influence from two nationalities that are closely connected to the Roman Catholic Church, it's not surprising that Bill Stringfellow, the late, legendary East Providence high school football coach, once said to me about East Providence, "In this city, they gave directions by churches." It also helps the sense of community that for the past sixty years, East Providence has been the largest Rhode Island city or town with only one public high school.

So, on October 5, it was "Townie Pride Night" in East Providence when the East Providence High football team was hosting Cranston East. It was the flavor of small-town America in a city of more than 40,000. Students from every one of the city's eight public elementary schools, the two middle schools, and East Providence High marched through city streets following the high school marching band and a couple of fire trucks into Pierce Memorial Stadium—"Home of the Townies." That type of pre-game activity can be distracting to a visiting team's game preparations, and this is a Cranston East team that doesn't need any added distractions.

Football has a great history in East Providence. East Providence was one of the original members when the modern R.I. Interscholastic League was formed in 1932; and from 1932–1980, East Providence was third to only Cranston/Cranston East and private school power La Salle for most Division I/Class A football titles won. Cranston East may have won the League's first official Super Bowl Division I title in 1972, but East Providence won two titles over the next eight years.

Even when the private schools became League powerhouses in the late part of the 20th and early part of the 21s century, East Providence was still one of the top programs in the League, winning three state titles in the first seven years of the 21st century. With six private high schools that field football teams within twenty miles of East Providence High, it's not surprising East Providence lost some football players to the private schools. But through the decades of the second half of the 20th century, and even into the early years of the 21st century, a lot of East Providence's top student-athletes, including football players, stayed home and attended East Providence High. They were players like Jamie Silva, who went directly from leading East Providence to the 2003 Division I state football title to Boston College, where he became a 2007 Associated Press first-team All-American.

But in the fall of 2018, East Providence was like a lot of 21st century cities and towns in the northeast, where many residents had lost confidence in their public school system over the previous decade or so. The second half of the 20th century was a golden era for many public school systems in Rhode Island, as well as other parts of the Northeast. The growth of the "Baby Boomers" had prompted an influx of new education infrastructure in the '60s, '70s, and even into the '80s. Also, at least in the northeast, teachers' unions had gained local and state political clout.

The passage of Title IX in 1972 had increased opportunities for females in high school sports, as well as in the academic areas of science and math. But by the second decade of the 21st century, that new educational infrastructure of the '60s and '70s was getting old. The Recession of 2008 sparked financial crises in cities and towns throughout Rhode Island, and support of public education became a victim of the resulting austerity involving both education programs and facilities.

East Providence High was a prime example. The high school was built in 1952, and over the decades, there wasn't much modernization to the building. When it was built, the school included a spacious six-lane swimming pool. For decades it had been the best high school aquatic facility in Rhode Island. But it had been neglected for decades. In the fall of 2018, that once outstanding swimming pool had been closed for six years because of leaks caused by cracks in the pool that were deemed too expensive to fix.

In the spring of 2017, a Rhode Island television station aired a news report that showed a crumbling foundation and broken pipes in a basement area under East Providence High. Studies show that when students have access to modern facilities that are easy to navigate, their educational outcomes are better. By the second half of the 21st century's second decade, it didn't take an educational expert to know that deteriorating physical school buildings and classrooms without modern technology do not create good learning environments at East Providence High School.

Also, while East Providence High students were literally watching their high school crumble beneath them, the private schools in the metro Providence area were intelligently staging an arms race of educational facility building, including new athletic facilities. It all made their schools more appealing to students and their parents. As parents lost confidence in the public school system, those parents who had financial options either moved out of the city to towns with better public school systems or optioned to send their children to private/parochial schools.

The increased financial aid made available at some of those private schools in an effort to create a more diversified student body was making a private school education an option for some parents who hadn't ever previously thought of sending their child to a private school. Later in the fall of 2018, East Providence residents would vote on a bond issue that, if passed, would fund the construction of a new high school, but as the Townies and Thunderbolts were set to kick off on Oct. 5, many long-time Townie faithful had lost confidence in the quality of an East Providence High education.

When a community loses faith in its public education system, student-athletes are often the first group of students who look for an alternative. With six parochial/private high schools that have extensive varsity sports programs within a fifteen-mile radius of East Providence High, good student-athletes who live in East Providence certainly have a multitude of alternatives to the city's public high school.

The once proud East Providence High football program certainly fell upon hard times in the second decade of the 21st century. From 2012 to 2017, East Providence High football only had one winning season, and their combined regular season record over that period was 14–33.

Victories Are Not Automatic

Hector Duran was worried as he stood on the field a few minutes before the kickoff against East Providence.

This is Duran's team. He may not be an offensive star like Rayven Deoliveira or Robenson Antoine, or one of the best defensive players in the state, like Jamari Mason, but Hector is the guy who pays attention to everything that's happening every day in practice. Just like he worries about being the only man in his house and what he thinks that responsibility entails, right now he's also worrying he's not doing enough to motivate his football family teammates to improve every day in practice.

He knows it could be easy for some of his teammates to think they have solved all the problems that surfaced in that regular season opening loss to Shea with victories the past two Friday nights. That certainly seemed to be what some of the other Thunderbolts are thinking. The nagging shoulder injury will keep Jamari Mason out of another game, but the prospectus of East not having his defensive contributions tonight didn't keep Mason from feeling all the early season problems had been fixed as the Thunderbolts were preparing to kick off against East Providence.

"We will take care of this one and set up a big game with Hendricken next week," said Mason, as he stood there wearing his ever-present headphones, watching his teammates warming up.

Maybe it's his daily routine of worrying, not just about his own status, but also that of his young siblings, that has conditioned Hector Duran not to take anything for granted. He knows this team isn't like last year's team. That just because they have won a few games, the victories will not keep coming this year unless this team improves.

For some players, there can be a point in their senior season when they start worrying about not having yet received any college offers or not having the type of stats that will earn them All-State recognition. But that personal lack of recognition is not what's concerning Duran. He's worried because he hasn't been seeing some of the things in practice this season that he saw last year. He is worried about his teammates doing their job, and if they don't do their job, HIS team is not going to make the playoffs. He's trying to make sure they do their job so his football family will stay together through a playoff run.

Sure, the schedule says that even if East doesn't qualify for the playoff in the first week of November, it will still have a non-league game with Cranston West on Thanksgiving morning. But the playoffs are this team's Holy Grail. If they don't make the playoffs, the season will be a disaster for many of the players. Duran is a captain. He feels responsible for his team—just like the man in the house feels responsible for his family.

"There doesn't seem to be any sense of urgency. They're thinking it's just going to happen," Duran said, as I stood with him on the sidelines watching the final few minutes of warm-up.

Duran knows it doesn't just happen. You don't grow up as the oldest son of a basically single mother who has three other children and think it is going to just happen. So, he calls the team together in a circle before they break to line up for the opening kickoff. I couldn't hear what he was saying, but from outside the circle, you could see the passion in Duran's eyes.

"What did you tell them?" I asked Duran before he headed onto the field.

"I told them they have to step it up," Duran said, a stern expression still evident behind his facemask.

The man of the family has issued his teammates a wake-up call.

Have They Figured It Out?

Cranston East took the opening kickoff and, directed by Rayven Deoliveira's passing and running, started marching down the field. They seemed to be picking up right where they had left off last Friday night, with the thrilling late touchdown drive to win the game against St. Raphael. Maybe Mack Hanley was right a few weeks ago when he said, "We will figure it out."

East had moved into East Providence territory, and when a diving catch by Robenson on a third-and-long pass was momentarily ruled a completion, it looked like the Bolts had another first down—this time in the red zone. But then, after an officials' conference, the pass was ruled incomplete. The Thunderbolts had to punt.

An average forty-eight-minute high school football game involves about 120–130 plays, so you wouldn't think one play in the first five minutes of a game could affect the outcome of the game. But as Tom Centore has learned, this is a team that still has to learn not to let a little adversity upset its rhythm.

"They are good kids. They're just immature," Centore said earlier in the season.

In the ESPN series *Rolling with Tide,* aired in August, Alabama coach Nick Sabin had said, "You will see what one play breaks you; what one play makes you lose focus." That's true—especially in high school football. That one play isn't always a great play by the opposition. In the game of football, where everybody has an assignment on every play, all it takes is one or two players on your team to allow that immaturity to result in a loss of focus, and the glitches start snowballing.

Within a few minutes after the officials changed the ruling on Robenson's reception, the game turned dramatically against East. An East lineman lost his focus and missed a blocking assignment, giving an East Providence lineman a chance to charge it and block a Deoliveira punt. That gave East Providence the ball near midfield. On the Townies' first play, a Cranston defensive back allowed an EP receiver to get wide open, and he easily pulled down a long touchdown pass.

Had one play—that lack of maturity after what some people felt was a bad call on Robenson's reception—caused the lack of focus that paved the way for the blocked punt? Then had that play led to another lack of focus in letting an East Providence receiver get wide open?

Cranston East was suddenly caught in an avalanche of miscues. After East took the ensuing kickoff, Deoliveira, who is usually unyielding when handling the ball, fumbled on a roll-out, giving East Providence the ball again. This time, EP had the ball deep in Cranston territory. A few plays later, East Providence scored again. It was 14–0 only five minutes into the game.

The Cranston East defensive made a few more mistakes the next two times East Providence had possession, and within three minutes of the second quarter, Cranston East was trailing 25–0. Even the most diehard East Providence fan hadn't expected this. East had defeated East Providence by 23 points last season.

Rayven Deoliveira may have some shortcomings, but to his credit he normally doesn't play like an angry young man. His game normally is very composed, the type of composure that comes with having immense confidence in his own talent. But when East Providence pulled ahead 25–0, Deoliveira seemed pissed. He knew much of the East Providence point-production had been spawned by his blunders—his blocked punt, his fumble. The next time East took possession, there was nothing composed about his game; he was mad, and he was determined to make up for his gaffes. It didn't take him long to make good on his mission.

With Deoliveira's running spearheading a comeback, the East offense finally settled down in the second quarter, and the Thunderbolts scored 14 points on two touchdowns and a 2-point conversion rush. Rather than facing a 25–0 deficit, East had cut its deficit to 9 points with a few minutes remaining in the first half. Both the Thunderbolts' offensive and defensive lines were starting to take control, and one of the big reasons was the play of Omar Reyes.

Unlike some other East players who, at times, were voicing their frustrations by complaining about their own teammates as well as the game officials, Reyes was playing completely under control. He was constantly working to keep his teammates engaged in the game, but rather than his usual restrained and understated demeanor, he was loud—yelling encouragement. That's the thing about football. There are so many different kids who can make a surprise contribution.

Unfortunately, with a few minutes remaining in the half, Reyes' helmeted head hit the ground on a tackle close to the East sideline. It wasn't a head-to-head collision, but Reyes came to the sidelines and told the coaches he was a little dizzy. He never lost consciousness and was always aware of what he was doing. Ten years ago—maybe even five—Reyes probably would have gone to the bench for a few plays, got some water, and told the coach he was ready to go back in. But not these days. Trainor Kate Chaffee doesn't wait for players to come to her with problems. She goes looking for them—especially when she sees a potential head injury.

Today, the minute a coach or a trainer becomes aware of a blow to a player's head that has the potential to cause a concussion, the player has to leave the game. Before the player can return to the field at any future time, he must see a doctor (not a trainer), be cleared, and also follow some additional procedures before he can return to play. So, Reyes spent the final few minutes of the half sitting on the bench while Kate conducted a series of tests.

The coaches don't get involved with the evaluation; whatever the trainer says is gospel. At halftime, Kate told Tom Centore Reyes was done for the night. Along with all the other problems, the Thunderbolts had now lost one of their best linemen for the rest of the night.

The good news was the Thunderbolts had cut their deficit to only 9 points, and the late surge should give East the momentum going into the second half. East Providence would get the second half kickoff, so East would need a big defensive play at the start of the half.

Robinson Antoine delivered it when he intercepted a pass near midway field on East Providence's first possession of the third quarter. The Thunderbolts immediately started a drive toward the touchdown that would make it at least only a 3-point game—with virtually the entire second half to play. That incredibly poor start, the worst start an East team had seen in years, could be wiped out.

The Bolts picked up a pair of first downs, moving the ball to the East Providence 18, but an incomplete pass and two runs left the Bolts still 5 yards short of a first down on an upcoming fourth-down try. Tom Centore didn't even talk to Isaiah McDaniel about having Jon Loy try a very makeable field goal that would cut the deficit to 6 points.

"You have to be positive. You have to think you are going to score every time you have the ball," Centore had told the team a few weeks earlier. This was the Bolts' chance to think positive.

The call was 57 Roger & Larry. It's designed for the quarterback to roll left. If he thinks he has the edge, he keeps the ball and runs down the sideline; if he doesn't have the edge, he looks for a receiver down field. Rayven obviously felt his offensive line had controlled the edge because he never really looked for a receiver down field. He had picked up 3, maybe 4 yards, when an EP defensive back moved up to a spot just inside the sideline just before the guy holding the first down marker. The D-back didn't keep charging forward; he just waited there for Deoliveira.

Rayven is one of the hardest hitting runners in the state. He had shown that two weeks earlier, when he had literally run over a couple of Portsmouth defenders in that big victory.

That's why he had been a first-team All-State running back in 2017. But now he is the quarterback, and maybe he now has a TV quarterback mentality. On the NFL TV games, you never see a quarterback going directly at an opposing defender trying to run over him like some high school quarterbacks do. The TV quarterback protects the product—steps out of bounds to avoid a big hit. For whatever reason, rather than trying to overpower a smaller defensive back, Rayven tried to step out of bounds just beyond the first down stick, right in front of the Cranston East bench area. The problem was the guy holding the stick marking where the first down was, dropped the stick and ran for his personal safety when he saw Rayven heading toward the sidelines. So, Deoliveira was somewhat guessing where the first down mark was.

Not surprising, the Cranston East players and coaches standing on the sidelines near the play felt Deoliveira had made it. But the official running toward the sideline from the middle of the field threw his bean bag where he thought Raven had stepped out. When he looked at the bean bag and where the stick mark was in the ground, the official ruled Raven had stepped out of bounds about six inches short of the first down. Cranston East didn't get any points out of a great scoring opportunity, and East Providence took over possession.

Now it became a question of how quickly could the Thunderbolts recover from disappointment? How much would they let one play disrupt their focus? For that's the thing about football. You need to get right back up and recover from disappointment. There's no time for self-pity; the next snap, the next test of your character, is only twenty-five seconds away. Those are the life lessons Tom Centore is referring to in some fashion almost every afternoon after practice. If you are not ready for the next play, something disastrous could happen.

That's what happened to the Thunderbolts. Rather than keeping East Providence pinned down deep in its own territory, somebody on the East defensive unit missed an assignment on East Providence's first snap when play resumed. The East Providence quarterback found a hole in the line and broke loose on about a 60-yard touchdown run. A minute earlier, Cranston East was 10 yards from pulling within a few points of the lead. Now, the Thunderbolts were 22 points behind.

Cranston East never regained its focus. East Providence scored another touchdown later in the third quarter, and another in the fourth quarter, upping its lead to 42–16. By midway through the fourth quarter, the outcome had become obvious. Cranston East would lose its second game of the season. Rather than going into a showdown against Hendricken with a 3–1 league record and be playing the seven-time defending state champion for a first place tie in sub-division I-A, East now needed to start worrying about making the playoffs.

A look of dejection had creeped across the faces of some Cranston East players. They were feeling sorry for themselves. There was still five minutes to play in the game, but most of the East players wanted to get off the field immediately. All except Hector Duran. Duran was still looking for a way to help his team. He had injured his foot late in the third quarter. So, he couldn't run with the ball or play linebacker on defense. But Duran still wanted to be with his teammates.

"Put me in coach. I can block," Hector yelled toward a group of coaches standing on the sidelines in front of the disheartened East players.

In an otherwise frustrating night, Duran's "never stop working" declaration gave Ken Simone's spirits a lift. But Simone wasn't going to endanger Duran's well-being.

"You're finished for the night, "Simone said to Duran, with an appreciative tone.

More than a Loss

Isaiah McDaniel was waiting at the end of the line of Cranston East players after the two teams had exchanged post-game handshakes at midfield. McDaniel was stunned by what had just happened. It wasn't just that East had lost a game; McDaniel had thought the Thunderbolts would win. East Providence had played a good game. The Townies had executed their game plan well and gave themselves opportunities for some big plays. For McDaniel, the really discouraging thing was the way some East players had started blaming their teammates for what was happening on the field rather than looking into themselves to understand what they had failed to do. McDaniel's frustration continued boiling up as the team headed toward one of the end zones for the usual postgame team meeting. McDaniel was so upset he didn't wait for Tom Centore or any other coach to start talking.

"What bothers me was the way you acted. It didn't show character," McDaniel shouted to the players in a frustrated tone.

For McDaniel, character is the tenet of football that should never—can never—waver. Players will make mistakes; players will lose focus from practice to practice and game to game. But the character of a player's persona can never fluctuate. Blaming a teammate for a team's troubles rather than looking into their own teenage inner-soul shows lack of character. For McDaniel, that's against everything Cranston East football stood for.

At a time in American society when the discussion on American life is often more centered on character and values as much—maybe even more—than issues and ideology, football may be more important than ever. For Tom Centore, character is the cornerstone of the program he has built.

For Isaiah McDaniel, character has been the constant ingredient in the mixture of that cornerstone. He played a role in laying that cornerstone fifteen years ago when he convinced some of his classmates to come out for a team when nobody wanted to play football at Cranston East. He knows how important being part of this program was for him and how important it can be for these kids today.

It's not just for the kids from the tenements on Cranston Street near the Providence city line or the kids from the duplexes in the old Cranston Print Works mill village. It's also for the kids from Edgewood, and the kids from the well-appointed capes in the sections of the city, like where Alex Corvese grew up. For different kids, it's different life lessons without their even thinking about it being an education exercise. It's a game that's fun to play. But those games are the weekly exams to test whether they have learned the lessons of character building; the lessons of thinking about the other guys; working to help a teammate rather than blaming him for the team's shortfalls. Now, in McDaniel's mind, the Thunderbolts have failed a test—and not just the one on the scoreboard.

Who Will Show Up on Monday?

"I'm worried about who is going to show up for practice Monday," Centore said to me as we walked together toward the team buses following the East Providence game.

Centore is worried about more than just some kids becoming disheartened by an unexpected, one-sided loss to East Providence. The next game on the Thunderbolts' schedule is next Friday night against Hendricken at Cranston Stadium. Hendricken is good and big—and the East players know it. Hendricken has a big, 6'7", 350-pound offensive lineman who had settled a national recruiting war when he committed to the University of Georgia a few weeks before the start of the season. Centore is afraid some kids might just say why bother.

Centore is also worried about more than just an upcoming game. Now it's the fate of the whole program that has him concerned. He has worked for fifteen years building the program, through all the changes in the student makeup at East. Now he's worried the program that has meant so much to so many kids—kids who need this football family—could be in trouble because some players don't understand character is more than a word in an SAT prep course.

"My father always said 'see who shows up on Monday,'" Tom Centore quipped about Tony Centore's appraisal of a team gut-check following a tough Friday night loss. "We'll see," Centore offered, with a tone of uncertainty in his voice.

CHAPTER XVIII

EVERYTHING AGAINST THEM, EXCEPT ON THE FOOTBALL FIELD

Monday was Columbus Day, a school holiday, so Tom Centore scheduled practice for 10 a.m. That would give the players who worked at the multitude of fast-food restaurants around Cranston a chance to make some much-needed money working hours they usually don't have a chance to work. That's one of the things Centore had to start factoring into his coaching strategy six or seven years ago. Cranston East football has never been a team of affluence. While there were always a few players from Edgewood, including some who lived in those big homes near the water, for generations the vast majority of Cranston East football players were the sons of parents who were squarely in the middle-class range of the economic standing. They were the type of kids who might work one weekend night to have some spending money in their pocket for a weekend date or to purchase some more advanced electronic entrainment device. But the coinage for their basic needs—a place to live, food, a teenager's basic wardrobe—was provided by their parents.

But for some East players, that started changing five or six years ago. Today, many of the Thunderbolts work—not only for their own indulgences but to help supplement the family income needed for shelter, food, and basic clothing.

"The difference between the kids here and the kids at West, is that at West they work because they want to. For them, it's just something to do," said Jarrod Clowery one day when I asked him to compare Cranston East players with their cross-city counterparts at Cranston West. "A lot of our kids work because they have to. Their income helps support their families."

That means Tom Centore schedules his holiday practice sessions not just for the convenience of football players but also for some family bread-winners. At most schools, all that would be needed for the players to get ready for a holiday morning practice would be for a custodian to open the school door so the players could get into the locker room, change into their equipment, and walk out to the practice field. But at East, there's also the question of scheduling a bus and bus driver to transport the players to practice, which is an added expense to the school's budget. That's not something they need to think about three miles away at Cranston West, but it's another case of the "that's just the way it is" sense of acceptance they have come to embrace at East.

So, Centore doesn't schedule a bus for Monday morning, which meant the players had to deal with bringing their equipment home and getting to the practice field on their own. What it all adds up to is there could be a lot of built-in excuses for why a player couldn't make practice on a holiday. Then, of course, there was also a discouraging loss like the one the Thunderbolts suffered at East Providence Friday night. So, Isaiah McDaniel was pleased when he walked out onto the practice field Monday morning and saw about 45–50 players there getting ready for practice.

"I'm pleased, maybe a little surprised, but very pleased," McDaniel said, with a sly smile. "Just about everybody who will be playing Friday night against Hendricken is here."

Different Challenges

Every high school football coach knows that when a team is successful, everybody wants to be part of it. It's when a team is struggling, when things aren't going well, that a coach can face his toughest challenges. High school football is so different than other high school sport. While a basketball coach has to deal with ten to twelve egos, and a baseball coach may have twenty to twenty-five players on his roster, many high school football coaches are dealing with fifty, sixty, or more teenage egos. Of course, that's nothing new. High school football coaches have been dealing with teenage egos for generations, including Centore since he became the East head coach sixteen years ago.

The last six or seven years, however, Centore's job as head coach has become more complex. As the demographics of certain parts of eastern Cranston began changing substantially around 2011 or 2012, Centore came to understand that more of his players were coming from single-parent homes; or there were kids like Dayshaun White, who was being raised by somebody other than a mother or father. Even in homes where there are two parents, the economic pressures on some of those parents means some players are working several low-paying jobs just to help put food on the table and pay the rent for an apartment in Cranston.

Unfortunately, some parents develop the mentality that they don't need to spend time dealing with their teenage son's anxieties because a fifteen- or sixteen-year-old boy is old enough to take care of himself. Centore knows nothing can be further from the truth for so many of his players.

"You are constantly checking on them; making sure they are doing the things they have to do," Centore offered about his daily routine involving his players. "Making sure they are in school; making sure they are at practice. It's challenging. It's a satisfying challenge when the players are successful, but it's a wearing challenge."

More and more, Centore has sensed some of his players weren't getting that positive reinforcement from home that's so important when a teenager is struggling with some of life's challenges. That's why the football field is so important. For some of his players, the football field is the only place they are experiencing success.

"A lot of our kids are new to the Cranston school system. They come from a poor school system in Providence, so they are behind academically when they get here," Centore offered. "They are being academically pushed here compared to what they were required to do in Providence. So many of them are having problems in the classroom. They are not feeling good about what they are doing in the classroom. Plus, for some of them, life is a constant financial struggle for his family. Everything seems to be against them, except on the football field. The football field is the only place they feel good about what they are doing. That's why this team is so important to them."

So, a season like the one the Thunderbolts are experiencing becomes a matter of worrying about more than the Friday night game plan for Centore and his staff. It's often said a field of athletic endeavor is an extension of the classroom; that high school sports stresses the same quality of commitment needed for success in the classroom. It's the focus, perseverance, and sense of purpose being developed on the football field that may help them survive in the classroom. So, Centore knows for a lot of his players the daily practice sessions are about more than just perfecting a game plan.

"When the team is struggling, other things in some players' lives get magnified," said Centore. "They need more attention in a lot of aspects of their lives. You want to help them. But it's hard because then you are not worrying about coaching as much."

It isn't just the star player who struggles with not being able to make the big play. In fact, more often than not, it's that kid who just wants to be part of the team, the kid who wants to be associated with something successful, who has a problem handling a team's lack of success on the field. For some high school football coaches these days, taking care of the kid who just wants to be part of the team is one of his most important roles, even though it usually doesn't have a direct influence on the scoreboard.

"You have to do more, and you don't have the time to give them because, as a coach, you are trying to get your team ready, correct some things in the game plan," said Centore. "That's the challenging part of it. The focus comes off the field a little more."

These days, the Thunderbolts' collective ego has definitely been wounded. They have lost two games most people didn't expect them to lose. Now—over the next two weeks—they will play two games most people expect them to lose: Hendricken Friday night and North Kingstown in two weeks. That means they could be looking at a 2–4 League record. If that happens, the Thunderbolts' hopes of making the playoffs will be in serious trouble.

The dream of another championship season may have evaporated by Columbus Day. But despite that bleak outlook, the majority of the players are there Monday morning. After Friday night's game, Centore had quipped one of his late father's football reality checks about seeing who shows up for a Monday practice after a tough Friday night loss. Now it's 10 a.m. on a holiday Monday morning, and just about everybody who will play a meaningful role in a big game Friday night is here.

Is It Hopeless?

Centore knows for a team like East, there can be a built-in excuse to take a "it's hopeless" attitude against a team like Hendricken. Hendricken won the state's major high school football title for seven consecutive years from 2010 to 2016. That record string of state titles finally ended in the 2017 Major State Super Bowl when La Salle posted a 1-point overtime upset victory over the Hawks, but now Hendricken has a talented and veteran team anxious to take home another Super Bowl trophy.

In Rhode Island, public school fans are constantly complaining it's unfair for a public school team to play a private school athletic juggernaut like Hendricken. They claim the private schools—with their unlimited student body geographic boundaries—get players from cities and towns from all over the state, even some students from towns in southeastern Massachusetts. Nobody knows how high the odds will be stacked against Cranston East Friday night better than Tom Centore. Centore has been dealing with the private schools' advantages since East moved up to Division I nine years ago. But Centore will not allow his players to accept a built-in excuse. So, when the two-hour practice finished around noon on Monday, Centore called the entire team to center of the field for the usual post-practice meeting.

"We certainly have our hands full Friday night," Centore admitted to the players kneeling in a circle in the middle of the field.

Despite the disheartening results of Friday night's game, kneeling in front of Centore was a circle of eager faces looking for a reason to think they have a chance to beat the unbeatable foe. Centore quickly gave it to them.

"If you are an athlete, and you are a competitor, this is the game you live for," Centore said, raising his voice a few octaves with every few sentences. "Nobody believes it can happen—especially after last week. Everybody thinks we are going to give up on ourselves."

Centore stopped talking for a few seconds as he looked around the circle of players in front of him—like a priest looking around his congregation during a Sunday morning sermon.

"I got tired of the text messages and emails over the weekend asking me what happened Friday night," Centore yelled, when he eventually resumed talking. "This is your chance to show them the Cranston football team never gives up on itself."

Omar Reyes returned to practice Tuesday after being cleared by a doctor of any ill-effects of the helmet-to-ground hit he had sustained Friday night. His presence on the field is important. When Centore first called the players together for a mid-practice meeting, one of the younger players kneeling on the outer perimeter of the circle had turned to a teammate to ask him a question. Reyes quickly turned to the two young players, gave them both a stern look, and raised his finger to his mouth indicating not to talk while the coach was talking. His work ethic is unmatched, and he is making more and more big plays every game. Now, even though he's only a junior, he's also becoming a leader—a quiet leader, but a leader.

That's the thing about the Thunderbolts. The contributions that build team character don't just come from the stars. They come from kids like Mack Hanley, who showed up with his arm in a cast every day for the first month of practice even though he wasn't a captain and knew he wasn't going to get on the field. Jarrod Clowery, whose season ended in the first game of the regular season, but he has been there every day at practice. Omar Reyes, who doesn't like to create attention, but he is coming to realize the younger players need to see his creed of discipline and respect for coaches in action. And of course, there's Hector Doran, the teenager who has more family responsibilities than most seventeen-year-olds; the kid who has never known a father figure but wants to be one for any of his teammates who need one.

Football Moms Worry

"How does your mother feel about you still playing after what happened Friday night?" I asked Omar Reyes about his head hitting the ground incident in the game against East Providence.

"She was a little iffy about my coming back this soon. But I'm okay," Reyes replied with a smile.

Every football mother worries, but Reyes' mother has seen all the positive things football has done for her son. She knows football has brought his leadership skills to the forefront. She knows football has helped make Omar, whose basic nature is to be laid back, a competitive kid.

But Mom still worries.

No Room for Lazy Learners

There had been three days of good practice sessions since the loss to East Providence, but now on Thursday afternoon, while the Thunderbolts were enjoying a rare opportunity to practice at the stadium, Isaiah McDaniel felt he needed to remind the team about one of last Friday night's problems.

"We can't take a play off because the play is going the other way," McDaniel yelled to the group of players standing in the middle of the practice field. "That's what we did last week against East Providence, then suddenly the play comes back your way and you are not ready."

Adjusting on the fly is one of the great tutorials experienced by high school football players. Some people say too many students these days are lazy learners. Today's teenagers know more information than any previous generation; but they are not open to critical thinking; not open to doing more than a couple of clicks on a search engine to find the answer to a question or solve a problem. They are growing up in a country where many people think the solution to every problem is give somebody an app rather than learning how to interact with other people. It's lazy learning. But you can't be a lazy learner in football.

"Do it again," Tom Centore yelled after he was not happy with the way the offensive unit had executed a run-through at Thursday's practice. When he still wasn't happy with the second try, once again he bellowed, "Do it again." It went on that way for thirty minutes, with Centore demanding two, sometimes three, repeats of a situation run-through. All week it seemed Centore had the undivided attention of most players at practice, and he was taking advantage.

It seemed the loss to East Providence had caused some players to take stock—suddenly they realize they may not make playoffs. All season the coaches had been telling them nothing will come easy this year. Unfortunately, they have come to start realizing it's true with two games coming up against the two toughest teams in the state. Centore still is not sure the team has bought into it as a whole, but at least now most of them are paying attention.

This Is Their Private World

It was 5:30 p.m., still a half-hour before complete sunset, but the sun had already dropped below the twenty-foot concrete wall of the Cranston Stadium west side grandstands. It left a reddish glow across the stadium's artificial turf as Centore called the whole team to the middle of the field at the end of practice. On the other side of that wall, rush-hour traffic had already started to clog Park Avenue, Cranston's main east-to-west artery. They are cars driven by Cranston residents with diversified concerns: a parent rushing home to put dinner on the table; a delivery truck driver intent on finishing his or her route; the elderly couple making a stop at either the CVS or Walgreen's drugs stores, which both front Park Ave a block from the stadium. But inside the stadium walls is a family experiencing a phenomenon that belonged only to the Cranston East football team. It's a team that doesn't look like any other team in Rhode Island, which for almost a decade now has been a source of team pride. Yet, right now, it's a team undergoing an identity crisis, and Tom Centore challenges them to ponder who they are.

"I know what happened last Friday night was not this team," Centore said in a solemn, but forceful voice. "We have an opportunity over the next few weeks to really redeem ourselves, starting Friday night."

At a time when many Americans seem unable to find a common language of expression, a common cultural of context for the past decade, the Cranston East football team has been a team of diversity with a common culture of character. Every weekday autumn afternoon, they test that culture through the common language of football.

So, Centore presents a challenge.

"Everybody wants to come here Friday night to see what kind of show they are going to put on against you. See how good that kid everybody is talking about really is. They want to see how he and his team push you around," Centore quipped.

Now, it's a matter of pride.

"If you are an athlete, you are not going to let them do that," Centore declared in a challenging tone.

"If you are an athlete, this is what you want," Centore offered.

Is beating Hendricken a long shot? Of course it is, and nobody knows that better than Centore. But when you have been coaching high school football players for twenty-five years, you know when things aren't going well, you need to find that tidbit of hope that keeps your coaching juices flowing. Centore might have found it the past few days with the enlivened practice sessions. All season, he has been upset about the lack of mental preparation. His coaching credo has always been you might not have the talent to be great, but you can always be prepared.

This year's team could have been the prime example of that attitude. It's a team that doesn't have the roster-wide talent of some previous East teams, but if they had been mentally prepared, they could have won a few more games. Centore has been blaming himself for much of that lack of preparation because he was so mentally occupied with his father's illness and death. But the reality is for weeks, some players didn't understand football is a game of doing things you might not want to do as an individual, but you do it because it will benefit the team. Now, Centore is seeing that sense of selflessness playing out in practice.

"We just have to get better on some little things," Centore continued to the players. "Last Friday was disastrous on specials. One thing I saw today was when I called for special scout, I had eleven guys run out for specials. That shows me a lot. We are down right now because of what happened last Friday night. But you know, one game doesn't define a program. We can come right back."

Centore knows his team is battling for more than just a playoff spot right now—it is a team battling for its soul. He knows the kids feel some people around the school, some people around the city, have already quit on them. Two league losses, and Hendricken and North Kingstown coming up—a lot of people in the city think this isn't a championship team like last year. Some people might think if you're not going to win a championship, why continue to put in all the hard work?

It doesn't surprise Centore that people who are not empathetic as to why young men play football could also think about not supporting a team when things start going bad. But Centore can't let his players quit on themselves because he knows once a player gives up on himself, he's done. Centore can't let that happen because he fears, for some of his players, it could become a life-long state of mind. So, Friday night has become more than a just a forty-eight-minute high school football game.

"Friday night, people are looking for us just to show up. We never just show up here," Centore said, his voice suddenly raising a few octaves. "We are going to compete. We are going to play hard, and you never know. Believe in yourself, and a lot of things can happen on the football field."

CHAPTER XIX

A POWERHOUSE WITH A PEDIGREE

Bishop Hendricken high school is a Roman Catholic-affiliated, all-boys school with about 1,000 students located in Warwick, only about ten miles from Cranston East. Compared to the other well-known Catholic high schools in Rhode Island, Hendricken doesn't have a long history. Some of the other Rhode Island parochial high school athletic powers have been in existence for at least 95 years, but Hendricken didn't open until the fall of 1959.

But while its institutional backstory may be thinner than the other Catholic schools in Rhode Island, Hendricken is definitely rich when it comes to sports lore. Hendricken fields teams in all of the fourteen sports the R.I. Interscholastic League offers in boys' competition, and since it joined the League in 1960, Hendricken had won at least four state titles in each Interscholastic League sport going into the 2018–'19 school year.

In the often called "major" boys' sports of football, basketball, and baseball, Hendricken had won a combined total of fifty-one state titles. All totaled in its fifty-eight years of Interscholastic League competition, Hendricken had won a sport's major state title 201 times by the start of the 2018–'19 school year. It's probably not surprising that an all-boys college-prep school, with almost 1,000 boys that can draw its students from any city or town in Rhode Island, as well as some nearby Massachusetts cities and towns, is an athletic powerhouse. When you factor in that Hendricken is the only all-boys school in Rhode Island; is a Roman Catholic-affiliated school in the state, with the most Roman Catholics per capita in the country; and also accepts students of any religious domination, it's not shocking supporters of public high school athletic teams in Rhode Island feel Hendricken has an unfair advantage.

With that type of athletic history, it's also not surprising that some Hendricken graduates have gone on to add to the Hendricken athletic mystique with their performances in the college and professional ranks.

Will Blackmon, now an NFL Network commentator, played four years at Hendricken in the late 1990s and early 21st century before immediately going on to a stellar collegiate football career at Boston College. He then played eleven seasons in the NFL from 2006–2016 for Green Bay, the New York Giants, Seattle, Jacksonville, and Washington.

Rocco Baldelli, who would be named manager of the Minnesota Twins in the winter of 2019, was starring for the Hendricken baseball team when he was drafted in the first round of the 2000 Major League draft. He signed a Major League contract the same month he led Hendricken to the state high school baseball title in June of 2000.

David Emma was a Hendricken ice hockey star before going to Boston College, where he was named the 1991 Hobey Baker award winner, the award presented to the National College Hockey Player of the Year.

The late Steve Furness was a star Hendricken football player in the late 1960s before going on to help the Pittsburg Steelers win four Super Bowl titles from 1974–1979 as member of the Steelers vaulted "Steel Curtain" defensive line.

The Rich Get Richer

Hendricken teams in the sports of football and basketball certainly had good teams for the first four decades of the school's existence, but nothing like the runs the Hawks football and basketball teams have enjoyed over the past fifteen years. At the start of the 2018 school year, since 2004, the Hendricken football and basketball teams had combined for a total of eighteen state titles: seven in football and eleven in basketball.

Part of that success might be traced to an education study Hendricken had an outside consulting firm conduct around the turn of the 21st century. One of the recommendations of the study was that the school needed to become more racially diversified. The school needed to make daily life at Hendricken look more like the world outside Hendricken's nice, suburban New England campus.

There was no question for decades after its founding, Hendricken was a school of mainly white boys going to school on a campus located deep in the heart of Rhode Island suburbia. The school's campus sits on thirty-four acres at the far southern tip of the city of Warwick, only a few miles from Narragansett Bay. The campus borders a working produce farm, whose corn stalks grow only a few yards from some of the Hendricken classroom windows.

While the school couldn't change its campus location, the report said the school needed to make its student body looked more like the 21st century world outside suburban Warwick. Translated, the school needed more faces of color in its student body. While some of the great Hendricken athletic teams of the 1970s, '80s, and '90s had players with faces of color, they were few and far between. In several seasons, when Will Blackmon was a star of the Hendricken football team, Blackmon was the only face of color on the team.

"I was the only one. It definitely was a different experience for me," Blackmon once told me about his being the only Black player on the Hendricken football team when he moved up to the varsity in his sophomore season in 1999.

Indeed, being the only face of color was a different experience for Blackmon. He had grown up in Providence attending elementary and middle school in a public school system that was composed of well over 50 percent minority students. When his father moved the family to the South Elmwood section of Cranston after Will's mother died of Crohn's Disease, Will became a minority member of his community. But he still had neighborhood friends of color, like Isaiah McDaniel.

If Blackmon had decided to remain in public school when he reached high school, his residence meant he would have been a Cranston East student—and football player. But the Cranston East football program had quickly gone into a tailspin after its surprising state Super Bowl title in 1987. By the time Blackmon was getting ready to go to high school, Cranston East football was in the pits, with their combined 3–31 record over a four-year period in the late 1990s.

"He wanted to play on a good team, and Cranston East football wasn't good back then," Wayne Blackmon, Will's father, told me about why his son told him he wanted to attend Hendricken.

"I just had to figure out a way to pay the tuition," said Wayne Blackmon, who was a correctional officer in the state prison system when Will was a high school student.

Hendricken was a difficult transition for Blackmon. Not only was he the only face of color on the varsity football team in his sophomore season, but he was also one of the few students of color walking the Hendricken corridors during the school day.

"It was definitely different," Blackmon told me with a sly smile about his early days at Hendricken. But Blackmon's quiet and infectious personality, combined with his enormous athletic talent, paved the way for an overall good high school experience for him at Hendricken. To this day, Blackmon still talks about how much the people at Hendricken did for him, helping develop both his athletic talent and his personal character.

To the credit of the people in charge of Hendricken at the time of the educational study—they paid attention. The school began an active effort to racially diversify its student body. In the fall of 2018, while an overwhelming majority of Hendricken students were still white, there were definitely more faces of color in the halls of Hendricken every day.

Of course, when a Roman Catholic-affiliated high school in the northeast determines it needs to add faces of color to its student body, one of the primary sources for finding potential minority students is from the inner-city Catholic parishes. Hendricken's primary objective in their expanded program of diversity may have been finding some young men of color who could benefit from the structure, discipline, and academic exposure the school felt it offered. But there's no doubt that a lot of those students of color were also good athletes.

Like a lot of Catholic schools throughout the northeast, Hendricken has definitely used its success in sports to market the school. Highway billboards, TV and radio ads, and print media advertising extorting the virtues of a Hendricken education—including "a highly successful athletic program"—are regularly seen throughout Rhode Island.

Became a Messiah

Despite being a Rhode Island high school superstar with future NFL-type talent, Will Blackmon could never lead Hendricken to a state football championship in his four varsity seasons at Hendricken (1998–2001). But while Blackmon may never have led the Hawks to a state title during his high school career, he has had profound influence enhancing the current Hendricken football reputation.

For more than a decade, young Rhode Island football players followed Blackmon as he went from being one of the nation's top college punt and kickoff returners to being a great NFL kickoff returner, then an outstanding defensive back, including an appearance with the Giants in their 2011 Super Bowl victory. It has certainly helped Hendricken's reputation that Blackmon, who in the fall of 2018 was beginning a career as an analyst on the NFL network, has taken every opportunity he has had to talk positively about his high school alma mater.

One of the pre-teen Rhode Island players following Blackmon's professional career was a young kid growing up in Providence named Kwity Paye. Paye was growing up in a public housing development in the heart of inner-city Providence when he started following Blackmon's career. He had been born in a West African refugee camp because his mother had been forced to flee her native Liberia to escape the horrors of a civil war when she was sixteen. But she managed to bring Kwity to America when he was an infant.

She was raising Kwity, and another older son, in South Providence, a section of the city where drugs and violence were all around the two young brothers. But their mother protected her sons by making sure they were always involved in constructive activities—especially sports. She made sure they were surrounded by good, positive-minded people, even if every day was a financial struggle. She also made sure her sons understood the value of education.

Even as a young kid, Paye had good size and excellent speed. So, it was no secret around the Rhode Island youth football ranks that Kwity Paye could be the next great Rhode Island high school player, and Kwity wanted to go to Hendricken because that's where Will Blackmon had played.

Hendricken had already begun a title run when Paye entered high school in the fall of 2013. But Paye's presence from 2013–2016 played a major role in Hendricken winning what would be a record seven consecutive state titles by the time Payne ended his high school career. When he was a high school freshman, Payne was about 6'3", 210 pounds, and he had sprinter-type speed. In fact, he was both a sprinter and shot putter for the Hendricken indoor and outdoor track teams in the winter and spring months. His running and play at defensive end led Hendricken to the state freshman football title in 2013. As a varsity player in his sophomore year, he had a break-out performance at defensive end in Hendricken's 2014 state Super Bowl victory over Cranston East.

By his junior year, Paye was being recruited by several Division I schools, and eventually he accepted a scholarship offer from the University of Michigan. Paye's earning a scholarship to Michigan put Hendricken football at a whole different level from any other Rhode Island high school football program. There had never been a Rhode Island high school football player who had been offered a scholarship by a nationally ranked Big Ten team. So, if you were a young football player in Rhode Island who thinks he has the potential to go big time, you wanted to play at Hendricken so you could become the next player drawing big-time college scouts to Rhode Island.

Coincidently, in the fall of 2018—in the same week Cranston East and Hendricken were preparing for their October 12 regular season meeting—out in Michigan, Paye, who by then was a Michigan sophomore, was being named the Big Ten Defensive Player of the Week.

Paye did more than just enhance the Hendricken reputation within the Rhode Island borders. Having seen how Paye was playing at Michigan, more and more big time Division I college football programs began checking out the Hendricken rosters to see whether there were any more "diamonds in rough"—especially big diamonds.

A Very Big Diamond

Xavier Truss wasn't an extremely big kid when he first started elementary school in his hometown of West Warwick, RI, a town of 29,000 about ten miles from the Hendricken campus. As a member of an African American family in a town that's 93 percent white, Truss was known in his hometown. But people really started noticing him when he began a growth spurt in the fourth grade. By the time he was in the eighth grade, he was 6'4" and 215 pounds. When he entered Hendricken as a freshman in the fall of 2015, he was 6'6" and 280 pounds. He played on the freshman football team, but the word was he was just a big kid with a gentle nature on and off the football field.

"When I was younger, I played football, but I didn't really like hitting kids. They called me the Gentle Giant a lot. I would hear things like "You're a teddy bear," Truss once told me.

It was in his sophomore season, in 2016, that Truss began to understand it was okay, when he was on the football field, to flip the switch from his normal gentle nature to that of an aggressive athlete.

"I needed a reality check from my parents and my coaches," Truss told me in the spring of 2018.

Watching Kwity Paye's work ethic up close, when Truss was a sophomore and Paye was a senior in the fall of 2016, also helped Truss' transformation. Paye was the star of the team, the best player in the state, yet nobody on the team worked harder than Kwity at practice.

"I think it was in my sophomore year when I moved up to the varsity and started playing with Kwity that I started to realize how much I had to work," Truss said. "Kwity really helped me. He showed me you have to be your best every day at practice. He told me it's what you're doing in the weight room when nobody is looking at you that's important. You have to make sure you are getting stronger. You always have to be working on your footwork."

So, Truss began working hard and as the old saying goes, "you can't teach size." By the start of his junior season in 2017, he was a 6'7", 315-pound dominant offensive tackle. By the end of his junior season, in 2017, Truss had become the subject of a national recruiting war. In August 2018, just before he was about to start his senior season at Hendricken, Truss announced he was accepting a scholarship offer from the University of Georgia.

That's what Cranston East would be facing Friday night—an undefeated team led by a 6'7", 325-pound offensive linemen who had big time college coaches coming to Rhode Island.

CHAPTER XX

YOU NEVER FORGET A
NIGHT LIKE THIS

Jonathon Loy's face was basically hidden behind the facemask of his helmet. But standing on the sideline in front of the Cranston East bench in the opening minutes of Friday night's game against Hendricken, you could still detect a huge smile on the senior kicker's face as he jogged off the field.

The majority of the fans in the Cranston Stadium stands had probably expected Hendricken would quickly blast out to a big lead after the opening kickoff and take the suspense out of the game early. But Cranston East had won the coin toss and elected to receive. The Thunderbolts, sparked by Rayven Deoliveira's running and passing, had steadily moved down the field—all the way to the Hendricken 15-yard line. But then the drive stalled, leaving the Bolts with a fourth and six.

Some of the players on the bench were uttering "go-for-it" in a low tone, not wanting Tom Centore to think they were trying to tell him what to do. But Centore felt getting an early lead against Hendricken might serve as a psychological advantage for the Thunderbolts, so he didn't hesitate sending Loy onto the field for a 28-yard field goal attempt. In the regular season opening game against Shea a month ago, Centore had opted to have David DaSilva, a soccer player who also was trying to become a football kicker, attempt a 40-yard kick for a game-tying field goal on the final play of regulation time. But that kick failed, and over the ensuing month, DaSilva hadn't been a regular at football practice because of his soccer commitments.

Loy, on the other hand, had been there every day. It's a lead-pipe cinch Loy was disappointed when Centore hadn't chosen him to kick the field goal attempt against Shea, but Loy never showed any umbrage toward his coach. He was right back at practice the following Monday, trying to get better.

"I would do anything for that man," Loy had said about Centore back in August when we talked about the positive influence football had been in the life of the grandson of a Laotian refugee who was trying to find his own identity in 21st century Cranston. The kid whose grandmother had waded through the rice fields of Laos while pregnant with Loy's mother wasn't going to let a little bruised ego stop him from working every afternoon to help make his team better. For a month, Loy never missed a practice, and now it was his chance to do something big for the team that has given him a new prospective on life.

So what if the most dominant defensive line in the state was coming at him? When Loy's kick sailed through the middle of the uprights with at least 15 yards to spare, the 1,000 or so fans on the Cranston East side of the stadium erupted in elation, sending Loy off the field with that a luminous smile evident behind the bars of his facemask.

There's no defined scientific way to precisely measure how much a moment like this can mean to a young man like Jonathan Loy. Loy had never expected to be in a position like this; never thought that one night he would have 1,000 people standing and cheering for him because of something he did on the football field. He was the quiet kid who never drew any attention to himself for something he had done. He might have gone through his entire life following that pattern, but then he went out for the football team when he came to Cranston East. He met a man named Tom Centore and said "yes" when a freshman coach asked him whether he wanted to try being a place-kicker.

If he hadn't decided to play football, he never would have been part of this football family, with all these guys who have so many different backstories. Being part of this football family has taught him things about life he never would have experienced by just living with his own family.

This moment of exuberance will fade. The fans sat back down and Loy, after a few minutes of receiving backslaps from teammates when he reached the bench, would refocus on the game and his team's quest to pull off a major upset. But in the days, months, even years to come, there will be brief moments when Loy will remember this night. The night he kicked the field goal to give Cranston East a lead against Hendricken. That's what high school football does; it presents a wide range of players with an opportunity to have a life-long memory, even if it was just one play on one night.

Not What the Fans Expected

Nobody was surprised when Hendricken came right back on the ensuing series after Jon Loy's field goal and scored a touchdown. Robenson Antoine did manage to come flying across from the right side and blocked the conversion kick attempt, however, so Hendricken was only ahead, 6–3. The Hendricken fans in the stands on the other side of the field didn't seem too upset about the missed extra point attempt. They had that look of confidence; some may say the same type of arrogance that NFL fans around the country have come to see on the faces of New England Patriot fans during the Tom Brady era. That "We let you stay in a game for a little while, but now we are going to take control" look.

But East was playing on a different level tonight. A few minutes before the end of the first quarter, Rayven Deoliveira tossed a pass to Chance McKinney, breaking down the right side, and McKinney broke loose on a 91-yard touchdown dash. At the end of the first quarter, Cranston East was leading mighty Hendricken, 9–6.

East was playing better than it had played in any game this season. But when a team has a veteran quarterback who can pass and a 325-pound lineman opening holes for speedy running backs, it's not surprising Hendricken was able to score two touchdowns early in the second quarter. But Deoliveira also directed a second quarter drive to another Cranston East touchdown. So, at halftime, the Thunderbolts were only trailing by five points, 20–15. If the Hendricken fans had come to the stadium expecting an early runaway so they could head home by halftime, they were wrong. This was a great high school football game.

"This is your chance to show them who you are," Tom Centore had challenged his team at practice a few days before the game, and under the bright Friday night lights of Cranston Stadium, that's what the Thunderbolts were doing. Tonight, it was a Cranston East football team that was laser-focused on one thing: proving it could play with Hendricken. It was a team following its coaches game plan to near-perfection.

Deoliveira was keeping the Hendricken defense guessing with his mobility and passing at quarterback, and Robenson

Antoine had delivered a couple of sensational pass receptions. Somehow, Hector Duran had found ways to get around the big Hendricken linemen from his linebacker berth, and Dayshaun White, Omar Reyes, and Cote Lietar were proving they were three of the best two-way linemen in the state.

Nobody had to tell the Cranston East players about the personnel advantages Hendricken had, with its ability to draw students from throughout the state. All the East players needed to do was look at their own team. One of the Hendricken players was the cousin of East sophomore Eric Thomas, and they both live in the same former Cranston Print Works Village duplex across from the East practice field. It was an example of how the private schools' geographic ability to fill a team roster with talented players could literally reach the edge of the Cranston East practice field. But nobody at East pressed the issue. It was just another case of the "that's the way it is" sense of acceptance of League rules that East coaches and players have come to live with.

Besides, for the first twenty-four minutes of a Friday night football game, nobody on the East team was thinking about being at a disadvantage. The Thunderbolts were playing on close terms with the best team in the state. Xavier Truss may have been the player people had come to see, but for the first twenty-four minutes of the game, Rayven DeOliveira and Robenson Antoine were the two most exciting players on the field.

Hendricken scored a touchdown on its first possession of the second half, but then East came back and scored, keeping the Hawks' advantage at only a touchdown going into the fourth quarter.

"Will making one bad play cause you to lose your focus on the next play?" Nick Sabin had asked his Alabama football team in the *Rolling with the Tide* documentary back in August.

That one play for Cranston came midway through the fourth quarter. Hendricken scored a touchdown, pushing its advantage to two touchdowns, and the frustration of Hendricken scoring caused the Thunderbolts to lose focus. Despite having a two-touchdown lead, Hendricken tried an on-side kick on the ensuing kickoff. The ball took a bounce on the ground over the heads of the Cranston East players on the front line, and none of the second line East players reacted fast enough to grab the loose ball. Hendricken recovered on about the East 45, and a few minutes later, Hendricken scored again. Two touchdowns within a few minutes. With only a few minutes to play, Hendricken was ahead 35–21

To its credit, East didn't stop trying to register the biggest upset Rhode Island high school football would have seen in decades. With a little over three minutes to play, Deoliveira was engineering a drive toward another touchdown, but the drive halted around the Hendricken 25 when the Hawks' defense made a nice stop on an East fourth-and-six and took over on downs.

A few seconds later, Rayven Deoliveira was standing on the sideline imploring his teammates on the East defensive unit to make the stops that would give the Thunderbolts the ball again. He desperately wanted to get back on the field and have the ball in his hands at least one more time. This was the game he had been thinking about since he knew he would be the Cranston East quarterback before the season started. The night he would prove to everybody that he was one of the best players in the state; the night people all over the state would be talking about Rayven Deoliveira.

Before the game, nobody thought it was possible that Hendricken would only be leading Cranston East by a touchdown late in the fourth quarter. But Deoliveira and his teammates played their best game of the season, and the impossible had seemed possible for the first thirty-six minutes of the game. Then there were those few minutes when the Thunderbolts lost focus. Now Rayven was standing on the sideline feeling hopeless. He had finally come to terms that there wasn't going to be the major upset he had dreamed about. Hendricken had the ball, and he knew they would run out the clock, ending the game. His chance to show he was the best quarterback in the state as he led his public school team to an amazing upset, was finished.

Couldn't Ask for More

A few minutes after the final buzzer sounded, the players from both teams passed along two lines at the center of the field, exchanging handshakes. As East players came to the end of the line, they turned and headed toward the south end zone for the regular post-game meeting. They knew they had played well—knew they had surprised a lot of people with their performance. But right now, it didn't seem to matter. They had lost the game.

The Thunderbolts walked toward the end zone with the numbers on the electronic scoreboard mounted on the concrete front wall of the stadium still shining brightly in front of them: Hendricken 35, East 21.

Ken Simone was the first to speak after all the players reached the end zone and took a knee. The glow from the lights mounted on the four stadium towers were still shining on the bright green artificial stadium turf. The fresh smell of an early autumn night filled the air, along with steam still coming off the shoulder pads and through the game shirts of some players who had been involved in the action right until the final buzzer.

"After last week, I was worried about you physically tonight; worried that you might get hurt," Simone admitted. "But tonight, you proved you can play with the best. Our team had the two best players on the field," Simone offered as a commentary on Rayven and Robenson's sensational performances. Then Simone looked toward Centore, who was standing silent looking at the faces of sixty to seventy disappointed teenagers. In time, probably even before they left the field, the Thunderbolts would come to realize they had done something special this night—something nobody outside their football family had thought they could do. They had given Hendricken a battle. But right now, the sting of not winning the game was still paramount in their teenage psyches.

A coach's post-game talk to a losing team is a scene carried out on thousands of high school football fields throughout the country every Friday night in September and October. They are all important, all meaningful, but especially after a game like the one East had just played—a game where a team had played well while battling overwhelming odds, but eventually lost. Cranston East hadn't won, but the Thunderbolts proved something important. They proved that if you make a commitment to a task and follow through with it, you might produce some surprising results. Of course, some people might ask, "What did East prove?" No matter how well the Thunderbolts played, they lost the game, and isn't winning the bottom line? But Centore wanted his team to understand an important lesson had been learned, a tutorial that will carry on in their lives well beyond the sting of tonight's final score.

"I want to thank you for your effort," Centore said with a disappointed, but positive look. "After last week, I was worried about how you were going to come back and play a game against a team like this. But you were within a touchdown with six minutes to go in a game against the top team in the state."

From where he was standing looking toward the other end zone, Centore could see Hendricken coach Keith Croft standing with his players who were kneeling around him. You would suspect Croft, a highly respected young coach whose fulltime job is a Cranston public elementary school principal, was congratulating his team on the victory. But you would like to think he was also crediting East with a great effort, a reminder to his team that it can never take an opponent for granted. Surely some of the Hendricken players were heeding their coach's warning about complacency. But it's a fair bet there are some Hendricken players and almost surely some Hendricken fans who are taking the approach that "Sure Cranston East made the game more interesting than anybody expected, but in the end, we won and isn't that what really counts?"

But Centore couldn't let his players leave the field with the idea that they weren't winners tonight. Regardless of what the scoreboard read. They proved the collectiveness of "We" that the Thunderbolts demonstrated tonight can produce results nobody expected.

"We couldn't have asked for more. You guys never stopped," Centore said, with the look of a coach celebrating a championship rather than a mentor trying to console his team after a tough loss. "You did everything we asked during the week. I am very, very proud of what you did tonight," Centore continued, as he moved his head around the circle of players, looking into the eyes of exhausted teenagers.

"This is a Cranston East football team," Centore shouted. "The way you played tonight; how hard you played; how well you listened. The officials tonight were the same officials who did last Friday's game. After the game they asked me how I turned this team around in a week. It wasn't me. You did it. You prepared yourself. You listened."

Centore closed out his post-game speech by telling the players not to become discouraged because they were now 2–3 in the league games that would determine playoff qualifying. He talked about the year when the Thunderbolts were 1–4 after the first five league games, but came back and made the playoffs. What Centore didn't say was that was six years ago, when it was a nine-game league schedule that determined playoff qualifying. This year, the Interscholastic had reduced the playoff qualifying schedule to only seven games.

Now, it's October 12. East is five games into its seven-game regular season schedule, and its chances for one of the five playoff berths in their eight-team sub-division are already in danger. It was starting to look like, in order for East to earn a playoff berth, the Thunderbolts might need to win their final two regular season games—and next Friday night they play North Kingstown, probably the second-best team in the state. Centore knows the playoffs have become a long shot, but now he's the coach of a team that seems to understand what being a football team means.

"You have North Kingstown next week. You are going to win that game on this football field. You are going to get into the playoffs, and you are not going to get beat," Centore yelled, with a look of determination that totally hid his concerns about facing a very talented North Kingstown team on this same field next Friday night.

CHAPTER XXI

EVEN THE GOVERNOR DOESN'T RESPECT THE THUNDERBOLTS

It's bad enough that the egos of Cranston East students often take a hit because some people in Cranston consider Cranston West the better of the city's two public high schools—largely because, overall, West students come from the more affluent areas of the city. But in October, the composite East student body's ego took a serious hit from the Governor of Rhode Island when Cranston East became the unwitting pawn in some negative TV advertising by Governor Gina Raimondo in her reelection campaign.

Allan Fung, the Republican mayor of Cranston, was challenging Raimondo, a Democratic, for the governorship in the fall of 2018. It was the second time Fung had run against Raimondo. In 2014, Raimondo had become the first female governor in Rhode Island history with a slim four-point popularity in a three-candidate field. In 2018, however, Raimondo was a heavy favorite in her reelection bid, but that didn't stop the governor's campaign directors from running negative ads blasting Fung.

One of those attacks was a TV ad of Fung's supposed under-funding of Cranston public schools. The voice-over on the ad declared something to the effect that Fung was overseeing "failing schools" in Cranston. It was typical political mumbo jumbo—the type of verbiage that probably could have been used by either candidate on an assortment of subjects. True, both Cranston East and Cranston West students failed to score well in some sections of the R.I. Comprehensive Assessment test, but so, too, had public high school students in all but a few of the state's wealthiest communities. The governor was the ultimate person responsible for the state's entire public school system, so the ad was just typical political posturing—until the governor's advertising team decided to use a picture of the front of Cranston East to accompany the voice-over of "failing schools" that was flashing across TV screens throughout Rhode Island.

The Raimondo campaign probably decided to use the photo because that same photo had been used in various media accounts the previous winter accompanying a story about how on a freezing, cold night somebody at Cranston East had inadvertently left a classroom window open, and it caused a water pipe to freeze and burst. The busted pipe caused extensive water damage in the school. If the Raimondo campaign was claiming Fung's under-funding was causing "failing schools" in Cranston, it could have used a picture of any Cranston school, including Cranston West. But the front entrance of Cranston West had been recently renovated. The photo of a newly remodeled high school doesn't make for the type of negative political images the governor's advertising team was looking for. So, they chose the photo of the front of Cranston East, which basically looks the same as it did when I was a student there in the 1960s.

You would like to think the Raimondo advertising team wasn't even thinking the ad might be an insult to Cranston East students. It was "just" a swipe at a political opponent—nothing personal about Cranston East students. But for many of the 1,400 Cranston East students, it was a huge insult. How could it not be? There is a picture of your high school flashing across the TV screen with the message "failing schools." The collective Cranston East student ego became innocent collateral damage in a political campaign, and East principal Sean Kelly didn't like it.

"I wasn't happy about it," Kelly offered about the ad shortly after its first appearance. "She was just here a few weeks ago, and she was talking about the great programs we have," Kelly offered about the governor. "Then she runs something like this. She better not come back here too soon."

The Best of the Best Almost Wasn't a Thunderbolt

Emma Boucher had conflicted feelings when she first saw the campaign ad.

In the fall of 2018, Boucher was a seventeen-year-old Cranston East senior, and she had admired Raimondo for several years. She was impressed Raimondo had become the first female governor in Rhode Island history. Boucher saw the governor, who had been the State Treasurer for eight years before she became governor, as an intelligent, well-educated woman who had grown up in a hardworking, middle-class family just like Boucher.

Raimondo had been an outstanding high school and college student and was now willing to help improve the lives of Rhode Islanders through civic leadership. It's what Boucher was envisioning herself doing some day in the future. Boucher was so enthralled with Raimondo that she had become a volunteer worker in the governor's reelection campaign. But when Boucher saw the ad with the picture of Cranston East and a voice-over declaring "failing schools," she was upset.

"That's not us. We are not a failing school. We are a great school," Boucher said to herself when she first saw the ad.

Nobody was a better judge of the quality of a Cranston East education in the fall of 2018 than Emma Boucher. Boucher was born in Boston, but basically, she has spent her whole life living in Cranston.

"I spent the first year of my life in Boston, but other than that year I have been in Cranston my whole life," said Boucher, a white teenager with a delightful smile.

She has lived her whole life living in the same well-maintained cape on a tree-lined street in a section of Cranston known as the Friendly Community, a few blocks from City Hall and Cranston East. For the first six years of her education, she walked to the public elementary school a few streets from her house, then for three years she took a school bus to the public middle school, in the Edgewood/Elmwood section of the city. Her middle-class parents stressed education, and she was the type of kid who loved to read and take on new educational challenges.

"Academics were always very important to me," said Boucher.

That's why four years ago, despite having spent every year of her schooling in public education, she was prepared to attend the parochial La Salle Academy for her high school career.

"I had loved going to public schools in Cranston, but I was thinking of my future, and I was a little concerned about going to Cranston East. I was worried what my future opportunities would be," said Boucher.

It wasn't anything in particular that she had heard about East. It's just that a lot of people were saying it was okay to go to the public school in elementary school, maybe even middle school, but the private high schools are better than the public high schools. The print and electronic media, social media, and the outstanding marketing by the private schools had all contributed to a question of confidence in public high school education. So, Boucher was all set to enroll at La Salle in the fall of 2015. But shortly before the school year was scheduled to begin, she talked to one of her father's friends, who was an administrator at Cranston East.

"My father's friend told me the teachers at both schools are going to be equally smart and equally dedicated to you. You will be able to take the same classes at either school," Boucher said.

"He said the difference will be some resources that will be available to you at La Salle. Like La Salle has beautiful athletic fields. We don't even have practice fields here at East. Here, we have to take a bus for an outdoor gym class," Boucher related.

But Cranston was Boucher's community—this is where her friends were. She thought about it and concluded that despite the lack of some physical resources, her whole community—the community in which she had thrived since kindergarten—was here.

"I had been in this community since kindergarten, and I had never had an issue. So why now?" Boucher asked herself.

She was also amazingly aware of the world outside her immediate surrounds for a fourteen-year-old teenager. She paid attention to the news; she watched, listened, and asked questions when her parents would view national and world media reports. She saw what America in the 21st century looked like. She lived only a few blocks from Cranston East, so she knew the composite face of the Cranston East student body. She saw it constantly when she and her friends would walk the half-mile from their neighborhood to the stores, restaurants, post office, or bank on the streets around Cranston East. She liked the diversity she was seeing at East. It was the same type of diversity she saw when she watched TV news accounts of people in parts of the country beyond the Rhode Island borders. Even at fourteen, she was thinking about preparing herself for an adult life of substance.

"Graduating from high school was not the prime focus. The focus was I would go to college and create opportunities for the future. What was my career path going to look like?" Boucher offered about her thought process going into high school.

She concluded East would be the best training grounds for a young woman who dreamed about making a difference in the world. So, she told her parents she had changed her mind and wanted to attend East.

"Were your parents concerned you might be jeopardizing your future by attending the public high school rather than the private school?" I asked Boucher.

"My parents weren't scared. They were always very supportive of me," Boucher told me. "They supported me in whatever direction I wanted to take. They didn't have any hesitation with it at all. I am so glad I made this decision."

Boucher has been an academic superstar since the first day she entered Cranston East. Taking virtually all honors and advance placement courses, she didn't receive a grade lower than an A in her first three years entering the fall of 2018. Although it wouldn't be official until the senior mid-year grades were calculated in January, in October there was little doubt she would be the No. 1 academically ranked student in the Cranston East Class of 2019, the class valedictorian. But she hasn't been just an academic "nerd." Her life has been a smorgasbord of activity and achievement. She was elected senior class president; she was a member of the girls' varsity tennis team; she was an All-State band member; and—in addition to campaigning for Raimondo—she was also spending nights and weekends in the fall of 2018 campaigning to convincing Rhode Island voters to pass a $250-million state education bond issue. This fall, she had applied to nine outstanding colleges, including schools like Brown University, Occidental College in Los Angeles, McGill University in Montreal, and Fordham University in New York City. (By early winter, she would know she had been accepted at most of them, including Brown.)

She had become every parent's dream. She has earned the opportunity to attend some of the top colleges in the country, and she didn't have to give up anything to attend her local public high school. She didn't give up her childhood friends; she made new friends, and she opened her world vision without leaving her hometown.

"Have you learned anything at East that you might not have learned someplace else?" I asked Boucher.

"I think so," she said. "I really like the life experiences. We have such a unique community here. In my French group, there are kids from all over the world; kids from all different languages. I know some people have questioned that. They think it would make for a disjointed high school experience. But I think it makes our community a lot stronger because of the appreciation for diversity in this community. I think I was really deliberate at wanting that. That's life. Life is broken up into different factions. You are going to have to interact with everyone. To learn how to harbor those relationships now is so valuable."

"Do you go to the football games?" I asked her.

"Of course," she said.

"The football team represents East. We are a majority-minority school," Boucher offered about white faces making up a large percentage of the Cranston city population, but minority faces making up a majority of the football team's roster. "This is what America looks like now, and this is what it is going to be in the future. It's very exciting to see everything we have been able to accomplish in the midst of all this diversity."

CHAPTER XXII

A TEAMMATE IS MORE THAN SOMEBODY WHO WEARS THE SAME UNIFORM

Maybe it was the strong showing in the losing effort against Hendricken that energized practice the first few days of the week of October 15. The drills were crisp, and everybody seemed to be paying attention to the coaches' instructions. But Quinn Lanigan thinks there's another reason why the practices have been so invigorated.

"I think some people are finally starting to realize we might not make the playoffs," said Lanigan.

For weeks, Lanigan, in his role as one of the four senior co-captains, has been trying to inject a cautionary mood in his teammates. Literally since the first practice in mid-August, Lanigan has sensed this team doesn't practice like last year's team did. It wasn't that last year's team was necessarily a great practice team. It wasn't one of those unique high school football teams that has a sense of intensity every minute of every practice. Even Isaiah McDaniel had told me earlier in the season about the differences between the 2017 and 2018 Thunderbolts.

"We weren't a very good practice team last year, but we had such great talent. I think these kids think they can be the same way, but they don't have that talent," McDaniel offered about the 2018 Thunderbolts.

Lanigan totally agrees with McDaniel that this year's team doesn't have the talent of last year's, but he feels it's more than that. While they may not have been intense every minute in practice, last year's team seemed to pay attention more than this year's team does. In Lanigan's mind, the guys on this year's team don't pay attention to details like last year's team did. Also, this year's team seems to dwell on its mistakes. They will make a couple of good plays, then they will make a mistake because they didn't pay attention to a detail. They will then dwell on that mistake, and then that mistake leads to another mistake. They also seem to take it personally when Centore highlights a mistake in practice or in a game. For Lanigan, one of the most important entities football has taught him is not to dwell on his mistakes.

"You have to learn from them and get right back in the action, in game or in practice," Lanigan offered about on-the-field mistakes.

"A lot of things can happen that you can either take one way or another," Lanigan continued. "When you got knocked down or drop a pass, you can take that and dwell on it or learn from it and become a better player. It's like life. When I'm in school and I fail a quiz, I can sit there and dwell on it, and it will affect my next couple of assignments. Or I can take it and say, 'You know what? I messed up, and I have to learn from it.'"

Tom Centore's constant message is that you have to be prepared for the tests on and off the field. If you pay attention in practice, you will not mess up in the game; if you study for the test, there's a good chance you will get a good mark. But there's also a human reality. People will make mistakes. Even if they prepare, they may not always get a good mark—maybe even fail the test. That's the allure of football. It's a game that produces success by preparing your assignment. But the game also teaches you how to handle failure, because in every life there will be some measure of failure. If you work, there can be success, but at some level there could also be failure.

"Coach Centore always talks about building character," said Lanigan. "That was his point. You definitely build character playing football. In football you have to accept the fact you are going to get knocked down. Accepting that reality is a big thing about football. But then you get up. You accept everything that happens and take it forward."

There's the classic Vince Lombardi line of—"It's not whether you get knocked down, it's whether you get up." But maybe a line attributed to the famous cookie maker Wally Amos even better defines the doctrine of most high school football coaches—"You may not be responsible for getting knocked down, but you certainly are responsible for getting up."

"When you play football, you share your success and failure with a lot of people every day," said Lanigan. "That's the great thing about being on a football team. It's that sense of brotherhood football players are always talking about."

Childhood Dream

Lanigan has become the personification of a young man who has the acumen to turn the annihilation of his childhood dream into a life enhancement lesson. He started playing youth football when he was about ten years old. Not surprising, with his speed and natural athletic talent his youth football coaches designated him a quarterback, and he was good at it. Even when he moved into high school, he was taking snaps. He was the quarterback of the Cranston East freshman team four years ago. Then, in his sophomore varsity season in 2016, in addition to playing safety, he was the backup to starting quarterback Justin Neary. That was fine with Lanigan. Neary, who was a junior that year, had blossomed into one of the state's top passers. So, Lanigan figured he would back up Neary again in Neary's senior season in 2017 while also getting in some playing time at defense. Then, with Neary having graduated in 2017, Lanigan figured he would be the starting quarterback in his senior season in 2018. It would be the fulfillment of his childhood dream. He would be playing quarterback every Friday night on the field he had walked past every day on his way to elementary school. The fact that Lanigan was a good-looking, personable kid who everybody likes would make the story an even better tale of gridiron Americana.

But last year, a metaphoric landmine was placed in Lanigan's smooth path to becoming the East starting quarterback in his senior season when Rayven Deoliveira joined the team. Quinn had known Rayven since their youth football days. Although they played for different Pop Warner teams, they were both talented young players—two of the best young players in the city of Cranston. Both were destined to be outstanding high school players, and when Rayven enrolled at La Salle in his freshman year, it looked like the two would never be high school teammates and never compete to be the starting quarterback at Cranston East. But then Rayven was expelled from La Salle in his sophomore year and ended up at East.

Despite Rayven having been one of the two quarterbacks alternating regular snaps when he was at La Salle in his sophomore year, last season at East there was never a question he would be a running back. Justin Neary had shown he was one of the best quarterbacks in the state in his junior season. He was the key to Tom Centore's high octane offensive philosophy of "You have to feel you will score every time you have the ball." So Neary would be the quarterback in 2017, and Rayven would be a running back, occasionally throwing a pass off an option.

Both Neary and Rayven were outstanding in their roles in the 2017 championship season. Neary was named the Providence Journal first-team All-State quarterback as he threw for 2,179 yards and 38 touchdowns; while Rayven also earned first-team All-State honors as he averaged 6.8 yards per carry on 118 carries, and also caught 20 of Neary's passes. He was the Division I scoring leader with 21 touchdowns.

But Neary graduated in the spring of 2018, which meant Tom Centore needed a new starting quarterback in the fall of 2018. Rayven had seamlessly moved into a primarily running role in 2017, but everybody knew he wanted to be the starting quarterback this season. For many young football players, that's the dream—be the "Main Man"; the guy who calls the play. It especially can be the case if the player has the type of talent and size that lends to being a quarterback. Of course, in Rayven's case, he had also been a starting quarterback at La Salle, one of the best Division I teams in the state, when he was a sophomore.

But Quinn Lanigan still wanted to be the Cranston East starting quarterback. He still wanted to live that dream of calling the signals for Cranston East under the Cranston Stadium Friday Night Lights the way he had watched Cranston schoolboys do since he was a little kid. After all, when you live a few hundred yards from Cranston Stadium, the Friday night high school football games are as much of your childhood as Big Bird and Power Rangers. But an injury had limited Lanigan's playing time last season, even in the defensive backfield. Rayven, on the other hand, was a returning first-team All-Stater. So Lanigan was disappointed, but probably not surprised, when practice started for this season in mid-August and Tom Centore had Rayven on the depth chart as the No. 1 quarterback.

Lanigan never sulked; he never questioned Centore's decision.

"If Coach Centore feels Rayven should be quarterback, then maybe it would be better for the team if I switch my position and play somewhere else. That's the decision you have to make for the betterment of the team," Lanigan said to me one day after an early season practice.

"That's the way you have to think if you want to have success for the team," Lanigan continued. "If I'm stupid and insist I want to be just the quarterback and end up on the sidelines, how am I helping the team—or myself. You have to do that because football is one sport where you can't be selfish."

Thousands of high school football players through the decades have had to make that same type of decision. Give up the dream of being "The Man" for the good of the team.

"You can't control everything in life," Lanigan added. "You can't always control decisions other people make, so you have to live with them and roll with the punches. You make the best of the decisions that are made for you."

So Lanigan began working on becoming an effective wide receiver on offense. He would never be the primary target—that was Robenson's role. But maybe Lanigan could help his team by making a few catches every game. After all, Rayven was going to need somebody else besides Robenson to pass to because Robenson would be seeing double coverage every game. Lanigan had also become the holder for conversion kicks and field goal attempts, along with playing deep safety on defense.

Anything he could do to help make this team better; anything that would make him a better teammate.

He had come to realize that real teammates aren't just guys who wear the same uniforms—especially on a team as diversified as East. In various degrees, he had grown up amongst diversity most of his life. The majority of his classmates in his elementary school—which was only a few streets from his house—were white. But there was a significant number of faces of color—kids like Robenson. When Lanigan moved into middle school, which again was only a few streets from his home in the other direction from his elementary school, there were probably more faces of color than white kids because the middle school boundary lines stretched down Cranston Street to the Providence city line.

When he moved to East, where his classmates included a significant number of kids from Edgewood, the composite face of the student body was closer to a 50–50 white/color split than it was in middle school. But regardless of where he was, he never really gave the diversity much thought. That's just the way it was.

Robenson had been one of his best friends since the day they'd first bonded on the elementary school playground. Robenson is a face of color; Quinn's complexion is white. They're friends, but even more important, they are teammates. There's no further explanation necessary why it works.

Lanigan always considered himself a good teammate; somebody who always tried to put the team's needs ahead of his own. But last spring, when it came time for him to make his course selections for the 2018 fall semester, he started thinking maybe there was a way he could be a better teammate that went beyond understanding the Xs and Os in Tom Centore's game plan.

"I know we are a unique team compared to the other teams in this state," Lanigan offered about the diversity of the East roster. "I'm a white kid, and most of the people in Cranston are white, but a majority of the guys on this team are not white. This year I took an African American history class just to expand my knowledge of the race of some of my teammates."

He's a seventeen-year-old, middle-class American high school senior so the reality is his life revolves around sports; his girlfriend; and where he will go to college next year. But he understands he is part of a generation whose future will be about more diversity and inclusion than any generation that has come before his. It's not something most seventeen-year-olds in 2018 were thinking about unless they were being exposed to it by some teacher. But Lanigan was thinking about it even before he started school this fall, and he understands that is because he's a Cranston East football player

"It frustrates me when kids live in their own reality and don't get to see what I get to see coming to Cranston East every day," Lanigan proclaimed. "They don't understand what it's like to be in a diverse environment like this. I couldn't be happier that I am in an environment like this."

Go East, Young Man

Are today's high school students under more pressure than high school students were a generation ago?

Sure, today's high school students are under pressure to avoid drinking, smoking (cannabis or tobacco), and drugs. But those temptations have been part of high school life since at least the 1960s. However, the ability to give teenagers the power to be a bully without actual physical confrontation, which today's social media gives some teenagers, has created a new realm of stress for many of today's high school students.

Jaevis Champagne-Carpenter is a sophomore Cranston East linebacker even though he lives in the Cranston West school district. Champagne-Carpenter even attended West last year as a freshman. But this year, he transferred to Cranston East. Some people in Cranston might find that strange. Cranston West is the supposed affluent school among Cranston's two public high schools. Through the years, there have been stories about families who lived in the Cranston East school zone, but the parents fraudulently used a grandparents' address in western Cranston so the teenagers in the family could attend West. But Champagne-Carpenter took the other route; he chose East over West.

"I don't know why he transferred. I heard it's something about a bullying situation," assistant coach Joe Madonna offered about Champagne-Carpenter one day at practice.

If it was a bullying situation, it's a safe bet it wasn't physical bullying that was being perpetrated on Champagne-Carpenter. He may only be 160 pounds, but Champagne-Carpenter is the proverbial "tough as nails" kid. In addition to being a football linebacker in the fall, he's also an outstanding wrestler in the winter. But Champagne-Carpenter may have looked a little different than most freshmen males at West. His complexion is white, but he wears little diamond earrings, and his comparatively short-trimmed haircut has the distinctive styling of individual self-expression.

"A kid can walk through the café in the morning wearing purple hair and nobody would even say a word," Ken Simone had said that first day of practice when I asked him what made Cranston East special.

Champagne-Carpenter doesn't have purple hair, but he does have a few streaks of red mixed with his blond-dyed hair.

"I didn't like it at West. I just didn't feel comfortable there," Champagne-Carpenter said, without wanting to elaborate on why he didn't feel comfortable at West.

"I feel comfortable here," Champagne- Carpenter added about East.

But while he feels comfortable with his new classmates at East, he is upset about something at his new school. He's not getting as much playing time in East football games as he thinks he should be.

Joe Madonna has a simple solution.

"You have to show the coach in practice that you deserve to play more," Madonna told Champagne-Carpenter, in his typical no-nonsense, "put in a day's-work for a day's-pay" style.

The Plan Has Changed

"My father said he knows he probably is going to have to pay for my first year of college," Jamari Mason declared to a few teammates shortly after joining the group on the sidelines of Wednesday's practice session.

"Yeah, he says now I'm going to have to walk-on at UMass next year, then earn a scholarship for the next three years," Mason continued. "So, he doesn't want me to play Friday night."

Nobody on the practice field seemed surprised by the proclamation.

The possibility that Jamari might not play a big game this coming weekend didn't have the impact it would have had a month ago. Last season, Mason had been one of the team's stars. He was one of the top outside linebackers in the state;

a first-team All-Stater. He was a big reason most East players had expected the 2018 season would be another year in which the Thunderbolts were involved in the hunt for a championship. But now, East has played five of the seven games that will determine the playoff qualifiers, and Mason has only played in one of those games. All of his teammates know it certainly has been a frustrating season for Mason, with the string of quirky injuries. They feel sorry for him. But it seemed some of Mason's teammates are also becoming frustrated with one of their captains. They are starting to think that Mason's injury rehab isn't as much about his getting back on the field so he can help the team make the playoffs as it is about what's best for Mason's long-shot chance to play Division I college football.

Week after week, while he hasn't been playing, he has been talking at practices. It hasn't been the type of encouraging messages delivered by Mack Hanley while he was standing on the sidelines for four weeks with his arm in a cast. Rather, Mason's talk has been a constant pointing-out of poor play by some teammates. There's no question, a lot of what Mason has been saying is justified. Lack of focus; poor execution—they are football sins the Thunderbolts have been committing all season. For a player who knows the game as well as Mason does, it can be frustrating watching this type of play. But some of his teammates seem to be becoming equally frustrated with Mason's constant critical comments.

If Mason had been on the field setting an example with his stellar play, it might have been a different story. Then his teammates would have felt he had legitimate reason to complain, especially since he was one of the team captains. But Mason hasn't been on the field making any contributions. Now he is saying he might not play in another important game even though he has been cleared by the doctor.

CHAPTER XXIII

FROM AMERICA'S BLUEST COLLAR
TOWN TO A GRIDIRON POWER

The town of North Kingstown, R.I. was once home to one of the country's largest U.S. Naval Air bases. At various times during World War II and the Cold War, there were five different Essex Class aircraft carriers, each with a crew of about than 2,000 enlisted men stationed at North Kingstown's Quonset Naval Air Station. There was also the Seabee naval construction battalion at Davisville on the outer perimeter of Quonset. That meant there were close to 3,000 naval enlisted men living in North Kingstown at various times throughout the 1950s and early '60s—making North Kingstown literally one of the bluest-collar towns in America.

But by the fall of 2018, North Kingstown had become an upscale southern Rhode Island suburban community. The town was also home to one of the best high school football teams in Rhode Island—the North Kingstown High Skippers.

The Quonset air station was decommissioned by the federal government in 1974 as part of defense cutbacks following the U.S. involvement in the Vietnam War. The closing of Quonset had a huge impact on North Kingstown. In the 1970 census, the population of North Kingstown was listed as 29,793. Ten years later—after the closing of Quonset—the official North Kingstown population was 21, 938. That was a 27 percent population decline over a decade.

It took some time, but to the credit of state and town officials, the naval land given to the state and town by the federal government has been turned into a thriving industrial park with an assortment of businesses, including one of the General Dynamics-Electric Boat submarine-building facilities. The timing of the closing of Quonset and the development of the industrial park corresponded perfectly with an extensive movement to the southern part of Rhode Island, by residents of the Providence metro area, in the late 1970s and early '80s.

North Kingstown, with miles of shoreline along Narragansett Bay, was perfect for the southern-ho movement. A lot of new, upscale housing developments rose on what once was North Kingstown farmland. North Kingstown did retain some of its blue-collar aura throughout much of the 20th century, but by the turn of the 21st century, it had become basically a community of white-collar professionals living in raised-ranches, nicely appointed capes, and big colonials. The population of North Kingstown increased by almost 20 percent from 1980 to 2000, pushing the population back up to just over 26,000. That's where it basically stood at the start of the 2018 football season.

North Kingstown high school, which has been in existence since the turn of the 20th century, has become a superlative example of how a public high school can keep most of a town's talented student-athletes at the town's public high school, if the town is willing to make a commitment to the public school infrastructure. Like a lot of public school systems, North Kingstown certainly has had its share of political educational bickering over the decades after the closing of Quonset. But one thing North Kingstown did right when other cities and towns in Rhode Island were skimping on funding for public education in the early part of the 21st century, was build a beautiful, modern-tech high school in 2001. It was a large financial commitment, but in retrospect it became a game-changer for the reputation of North Kingstown public education.

The new North Kingstown High building alone was not the only reason North Kingstown was considered one of the top public high schools in Rhode Island in the fall of 2018. Good faculty and solid academic programs are the core of any outstanding high school, but the new infrastructure was a sign of confidence in a public school system when other cities and towns were not investing in their public high schools.

In the fall of 2018, there hadn't been another new public high school built in Rhode Island since North Kingstown built its new high school in 2001. So, while state media reports were telling stories of public high schools in places like East Providence and Newport literally crumbling at their foundation, North Kingstown High students walked into a twenty-foot-high, glass-walled center lobby with national news feeds running along a video banner; an inhouse TV station; and 21st century technology in most classrooms.

At the start of the 2018-2019 school year, for better than a decade, many private high schools in Rhode Island had been in an arms race of building and improving their infrastructure in order to attract new students. Unlike most public high schools, the new high school gave North Kingstown a chance to match the private school infrastructure improvements. That played a big role in North Kingstown keeping the town's top student-athletes at the town's lone public high school, and it wasn't just good football players. North Kingstown High girls' teams have been some of the most successful female teams in Rhode Island state, public or private, for several decades. In the twenty-eight-year period from 1990 to 2018, North Kingstown girls' teams had won a combined total of twenty-six of Rhode Island's major high school girls' titles in the sports of soccer, field hockey, volleyball, and cross country. North Kingstown, however, had never won a major state football title since the official state football playoff system began in 1972.

But in 2015, Joe Gilmartin, a one-time assistant North Kingstown football coach, took over as head football coach and started reviving a program, which had its up and downs in both Division I and Division II over the decades. In 2017, North Kingstown won the Division II state title, which caused the Interscholastic League to move North Kingstown up to Division I competition for the 2018 season. Gilmartin, a long-time assistant coach in various programs throughout Rhode Island, had revived the NK program to the point where he had 100 players, grades 9–12, on the roster at the start of the 2018 season.

So much for the idea that high school football in America is in trouble.

Gilmartin's revival of North Kingstown football was a multi-faceted campaign. In Gilmartin's mind, one of the most important factors was that, after having been a teacher at other schools, he had become a teacher at North Kingstown High. Having a coach who is also a teacher in the school building is important for any high school team, but especially for the football team that has close to 100 males on its roster.

"I don't need a desk; I need a golf cart," Gilmartin once told me with a laugh. "I'm all around the school all day. The guys know I'm going to be in the corridors all the time keeping an eye on them."

A well-established North Kingstown Pop Warner tackle youth program has also been a good feeder system.

"We have been fortunate that the community trusts us with their children," said Gilmartin.

North Kingstown may also be at the forefront of what could be a key to the survival of American high school football. In addition to the tackle Pop Warner program, the town recreation department also runs a youth flag football league that has about 400 kids (boys and girls) involved.

"I think the biggest detriment to football is contact over time," Gilmartin said one day when we were talking about the future of high school football. "This way kids are learning the game without the tackling."

Also, each spring Gilmartin and his staff run a "transition to tackle football" program for the town's eighth graders who think they might want to play high school football when they reach the ninth grade.

"When they get to high school, a lot of the kids who played in just the flag league wanted to play for the high school team because football is an exciting game," Gilmartin offered.

Now in its first season in Division I, North Kingstown hasn't wasted any time showing it's ready for Rhode Island's answer to big time high school football, with victories in four of its first five DI league games.

He's Better Than the Coach Thought

It didn't take long after the opening kickoff Friday night for Ken Simone to confirm what he had thought was the case after studying game films of North Kingstown's first five games. North Kingstown was a very good football team, especially with Dylan Porier at defensive end. Porier is a 6'2", 255-pound senior who had already committed to the University of New Hampshire, and he wasn't wasting any time showing a Cranston East homecoming crowd that he definitely had D-I college talent. Very quick and very athletic, Porier was putting constant pressure on Rayven Deoliveira any time the Thunderbolts' quarterback attempted a pass while also controlling the edge on his side of the field against East runners.

Porier is a prime example of a player who can make other players better, both because he is individually talented and also because he sets the tone for a team's work ethic with their own diligence on the practice field. If Porier, who is probably the best overall football player in the state this season, pushes himself to extremes in practice every day, the other kids on the team are going to push themselves, too. It happens in every team sport, but especially in football where one player can influence so many other players with his work ethic.

Porier is also one of those outstanding multi-sport athletes you once saw a lot in high school sports. But these days, more and more good athletes are optioning for sports specializing. They are seduced by the lure of specializing because they—and often their parents—feel that if a young athlete eventually wants a college scholarship, the kid has to start specializing at a very young age. So, they join one of the "travel" youth basketball, baseball, soccer, or lacrosse teams that played games and/or train winter, spring, summer, and fall when they are nine or ten years old. Even if some kids might have played another sport a few months a year in their pre-teen years, by the time they reach high school, they are dedicating all their energies to the sport they think will be their ticket to attracting the attention of some college coaches.

Many high school sports have seen the loss of multi-talented athletes over the past few decades because of sports specialization, but probably none as much as football. Fortunately for North Kingstown fans, Poirier has spread his athletic talents between both the football field and the basketball court.

"I knew he was quick off the corner; but in person he seems ever quicker than what I saw on film," Ken Simone, the Thunderbolts' defensive coordinator offered after watching Porier spending a better part of the first quarter in the Cranston East offensive backfield.

Despite Porier's outstanding talent, the East coaching staff felt the Thunderbolts were ready for North Kingstown. They had laid out a game plan that accounted for proper protection for Deoliveira, even with Porier's explosive speed coming in from the corner. The problem was the Thunderbolts were not executing the game plan. Normally North Kingstown was only rushing four defenders, and the East game plan had allowed for blocking as many as six rushers. But the East offensive linemen were missing their assignments, so the North Kingstown defense was completely shutting down the East attack.

Time and time again, Deoliveira was caught in the backfield before he could even begin running an option. To make matters worse, the East defense was also having some problems. Midway through the second quarter, Omar Reyes—the kid who never complains, the kid who is always encouraging his teammates to work harder—comes up to assistant coach Joe Madonna on the sidelines and declares, "I wish we had a corner who knows how to play this game," Reyes screamed. "We are doing the job up front, but then our cornerbacks let them complete a 25-yard pass."

It's not Reyes' nature to complain, not his style to blame somebody else. But football is such a physically exhausting sport, it can frustrate you into thinking you are working harder than a teammate. Football teaches you to work through that sensation; you have to encourage rather than criticize. That's the gospel of football. Unfortunately, the Thunderbolts were not practicing the gospel according to Tom Centore.

Still in the Game as the Band Warms-Up for the Halftime Show

Despite several miscues from the East defense, the Thunderbolts "only" trailed by 14 points with about a minute to play in the first half. Thursday afternoon, Jamari Mason had come to practice and told his teammates that morning he had told Tom Centore he could play Friday night. Apparently, he decided trying to help his teammates was more important than a long-shot chance at a walk-on scholarship offer. Centore was certainly happy to hear Mason was ready to play, but because Jamari hadn't actually practiced any of the run-through this week, Centore told the assistant coaches he wouldn't start Friday night. "We will just use him in some situations," Centore said to the coaching staff after practice Thursday afternoon.

But it had only taken a few North Kingstown offensive series for those "situations" to occur on a regular basis, and not surprisingly Mason was making some good plays from his linebacker berth. All things considered, only being 14 points behind at halftime wouldn't have been that bad. Centore just wanted to get off the field so the coaching staff could start making halftime adjustments.

North Kingstown had possession and was moving the ball as the final minute of the first half clicked off the scoreboard clock. The Skippers had moved the ball to the Cranston 30, but by then, there were only eight seconds remaining until halftime. Probably only one more stop, and East would go into halftime only needing to make up a 2-touchdown deficit in the second half.

It was obvious North Kingstown would try some type of pass-play on what probably would be the last play of the half. So, the East secondary was set up to make sure it didn't give up a 30-yard touchdown bomb on the final play of the half. The Thunderbolts could afford to give up a short reception, and as long as the receiver was quickly tackled, the half would end before North Kingstown could run another play.

The NK quarterback did complete a pass on that final play, but it was only to the 15-yard-line, and there were at least four Cranston East players between him and the end zone. Surely one of those East defenders would make the tackle that would end the half. But, somehow, nobody made the tackle; nobody made sure of that last stop; nobody kept working to the final second of the half. The receiver broke away from the defenders and raced into the end zone just as the scoreboard started flashing all zeroes.

Tom Centore couldn't believe East had given up another touchdown on the last play of the first half. He stood a few feet over the sideline onto the field watching the North Kingstown players celebrating. Even though time had expired on the clock, Centore was forced to stand on the sideline watching North Kingstown kick the conversion point before he could start walking off the field for the halftime break. He was trying to think of what he was going to say to his players as he headed for the maintenance department storage room under the grandstands, which the football team uses for halftime meetings when the weather started getting chilly later in the season.

Once again, Centore feels he is fighting for the soul of his team. He was discouraged. East had lost to Hendricken last week, but the Thunderbolts had played well. Most of the players were following instructions—staying focused. It seemed his team was finally coming together after the debacle against East Providence. But now those problems of the East Providence game were coming back—lack of focus, missed assignments, no second effort.

Centore stopped and waited for all the players to pass by him on their way into the room under the stadium stands. Finally, the coach walked behind the last of the players into the room and told somebody to close the eight-foot-wide green wooden door that separated the outside world from a football family.

"They are doing nothing defensively you haven't seen," Centore said, as he started speaking in a disgusted tone. "You're not executing on what we have to execute with the protections. We asked you to double the One technique—you forget. We ask you to double team to block Number 76 [Porier], and you forget the second man. I think it's because some of you have tuned yourselves out. You know what happens if you don't do what you're supposed to do. That's when guys get hurt."

Once again, Centore is bringing the game into the classroom.

"You ask yourself how things are going through the week, and it carries through into tonight," Centore declared. "It's the same thing, gentlemen. Why do you fail a test? Do you study? No!"

Centore is on a roll, and now he takes a Friday Night football game beyond the walls of Cranston Stadium. His primary concern at the start of the night was to win a football game. Now the reality is, when you are trailing a well-coached, talented team like North Kingstown by 21 points at halftime, the chances of having the highest numbers on the scoreboard at the end of the night are minuscule. You would need help from the opposition, some kind of letup by North Kingstown, and it's a virtual guarantee North Kingstown coach Joe Gilmartin is on the other side of the field right now warning his players about such a let-down. After twenty-five years of coaching high school football, nobody understands that type of football reality better than Centore. But Centore does not want some early setbacks to cause his players to give up on the game—give up on life—while there's still time to play.

"It is the same thing about life. We are not doing it out there on the field tonight because we are not doing it during the week," Centore proclaimed.

Then Centore goes silent for a few seconds, giving the players a chance to reflect on what their coach was saying.

"I don't see that same football team that played here last Friday night. I just don't see that focus," Centore said.

Centore's tone was measured. He's wasn't screaming; he wasn't throwing the nearby twenty-gallon trash cans against the wall for emphasis. It's a football game pep talk, but like most of Centore's pep talks, it's leading back to a life lesson.

"Those are the things I'm talking about. Doing the right thing every day of your life will lead to better things," Centore said, as he looked around the room trying to make direct eye contact with some players.

Some of the players had found seats on the portable wooden benches that lined two walls of the room, but others just sat on the cement floor. All of the players' heads were bowed. They knew they were failing their coach, the man who puts so much time into making them better football players; the man who cares about every one of them as a person, not just as a football player.

"I don't need to tell you they are playing a one-three," Centore offered about North Kingstown's defensive scheme.

"They are doing exactly what we showed you all week," the coach continued.

"Everything you were taught during the week, they are doing. Would anybody like to tell me they are doing something different? Go ahead, raise your hand, and tell me they are doing something different," Centore said.

Throughout the room, the bowed heads were shaking from side-to-side, validating Centore's appraisal of the situation. Centore's eyes scanned the room, then he resumed his football sermon. But now it's going beyond making tackles and solid blocks.

"Things in life go against you when you don't do the right thing," Centore pronounced.

"Beyond the Xs and Os on the field, learn that about life," Centore continued. "Don't blame other people for your faults and your shortcomings. When you start looking inside yourself, things start to change. That's what will happen in your life. When you stop blaming other people and stop being an excuse maker, things will change in your life."

Then Centore looked at his players and issued a challenge— a test that will have far more long-range implications than the final numbers on that scoreboard out on the field.

"Now you have an opportunity to battle through the adversity we just faced through the end of the first half, or you can quit in your mind," Centore declared.

"We are going to test your character in this half. How are you going to handle what they throw at you in the second half? That's my question," Centore proclaimed. "How are you going to handle it? Are you going to show some guts, or are you just going to let it happen to you? That's what you need to find out about yourself in this half."

The Scoreboard Doesn't Record Moral Victories

Right from the second half kickoff, Centore could sense a different purpose in his team, a different attention to focus. Throughout the twenty-four-minute second half, the two teams played on virtually even terms, a complete contrast from the first half. The East offense came alive and scored three touchdowns. The Thunderbolts' defense was much more focused. North Kingstown, however, is too talented to be shut down by any team. So, while East couldn't cut into its halftime deficit, the Thunderbolts also wouldn't let North Kingstown put the game away early in the second half. Even in the fourth quarter, they were playing with abundance, certainly not a team that had "packed it in" at halftime. They had accepted Centore's challenge of "showing some guts" in the second half. They did it the "right way"; they played for each other. But North Kingstown was a very talented, well coached team, so when the game ended, North Kingstown was leading, 42–21.

About five minutes after the final whistle, Centore stood on the field with his players kneeling around him in their white game shirts, their helmets resting on the ground beside them. Their faces had a look of anguish. Nobody knew for sure, but the talk had been East would need to win its final last two regular season games to make the playoffs. Now they had lost one of those games. Nobody would be more upset if the Thunderbolts didn't make the playoffs than Centore, but Centore had just seen a commitment by his team—a refusal to "pack it in" when it would have been very easy to do just that. His team didn't quit, and Centore couldn't let his players leave the field without their realizing what they had just done was special.

"We asked you to commit. Not to give up, and you didn't," Centore declared. "You played a great half of football. I know you are disappointed, but you should be proud of what you just did."

It was all the right lines. All the things an adult should say to teenagers to make them feel better about themselves. But when you are a sixteen- or seventeen-year-old high school football player, who has been dreaming of another Super Bowl appearance; when you never really thought about not being in the playoffs—this hurts. It puts a hollow feeling in your stomach. All the words the coach said, all the "feel good about yourself" psychology, doesn't change the final score. They know it shouldn't have come to this. There are legitimate excuses for why it has happened—those mixed-up few weeks of practice at the start of the season when Tom Centore wasn't there many afternoons because of his father's physical condition; Tony Centore's death the week of the Shea game; and the freakier injuries throughout the season.

But all that doesn't matter right now. The bottom line for the Thunderbolts is—this hurts.

CHAPTER XXIV

THERE'S STILL A CHANCE

When Cranston East lost to North Kingstown Friday night, dropping its Interscholastic League playoff qualifying record to 2–4, most people figured the Thunderbolts were out of the playoff picture. But League parity was working in Cranston East's favor. Tom Centore had spent the weekend figuring all the playoff scenarios, and the way he figured it, the Thunderbolts still had a chance to be one of the three teams finishing in a three-way tie for the final two of the four playoff berths in Division IA.

If a three-way tie became reality, the playoff berths would be determined by a tie-breaking formula that nobody in the state ever seemed to understand. So, Centore hadn't even tried to figure out a tie-breaking scenario because the only way East could be involved in a tie was if the Thunderbolts upset Cumberland Friday night in Cumberland. That would be a massive task for a Cranston East team that had lost three straight games. Cumberland not only had a .500 record against Division I competition, but Cumberland is also big and strong.

"They were one of the hardest hitting teams we played all last year," Ken Simone offered about Cumberland.

Tom Centore understands the challenge facing his team.

"We have our work cut out for us," Centore offered about the Thunderbolts' upcoming game, as he headed off to watch game films with the players and assistant coaches on Monday, October 22.

It isn't just the possibility of not making the playoffs that has Tom Centore concerned as the Thunderbolts head into the final week of the regular season.

Centore knows that when the team is not winning, some of his players will tell him they're okay, but they're really not—not even close.

"For some of these kids, the winning in football is the only place they see reward for their work," Centore offered about his team. "The guys who came from Providence over the past few years are still playing catchup in school, so they are struggling in the classroom. They don't see any rewards in the classroom, so they see the football field as the only place they can excel, the only place they can feel good about themselves. Some of them don't get much encouragement from home because their parents are struggling themselves."

So Centore and his coaching staff are often spending their afternoons worrying about more than improving speed off the snap or more defensive discipline on option assignments.

"Some kids need more attention, and I and the other coaches can't always detect that," Centore offered. "But you can work it out within the team if you have the right mix of kids."

That's why Mack Hanley is so important to this team, even if he has only played about 30 percent of the offensive downs this season and only one or two plays on defense.

Hanley never says a lot, but he is there every day—often talking to kids on the team who normally don't get a lot of at-tention. After practice, Hanley usually goes home and sits down with his parents and two younger brothers at the dinner table in their Edgewood home. Some of the other kids on the team will grab a burger at the Burger King across the street from the high school before walking home to their rented apartment on some road off Cranston Street near the Providence city line. They come from different circumstances, but for two-to-three hours every afternoon, the Thunderbolts are together communicating—Mack Hanley, the high honors, Irish kid from Edgewood talking on the side of the practice field with the young Dominican sophomore, who moved to Cranston from Providence a few years ago and is struggling in the classroom.

Hanley doesn't create any big spectacle; he doesn't have any long, heart-to-heart discussions with the young sophomore. It's just a conversation between teammates while they are waiting to do a drill or standing watching a defensive unit run-through. But it's the senior from Edgewood making connections with the young kid from Cranston Street on the sidelines of the practice field. They are teenagers who have different backstories, proving every kid has value to this team—simply because he is a teammate. It's the conception that you don't necessarily have to "live in another man's shoes"; you don't need to have lived a teammate's family experiences to want to be a good teammate. You just need empathy for your teammate's situations. You need to want to help in any way you can; and not because you feel sorry for him, but because he is a teammate.

"The better teams are the teams where more kids are connected," said Centore. "This school needs this football team. It shows a large number of kids from different backgrounds can connect while having fun."

Never Quit on Yourself

Like most days, Hector Duran was ready to start practice Tuesday afternoon long before Isaiah McDaniel blew his whistle to signal the beginning of the stretching routine.

He's only seventeen years old, but in his mind, Duran is the father figure for this year's East football team. Duran believes one thing a good father always tries to install in his child is fortitude. Other people might lose faith in your ability to accomplish some quest; but you never quit on yourself—or your teammates.

"I know some people around the school have given up on this team," declared Duran. "But you can't give up. We have a lot of work to do, but if we play as a team, we can make this thing work."

Duran has every reason to lament his circumstances in life. He's the kid who has never really had a father; the kid who lives in South Elmwood with the Amtrak mainline and U.S. Rt.95 within a few hundred yards of his front door. He's the kid who feels it's his responsibility to help his mother and grandmother raise his younger siblings. He could be a bitter teenager. Instead, Hector Duran is the eternal optimist.

"I feel like I have to be the big brother to some of the young guys on the team," Duran said. "I'm the one who has to say, 'Hey, we can do this.'"

Football practice at East forces people from different backgrounds to communicate without their even realizing they are being forced to do it because football, even football practice, is fun. The fact that the game is fun is what first drew Duran to football. Now the game has become his persona—a way to examine his inner character.

"I have been playing football since I could remember. At first it was just fun. Now, it has gotten to the point where football is my home," said Duran, flashing a broad smile. "I feel at home on the field. There is something about football that makes me feel whole. I feel I belong here."

Now Duran believes, as a team captain, it's his responsible to try selling his teammates hope—the hope that they can turn around three weeks of frustration and disappointment by Friday night. Every afternoon at practice, every day in the school corridors, Duran has been preaching his gospel of self-confidence to his teammates. If you believe in yourself, if you do what you know is the right thing, sometimes you may hit a rough stretch, but you will get through it. But losing week after week can take a bite out of a teenager's soul. So, Duran's mantra is you don't stop working while there's still a chance.

Things in life don't always come out the way you planned it. Most East players certainly hadn't planned on going into the final weekend of the regular season desperately fighting for a chance at simply making the playoffs. But it is what Centore has been talking about all season; this is what he was thinking about back in the first few weeks of practice when he said, "I'm worried about what's going to happen when things go bad, and things will go bad."

Now, it's almost two months later, and things have gone bad. There have been three straight losses, and now any hope of salvaging this season by earning a playoff berth rests on beating a very good team on its home field. The bottom line is it's about a game—about a group of football players keeping alive a slim chance of making the playoffs. But as Tom Centore has often evangelized in his end-of-practice dialogues with the players, it's how you rebound when you get knocked down that will matter in your life.

Centore's aspiration is that when a kid finishes playing for East, he will be better equipped to know what loyalty and faithfulness means—what it means to care about someone other than yourself. Hopefully, someday, the execution of those weekly game plans will translate into love for a family—a wife, children—as well as the ability to understand the importance of relationships with people outside your family. These are the types of relationships that will make you a productive member of your community, a good employee, and, maybe, a good employer.

Hector Duran understands Centore's football gospel and has been a devoted disciple of Centore's teachings since Duran became a Thunderbolts starter in his sophomore season. But right now, Hector is just trying to show his teammates how to translate those wisdoms into winning a football game Friday night.

Just Being Part of the Team

Quinn Lanigan has come to understand that being a Cranston East football player can affect your outlook on life.

"I'm in a great situation with my home and my family," said Lanigan. "But you realize some kids here don't have the greatest home life. When they are playing football every day after school, they don't have to think about home or school. You're just on the field, being part of a team."

Delivering under pressure, learning to deal with the stress associated with important games, is a nuance of football that Lanigan has always loved. However, Lanigan has also come to realize that for some of his East teammates, stress is a constant in their lives, and the football field is their safety zone from stress and anxiety.

"There's a lot of stress out there for some of our guys," added Lanigan. "There are a lot of kids who have responsibilities outside school. They have to work to pay for their own phones; they have to help around the house. That sucks because it takes away from football."

Witnessing his teammates' challenges has prompted Lanigan to do some personal soul-searching.

"It makes me appreciate what I have. How I have it good," Lanigan admitted.

That senior season personal revelation has changed the way Lanigan has approached every practice this fall.

"It has made me realize if I'm coming to practice every day and not really trying—what am I?" Lanigan asked of himself.

"If you are not doing what you are doing at practice for somebody else other than just you, you are not doing it at all. That's what football teaches you," concluded Lanigan.

High school football is two to three hours of practice every afternoon building relationships with people. Then you have a chance to play a game with those people on Friday night while the whole school is watching. For four months a year, five or six days a week, you talk; you sweat; you exhaust yourself in the dirt with some kids you might not have ever known if you didn't play football.

"If you are a person who wants to be a part of something with a group of people who have shared interests, football probably is the best sport to play," said Lanigan.

"You gain popularity by playing on the football team," Lanigan offered. "There are some kids here who didn't have a lot of friends when they first started high school. They join the football team, and by end-of-season, there are ten other kids from the football team who they are hanging out with every day. Little things like that go a long way."

He's one of the more popular students in the school, so Lanigan has plenty of friends. But football is helping him better understand the dynamics of leadership.

"As a captain this year, I see a kid who doesn't really care that much about football, but he's playing just so he can be with his friends," Lanigan related. "When I see that kid do something good in practice, I will say something to him; tell him he's getting better. A little thing like that might help him care more about football; it might make him feel like he's helping the team.

"With all the kids who are out here at practice, it's easy for some of the younger kids to think the coaches don't see what they are doing in practice," Lanigan professed. "But they don't realize—football coaches see everything."

He Has Made His Coach Proud

"I'm so proud of that kid," Tom Centore said, as Anthony Migliacco walked past us on the practice field on his way to the parking lot for the bus ride back to the school after practice.

Migliacco is the epitome of "low profile." A face of color, he is a kid who never says much in team huddles and never questions a coaching strategy. He's also a player who never sees his name in the game stories that appear in the local weekly newspaper. But as the regular season headed into the home stretch, this week, in Centore's mind, Migliacco has become one of the most valuable players on the team. He has become an unsung hero because he is the kid who, back in the first week of practice, answered the call when Centore pleaded, "I need somebody who can snap the ball."

Migliacco became that guy, and in his usual low-key manner, he didn't make a big deal about becoming a center—a position he had never played. He just went to Centore and told him he was willing to try being a center. The result is he has made virtually every snap this fall at practice and in games.

"He must have taken 1,000 snaps so far this season," Centore offered. "He has not missed a day of practice."

Migliacco has been on the team for four years; always there but not seeing a lot of playing time until this season. He didn't play football before he came to East, so he has been slowly—and quietly—improving his game. Even after four years, Centore still doesn't know much about Migliacco's home life because the kid doesn't talk much; he never complains about anything. But Centore has always suspected he was a kid who might have needed a little help finding his way through a critical time in his life.

"He's a good kid," said Centore. "He was having some difficulties with his grades when he was younger, but he worked at improving them."

It has all turned around for Migliacco this season. Now he's a starter on the football team, and he had become a solid student in the classroom. He's the kid who has flipped the switch and learned how to become a contributor.

What Makes a Teenager Flip the Switch?

For generations, high school teachers—and coaches—have asked themselves what inspires a teenager to flip that personal switch, which electrifies the idea of improving their life by working hard at something. Is it some book or movie or inspirational speech by a celebrity or professional athlete? Is it the cumulative efforts of a teacher's classroom discussions over a school year? Or is it a season of a high school football coach relating an afternoon practice session to a life-lesson?

The possibility that football might have helped inspire Migliacco to flick that switch is Tom Centore's reward for his fervent love of coaching high school football.

"I couldn't be happier for a kid," said Centore. "It's amazing how much he has matured. He has become responsible."

As Sandra Bullock's character said to a young Michael Oher in the movie *Blind Side*—"Protect your family, Michael." Considering in the fall of 2018, *Blind Side* was a nine-year-old movie, there's a good chance Migliacco had never seen the biographical sports drama.

But Migliacco could certainly relate to the domestic football reference.

"This team has become like a family to me," Migliacco told me one day as we walked off the field after practice.

CHAPTER XXV

"HE'S PASSIONATE ABOUT IT"

"Why did you allow your son to play football?" I asked Bo Cassidy-Bou, the mother of freshman defensive back Jordan Bou.

It was Monday afternoon, and with the varsity team members at the high school watching film, I decided to go over to the stadium to see the East freshman team play its last game of the season. With all the conversation about the potential for head injuries and national media accounts claiming more and more mothers were keeping their sons away from football, I was hoping to talk with the mother of a freshman football player to discover why she'd consented to letting her son play football.

It's not difficult to determine who is a mother at a freshman football game in Rhode Island, or probably in any New England state. Maybe in Florida, Texas, or some midwestern states, the stands at freshmen football games are crowded with long-time devoted fans of a high school football powerhouse eager to get a look at the team's future stars. But that's not the case in New England. In New England, you can almost be certain the few women in the stands at a freshman football game are either mothers, grandmothers, or some aunt.

My question had Bou looking at me with uncertainty.

"I was skeptical about letting him play," Bou finally offered. "But he's passionate about it. As a mom, I'm not going to take that away from him. Plus, it keeps him out of trouble. It keeps him focused, and it keeps him disciplined. I would rather see him doing this than doing something stupid."

Jordan Bou is an exception on the Cranston East team. He is one of the few players who started playing organized football long before he entered high school. He started playing Pop Warner when he was ten years old. Even then, it was a later introduction to organized football than Jordan wanted because of his mother's trepidations about his starting when he was younger.

"He had been bugging me since he was five years old, but even when he was ten, I was a little skeptical about it," Bou's mother related.

It didn't take long for Jordan's mother's concern about an injury to be realized. In the fall of 2016, when he was twelve years old, Bou broke his leg playing football. The injury kept him off the football field during the 2017 season. But once he had medical clearance to play again, there was no question he would be back on the field this fall playing for the East freshman team in 2018.

"He's been training the whole year to be ready to play again this season," his mother offered about Jordan. "He loves football. These boys are like his brothers. I don't have to talk to him about going to practice. He is very passionate about it. I can't take it away from him just because I worry about him."

A Monday afternoon freshman football game spawns a family ritual. You see it at a lot of freshman or junior varsity games around the country where there's a limited number of fans in the stands. The kid's mother sits in the stands patiently watching the action, or maybe talking to another mother while the father walks along the nearly empty stands or the field sideline following the action as it moved up and down the field.

Bou's father, Seayha, played high school football at Central High in Providence at the turn of the 21st century. He never pushed his son into the game, but he wasn't surprised when Jordan said he wanted to play football. Although he played a variety of sports growing up, football is the sport that has stirred Jordan's competitive juices. His father likes that his son is part of a team, and football is the ultimate team sport. While there are certainly physical dangers in the sport, these days there can be more serious dangers for a teenage boy than a sprained ankle or a broken arm.

"He's doing something safe," his father offered about his son, avoiding some of societal menaces while he is on the football field every afternoon. "I would rather have him doing something like this than not knowing what he is doing. He's in a good team atmosphere. When you are on a team like this, you feel you are doing something special."

His father only graduated from high school sixteen years ago, but he knows a teenage boy's world has dramatically changed over those nearly two decades since his own high school days.

"I think it's even more important today for a kid to be on a team like this than it was when I was in high school," said Bou's father. "These days, social media can suck a kid into trouble. It can almost eat a kid alive. You have to stay between them and social media for a child to behave the way you want any child to behave."

That's the thing about football. It helps a young man understand the value of purpose, but the purpose isn't just you—it's what you can do to help the team. That's why the team is so important," added Seayha. "Football makes you feel like you have a role, but that role is being part of the team."

His son has only been a high school football player for a few months, but Seayha has already seen that personal growth—that understanding of "team" in his son.

"He's never been a defensive player. He has always been a running back," Seayha related about Jordan. "Now he's a defensive player, and he has learned how to adopt to the defensive side of the game. He's actually learning to appreciate defense. It's not even what position it is. It's about adapting to something else; it's realizing there's always something more that could give you an opportunity. You get an opportunity; you work hard and take advantage of that opportunity."

It's one of the shrouded benefits of high school football that doesn't appear on the scoreboard. It's a game where there are many different positions for a kid to try; so many different ways a young man can find a way to feel good about himself.

One of the Thunderbolts' Best

Jordan Boo wasn't the first member of his extended family whose life had been enriched by playing for the Cranston East football family.

It was eight years earlier that I had met Erik Bou, Jordan's second cousin.

At the time, Erik was an eighteen-year-old, first-generation Cambodian American, who had graduated from Cranston East a few weeks earlier and was headed to Bates College, the academically prestigious NESCAC Conference school in Waterville, Maine.

On the surface, it looked like a simple formula for a ride to the American Dream—a multi-talented athlete and good student gets accepted to an elite college.

But there was nothing simple about Erik Bou's life.

Bou and I sat one morning in the summer of 2010 in a small restaurant in Edgewood so he could tell me the story of how sports, especially playing for Tom Centore and the Cranston East football team, had changed his life. It was a story I would later write in a *Providence Journal* column.

Bou told me how his mother's first husband had been murdered in the "Killing Fields" of Cambodia, in the 1970s. He told me how his mother had escape from that war-torn country on foot, walking along the mountainside carrying her infant daughter, Bou's older stepsister.

He told me how his mother later endured the hardships of a difficult marriage to a second husband in America, Bou's father. There was family turmoil that eventually found his mother divorcing Bou's father because she wanted a better life for her children. Bou told me that despite all her hardships in life, he never saw his mother cry until that day a few months earlier when he told her he had been accepted to Bates.

"When I told her I had been accepted at Bates, she cried because she was so happy," Bou told me that day.

His story was a tale of a kid who, the year before he entered high school, suddenly realized he couldn't let his mother's courage and sacrifices go to waste. So, he went from barely making it in the classroom—a kid who didn't really care much about even going to school—to being a National Honor Society member and Cranston East's nominee for the award as the top male senior student-athlete in the state of Rhode Island.

And while he wasn't quite sure why he suddenly began working toward that day that would bring tears of joy to his mother's eyes, he knew it never would have happened without his involvement in high school sports, especially football.

"Sports teaches you to make the most of your abilities," said Bou, who played both football and boys' volleyball during his high school career at Cranston East. "I never would have accomplished what I did if I didn't play sports."

His mother never said a lot about the anguish of her first husband being killed by the Khmer Rouge; her escape from her homeland; or her eventual journey to America and her abusive marriage. But occasionally, in passing, she would tell her son some of her stories.

"It was unheard of for a woman like my mother to divorce her husband, because she worked in a factory making minimum wage and spoke no English," Bou related. "But I was just a baby, and she did not want me to go through all the hardships that my dad was putting the family through."

But while his mother knew she wanted better for her children, it's not always easy for a newcomer to understand that in the American education system, there are different levels of success.

Bou had grown up in a home where he didn't speak English until he was almost five years old. His mother had remarried, bringing younger step-siblings into the family when Bou was in his pre-teen years. Often it was Erik's responsibility to babysit while his mother and stepfather worked. School became a place to exist, not necessarily a place to excel.

"I just went to school because it was where you were supposed to be. I never did my homework," Bou said. "I was a lazy kid. I would play video games; I would go outside and just hang around. When I was in the seventh grade, I got a couple of Fs. I probably would have just done enough to graduate from high school, then try to get a job."

But when he was in the eighth grade, he started thinking more about his background—more about the stories he heard growing up, about what his mother had sacrificed; and he began thinking his "just being in school" wasn't enough.

"Suddenly, it just clicked. He looked around at the other kids and realized he could do better," said Tom Centore, who was both Bou's football coach and a guidance counselor at East.

Bou's new interest in school in the eighth grade coincided with his introduction to organized sports.

He had been an active kid growing up, but he never played organized youth sports. It just wasn't part of his family's social DNA. But in the eighth grade, some of his friends were playing for a local youth football team. So, he asked his mother and stepfather if he could play.

"I was afraid to ask because it was lot of money," Bou said of the approximately $150 registration fee at the time. "But I asked, and they said I could."

So, he played a year of youth football and enjoyed it. The first thing he did when he enrolled at East as a freshman the following year was join the football team. The game of football was giving him a sense of purpose, an understanding of achieving goals plus structure and discipline in his daily life. All that, and it was fun, too.

"The football team is like a brotherhood," Bou told me. "We all work together for one goal. The coaches were always talking to us about getting our work done in school and on the field."

Bou had found a love of football and a desire to excel in the classroom.

"I started doing my homework," Bou said. "Once you start doing your homework, it becomes a habit. You do your homework every day, and it makes you feel good. I'm close to my mom, and I wanted to make her proud."

Centore wasn't surprised football helped pave the road to Bou's academic success.

"He's such a competitive kid. He hates to lose," Centore had offered about Bou back in 2010. "He took that competitiveness from the field right into the classroom."

In his freshman year at East, only two years after he was getting Fs in middle school, Bou earned seven As and two Bs in college prep courses. By his sophomore year, he moved from simple college prep courses to honor courses. By the time he graduated from East, he academically ranked in the top 11 percent of his graduating class; he was an all-division football player and a member of both the World Language and National Honor societies.

His mother and stepfather were loving parents, but there was no hand-holding, no snow-plow parents clearing the way for his journey to an elite college. His success was a product of his own convictions, his desire to reward his mother for all her sacrifices, and a work ethic that he first learned on the football field.

Bou went on to graduate from Bates in 2014, and in 2018 was working in finance. His name is not listed among any of the Cranston East football record holders, but in many ways, Bou is one of Cranston East's greatest success stories.

Even in the fall of 2018, mention Erik Bou's name, and a smile comes to Tom Centore's face.

CHAPTER XXVI

SOMETHING ABOUT MARY

The town of Cumberland, R.I. is an upscale, well-manicured suburban community, and Cumberland High is the town's lone public high school. Located in the northern section of the state, Cumberland is a town of about 33,000, making it one of the largest towns, population-wise, in Rhode Island. Cumberland's western town line borders the Massachusetts state line, only about forty miles from Boston. So these days, in addition to being a Providence commuting suburb, Cumberland also has become a Boston commuting town. The result is that in 2018, Cumberland had become even more of a prime upper-middle class suburban town than it was only a decade earlier.

Between the 2010 census and the fall of 2018, the population of Cumberland increased 5.5 percent compared to only a 0.65 percent increase for the overall Rhode Island population.

American movie-goers first heard of Cumberland High when it was identified as the high school in the opening scene of the movie *Something about Mary* starring Cameron Diaz. Pete and Bobby Farrell, the American film director brothers who directed *Something About Mary*, grew up in Cumberland,

and the Farrells have never forgotten their roots—referencing their hometown and home state in several of their movies.

Like a lot of other Rhode Island suburban communities, Cumberland is very white. In the 2010 U.S. census, 92.8 percent of Cumberland's 33,000 residents were white; while only 4.5 percent were Hispanic/Latino; and 1.5 percent were African American. In the fall of 2018, those demographics hadn't changed much. The Cumberland High student body reflects the town's population, so—like most Rhode Island suburban public school teams—the composite look of the Cumberland football team is different from the look of the Cranston East Thunderbolts.

Despite being one of the ten largest Rhode Island high schools for most of the past half century, Cumberland High hadn't enjoyed much success at the top level of Rhode Island high school football. At the start of the 2018 season, the school had never won a Division I (top division) state football title in the forty-five-year history of the official Rhode Island high school football playoff system. In fact, Cumberland didn't even play in the top football division for the first thirteen years of the 21st century.

Cumberland was finally pushed up to Division I in 2014, but coming into the 2018 season, Cumberland hadn't had a winning regular league season in those five years of Division I competition. But in 2018, a new mindset for the program was starting to produce some positive results.

As the 2018 regular season moved into its final weekend in October, Cumberland was poised to have its first Division I winning regular season in the 21st century. All Cumberland needed for that winning season was a victory over Cranston East Friday night at Cumberland, and based on comparative scores against common opponents, Cumberland was a heavy favorite to register that historical victory Friday night.

Same Old, Same Old

The first half of the Cumberland game didn't give any indication the contest was going to produce any different result than the disappointing final scores the Cranston East football team had experienced over the past month. On its first three offensive possessions, East moved into Cumberland territory, but all three possessions failed to produce any points.

For a team that had lost three straight games, this could be a reason for the Thunderbolts to quickly start feeling sorry for themselves. They had worked hard on those first three possessions, but they had nothing to show for it. For some of the Thunderbolts, that seemed to be the story of their lives. They would try doing what the teacher asked, but because of their poor academic preparation when they had been living in some other city, they weren't experiencing classroom success. So, they would become frustrated.

Now, despite having played twenty-four minutes of good, solid football on another team's field, the Thunderbolts were trailing 12–7 at halftime. The frustration was about to consume the Thunderbolts' psyche. It was the final week of October. They had been together as an official team for almost eighty days. They had heard hundreds of directives from coaches, but at halftime, Ken Simone still needed to go back to Tom Centore's message on that first day of practice.

"You are not trusting the guys next to you on the line," declared Simone.

Simone had seen some players leave their assignment because they didn't trust that the guy next to him would carry out his assignment. So instead of having one problem because one player was leaving his assignment open, they had two problems because two players weren't focusing on their job.

"You have to trust the person next to you; the person next to you has to trust you," Simone implored.

Once again, the Thunderbolts were being reminded that trust is the cornerstone of football. It doesn't matter if you're a team rolling toward an undefeated season or a team struggling through a losing season playing a game most people didn't think you have a chance to win. If you have trust in the guy next to you, you have a chance to be successful. If you have trust in your teammate, and he has trust in you, that consortium of faith might produce something special.

It will not be a touchdown on every play; maybe not even a team victory at the end of the game. But there's a good chance there will be a feeling of satisfaction. It's the security in a very unsecure world for a 21st century teenager that being part of a high school football team can give a kid. That's what separates football from other high school sports.

There is an average of 120–130 defined plays in a high school football game. That's constant opportunities to prove that if you trust the guy next to you, together you might accomplish something you didn't think possible.

Not to raise sports competition to a level it doesn't deserve, but at a time when America political leaders—and other segments of American society—can't seem to work together in the quest of positive results, here on a football field in a suburban Rhode Island town a bunch of teenage males from different backgrounds were trying to show what can be accomplished if you do your job and put your trust in the guy next to you.

Their composite look is different from every other high school football team in Rhode Island. All season they had encountered problem after problem, but on this Friday night they are trying to show what Cranston East football is all about.

It would have been easy for some Cranston East players to find a reason not to keep trying to fix the season's problems this late in the year. After all, even if East does come back tonight and pull off an upset, there's no guarantee the Thunderbolts will make the playoffs. It had been a season in which fate seemed stacked against this team's being successful. The coach's beloved father dies two days before the first League game of the season; one of the best linebackers in the state misses four of the first five games because of quirky injuries; and the offensive and defensive lines never had a chance to reach their potential because of injuries. Yet when Hector Duran stands up during the halftime meeting and declares, "We can still do this," his teammates trusted him.

A Collective Turn-On

All season Tom Centore has been talking about seizing the intensity the game of football offers. But week after week, his team hadn't collectively bought into the concept. Suddenly, for some reason, at the start of the second half, they had become enthusiastic consumers of Centore's sales pitch.

A football team doesn't turn a game around in the second half because one or two players suddenly decide to begin focusing on the coach's instructions. That's the thing about football—it takes a collective "turning on" of the switch to bring about a change of fortune. It takes focus from end to end on the line, blocking in the backfield, and trust and coordination in the secondary. It wasn't that East had played poorly in the first half. It was just some little things that were missing, which could have made a difference in the first twenty-four minutes. They were missing because—as Ken Simone had referenced—some people were worrying about doing other people's jobs rather than totally focusing on taking care of their own responsibilities.

The thinking is simple. If eleven players completely focus on their own assignment on every play of a game and don't allow their attention to be diverted by other people's actions, a football team has a chance of being successful. It's the message Centore had been preaching almost every day at practice—whether the subject was the Thunderbolts "Jet" offensive scheme, a school academic assignment, or life beyond the halls and playing fields of Cranston East High.

Finally, on a chilly late October night, the message seems to be resonating.

Jamari Mason was doing a great job sealing the edge, keeping Cumberland's speed guys from getting outside. He seems totally focused on doing his job rather than diverting his attention toward berating a teammate for a sloppy play.

Also, Dayshaun White was dominating on the defensive line. White's foot had been twisted under a pile-up in the first half, and it had been aching ever since. But White never said anything to trainer Katie Chaffee or any of the coaches. He wanted to keep playing, and he was afraid if he told Katie he was hurting she might tell him he needed to sit out the second half. This is the guy who—in the words of his teammates—had been a "dickhead" when he was a freshman; the kid who, when he first got to Cranston East, didn't care about anybody but himself because he was mad at the world for the shitty family situation he had been dealt. He's the kid who wouldn't listen to any adult giving advice until he met Tom Centore. Now that young man wouldn't leave the field, even though he was in pain, because he felt his teammates were depending on him.

Hector Duran was playing his usual "Never stop trying" style. Even after weeks of frustrating losses, he has refused to "throttle back" his aggressiveness and enthusiasm. There he was rushing in from his linebacker berth and pushing his way past offensive lineman who were forty or fifty pounds heavier and four or five inches taller than him.

But even on a night when team harmony is faultless, this may be a team that just doesn't have the talent needed to register a statement victory. Late in the fourth quarter, the Thunderbolts, trailing 26–22, had a chance to take the lead as they moved the ball inside the Cumberland 25-yard line. But they couldn't get into the end zone, eventually giving up the ball on downs. That gave Cumberland the ball deep it its own territory, somewhere around its own 20-yard line.

That's always precarious territory for a team holding a slim lead, but the clock was in Cumberland's favor with just under two minutes to play. If Cumberland could keep the ball on the ground and pick up just one first down, they could run out the clock. East will not get another chance to make up its four-point deficit. A season of frustration would end with one final insult—about 20 yards short of a winning touchdown.

Cumberland immediately started milking the clock with a pair of runs. But the East defense did a pretty good job, giving up a combined total of only 6 yards on the two plays. But Cumberland was still in a commanding position. If the home team could ground out 4 more yards on its third down play, for all intents and purposes, the game was over. Even if East did stop them short of the first down on the third down play, Cumberland would just punt the ball on fourth down and, unless East got a rare good punt return, the Thunderbolts would need to move the ball 50 or more yards for the winning touchdown in less than a minute.

Ken Simone knew his defensive unit was tired. It had been a tough, physical game against a big team. Simone felt he needed a comparatively fresh body out there for the Cumberland third down attempt, so he sent in Mack Hanley at an outside linebacker spot. It would be only the second time this season Hanley had played on defense.

All season, Hanley had been hoping the coaches would give him a chance to play defense. He knew he didn't have any defensive game experience, but he always thought he could play defense. Defense is a game of strategies—a thinking man's game—and Hanley is a good thinker. Even before the season had started, Hanley felt he might be helpful because of the team's lack of experienced defensive players, especially at linebacker, the position Hanley saw himself playing. With that lack of depth at linebacker, and Hanley's work ethic, eventually the coaches would probably have given Hanley a chance to earn a starting spot on the defensive unit.

But when Hanley broke his hand only a few days after the start of practice, it limited his chances to work his way onto the defense. By the time he was able to return to action midway through the season, the coaches felt it was too late to teach Hanley how to be a linebacker. So even though he felt he could help the defense, Hanley didn't question the coaches' decision. It wasn't Mack Hanley's way to question a coach, even if Hanley felt he could help the team by playing defense. But his natural intellectual curiosity required Hanley to pay attention when Simone would go over defensive assignments in practice. So, Hanley knew the defensive schemes. Only one other time all season had Simone told Hanley to go on the field with the defensive unit, and even that was for a basically meaningless play late in a game a few weeks ago. But now Simone needed a fresh body in a critical situation—maybe somebody who could make something happen. So, Simone looked at Hanley and told him to go in at linebacker.

On the third down play, the Cumberland runner cut off left tackle in search of some open space. But an East lineman grabbed enough of the runner's arm to slow him down. Hanley darted into an open space from his linebacker berth and hit the runner in the mid-section. Just as the runner was headed to the ground, the ball slipped out of his arm and hit the ground. Hanley saw the loose ball bouncing on the ground and quickly dove on it. A couple of Cumberland players pounced on Hanley's back and tried clawing the ball away from him. Fostering every bit of strength he could muster from his 210-pound body, Hanley fought off the attempts to steal his prize recovery.

Eventually, an official blew the whistle and declared it was Cranston East's ball on the Cumberland 18-yard line. It was the type of moment Hanley had envisioned all those afternoons he showed up at practice with a cast on his hand, but he wasn't sure if it would ever happen. He would stand at those practices for hours listening to the coaches' instructions without being able to actually take part in a drill. He wasn't there because he was dreaming of some day being the star of a game. He was there because he felt, even with his injury-shortened season, there still might be a time when he could help his teammates.

Football would never be Mack Hanley's voucher to the spotlight. For Hanley, playing football for Cranston East was a passion without expectations of celebrated satisfaction. Hanley kept coming back every afternoon with that cast on his hand because, maybe some Friday night he might be able to do something that would help HIS team enjoy some measure of success—even if nobody noticed it. Now he had done something everybody noticed.

You could say the fumble was a gift, an absolute football gift, for Cranston East. A Cumberland team that was basically in control of its own destiny handed the ball over to the Thunderbolts only 15 yards from its own end zone. But the reality is—football gifts happen. Football coaches prefer to call them opportunities. The key is to be ready to accept your gift/opportunity. A cardinal rule of football is—be ready to take advantage of opportunities.

The Thunderbolts could have bailed out earlier in the game when they had been frustrated by not taking advantage of some golden scoring opportunities. Some teams that had gone through the type of season East had encountered up to this point might have, but the Thunderbolts didn't.

They don't have a name for it. Nobody talks about "Bolts Pride," but it's there. It's more than just what this single victory might produce. It's pride in something that has been built by the Cranston East football family over the past decade or so. They don't parade it around their city; they don't plaster it on a tee-shirt to be sold in one of the Garden City boutique clothing stores. Most Cranston residents don't even understand how unique one of their city high school football teams is. It's only the Cranston East football family who know it's a team that looks different than the other public school teams they play. Even the East players don't think about it that much. For them, it is what it is. But they are proud of what has been built—what they are part of, as Alex Corvese had told me earlier in the season about the reaction of his college teammates when he told them about his high school team.

"When I was in college, I told the guys on my team that I had been one of only two white kids on the starting offense on my high school team. They didn't believe me."

Now the Thunderbolts' chance for an upset, which most fans thought was dead only a few minutes earlier, was back on life-support. East still trailed by 4 with 1:41 to play, but now they had the ball and were only 18 yards from the Cumberland end zone.

Of course, with this year's Cranston East team, being in scoring position doesn't guarantee any points on the scoreboard. Not wanting to take a chance with a pass, Centore called three sweeps with the following instructions: If you don't have an open edge, get out of bounds before you go down. The Thunderbolts' runners did manage to get out of bounds each time, but the 3 runs had only produced a total of 6 yards. That left a fourth-and-four from the 13 with about forty-five seconds to play. They had only gained 6 yards in 3 plays; now they needed at least 4 yards on 1 play. Was it going to be a final case of "coming close, but not being able to deliver the big play"?

Alabama coach Nick Sabin once wrote, "You must be prepared for adverse situations. Have confidence in your plan, but be ready if it falls." Rayven Deoliveira probably never read that Sabin quote, but fortunately on this night, Deoliveira, who always seems to be confident about his ability, was ready when the coach's first plan for the winning touchdown failed.

On the fourth down, Centore called for a quarterback roll-out. Apparently, Centore felt it would give the Thunderbolts two chances to pick up the 4 yards. Deoliveira's first response was to quickly look for an open receiver. If nobody was immediately open, he could try to beat the on-rushing Cumberland defender around the right edge and at least pick up the 5 yards needed for a first down. It's a play that had probably been called at least five times a game this season; but time and time again, it seemed Rayven's first thought had been to run the ball rather than look for a receiver. It seemed he never really grasped the concept of seeing the field the way the coaches wanted him to see it. As Alex Corvese had said about Deoliveira that first week of practice, "He definitely has all the tools. We just have to have him thinking as a quarterback."

Deoliveira took the snap and made a quick look down field. Apparently, he didn't immediately see anybody open because he quickly started rolling around the right side. But a Cumberland linebacker had found a gap in the East offensive line and was already in the Cranston backfield just as Rayven started making his turn up-field. The defender reached out and grabbed Rayven's shirt. It could have been enough to stop Deoliveira's forward progress. There had been times this season when Deoliveira had seemed to quit on a play like that. Maybe he had adopted "the quarterback needs to protect himself from injury" mantra you see on Sunday NFL telecasts rather than bulling his way for a few yards like he had done so often last year when he was a running back.

There were times this season when some teammates seemed to be losing confidence in Rayven's ability to come up with the big play. But this time, Deoliveira wasn't playing it safe. He never let his legs stop pumping and eventually broke out of the grasp of the defender. Deoliveira could have tried bulling his way for those 5 or 6 yards for the first down. But, after a season in which he often tried to do it by himself—thus demonstrating the self-survival mode that had been the core of his existence through most of his teenage years—this time Rayven looked for help from a teammate.

Deoliveira looked down field and saw Chance McKinney cutting across from the right side a few yards inside the back of the end zone. Rayven fired a low bullet-pass; McKinney left his feet, and while in a full body length extension made a diving catch for a touchdown. The kid who was at East because his mother wanted him in a safer environment had just delivered—big time. McKinney had been on a good team at Central, coached by a good coach, and most of his teammates were faces of color like him. But he found a new football family on this East team. Now, McKinney may have put that team in the playoffs with the biggest catch of his football career.

McKinney's touchdown gave the Thunderbolts a 28–26 lead, with thirty-four seconds to play. A few minutes later, after a wild celebration by East players in the Cumberland end zone, Jon Loy came trotting onto the field to boot a conversion point. But this was a season when even a triumphant moment could turn into misfortune.

Quinn Lanigan was kneeling down in his usual spot as the holder for Loy's conversion attempt, ready to take the snap from Anthony Migliaccio. The trio had been one of the few East football consistencies all season: Migliaccio making an on-the-mark snap, Lanigan putting the ball on the ground and perfectly spinning the laces so they are facing away from the kicker, and Loy booting the conversion. Loy had already hit 25 conversion attempts this season. But a second before Migliaccio snapped the ball, a Cumberland lineman crashed through the East line. It would be an offside penalty, but the officials didn't have time to blow the play dead before the ball was heading back to Lanigan.

The illegal, quick start gave the Cumberland player a chance to break-in on Lanigan, and it was obvious he would block Loy's kick. But Lanigan wasn't sure there was going to be a penalty called, so rather than just stand up and move out of the way, he picked up the ball and tried rolling-out for a 2-point conversion attempt.

Lanigan's cleat caught on the artificial turf, and he stumbled forward. A charging Cumberland lineman hit the off-balance Lanigan at full speed, and Lanigan crumbled under a pile of bodies, with one leg lying at a gruesomely different direction than his other leg. It was immediately obvious Lanigan was seriously hurt. His face was hidden behind his facemask, but as his helmet rolled from side to side, it was easy to picture that inside the helmet, Lanigan's face was clenched in pain. Kate Chaffee had immediately rushed onto the field and began treating the lower portion of Lanigan's leg, but almost immediately she signaled for the rescue squad to be summoned.

The rescue squad arrived within a few minutes, and eventually Lanigan was placed on a stretcher and rolled off the field. Some of his teammates reached down and extended their hand to touch Lanigan in a show of support as he passed by them; others just stood there, their heads bowed. They all knew Lanigan's high school football career was finished. The kid who was all about doing whatever was best for the team wouldn't finish his high school career on the field on Thanksgiving Day. Given another conversion attempt, when play resumed, Loy calmly booted the ball through the uprights, increasing East's lead to 29–26.

There were still about thirty seconds to play, but a good effort by the East special teams unit on the ensuing kickoff and couple stops by the defensive unit closed out the game.

Maybe fate was finally starting to smile on the Thunderbolts.

Sometimes You Make Your Own Luck

"Great game," I said to Mack Hanley after he finished the post-game handshakes with the Cumberland players and started heading toward the end zone for the post-game team meeting with Tom Centore.

Maybe this was the type of game Hanley was thinking about earlier in the season when he said this season, for the first time in his football career, he really felt a connection with the team because he finally knew the game well enough to make a contribution.

"Thanks," Hanley said. "What are the odds? I play defense on two plays all season, and I make one of the most important plays of the year. I'm a very lucky person."

"This took heart," Hector Duran yelled to me, as he ran toward the south end zone to join his teammates who were waiting for Tom Centore.

Duran was holding his helmet, and his face was beaming. It was one of those halcyon days of youth; one of those idyllically happy moments that will be embedded in Duran's memory for years—maybe for decades to come. The night his team beat Cumberland when nobody thought they could. Generations of high school football players have those type of triumphant moments stored in their memory banks; maybe retrieved at some later time when the former player's psyche needs a little uplift.

Regardless of how this season eventually plays out, this will be one of those moments for Duran. He's the teenager who took it upon himself to become a father figure to some of the younger players on the team. "Become the father figure I never had" was the way Duran described it a few months earlier. Now Duran was walking toward his football family gathering in the end zone with the smile of a happy teammate—and proud father.

For This Team, the Game Doesn't End at the Final Buzzer

There was no need to ask Tom Centore how he felt in the minutes following the game's final buzzer. The grin on his face said more than 1,000 well-written words could chronical. The last three games had added to the frustration in a season of stressful moments. The death of his father two days before the regular season started; his conscious-probing moments when he questioned whether he should have taken a leave from coaching this season in order to spend more time with his father in his final month; and Centore's concerns about his own health after he collapsed on the field at the Shea game.

But tonight proved it was all worth it.

Games like this are why men like Centore coach high school football. There was no championship trophy going to the winner. In all honesty, Centore has serious doubts it will even be enough to put the Thunderbolts in the playoffs. He had done his own calculation of the playoff scenarios, and he knew it would take some major upsets in other games being played tonight for East to be a winner in the playoff tie-breaking formula. But this game was evidence that the improbable could happen for a high school football team. It had been a test of trust and character for the Cranston East players—the core of Centore's coaching doctrine.

Centore stood in the end zone. Looking up at him where sixty or so young men who hadn't quit when a lot of people thought they would. Centore wanted them to understand how proud he was of them. This is what he has been looking for all season—focusing on their jobs; never quitting even when it seemed hopeless. It would have been easy to pack it in, but they didn't. They had shown what a football family can do when they trust in each other.

"What you did in terms of never giving up, doing what we asked you to do in the second half, was amazing," Centore said.

"Even after we had chances to get into the end zone and didn't, you didn't give up. Then Mack makes the big play at the end. You needed to do something to have a chance, and you did it. That's what a football team does. Nobody thought you would come up here and beat this team, but you did it," Centore continued, the smile cascading off his face.

"I'm really proud of what you did. What a game!" Centore pronounced. "That's Cranston East football. Now leave here and enjoy this the right way."

Even in the euphoria of his team's biggest victory of the season, Centore is concerned about the image of Cranston East football. They are on the road in a town where a lot of people think of Cranston East as a city school, with all the city school stereotypes, because of the composite face of the team. It's as if—for some people—the stunning victory isn't enough to prove East is a team of character. His players have done the job on the scoreboard; now they have to leave the field, the parking lot, and the town showing "class."

Centore wants them to understand that what needs to be done goes beyond just winning a football game. He wants them to be a success in life long after the score of this game fades from most of their memories. Over the years—the decades—that will mean living a productive life; being a good father. That's all part of Cranston East football.

But right now, their coach also wants them to enjoy the thrill of winning a big Friday night high school football game.

CHAPTER XXVII

YOU DON'T WANT TO LEAVE THE FEELING

The trip back to Cranston on the two school buses following the Cumberland game was the most euphoric journey of the season for the East players The return trip following the victory over Portsmouth back in September had been filled with the sound of boisterous teenage chatter that's common on a bus ride following a victory, but that was early in the season, before the Thunderbolts knew the strange quirk of fate the season had in store for them. Friday night, the Thunderbolts had exorcised many of the demons of the past two weeks with their performance against Cumberland.

Tom Centore sat in the front seat of one of the buses, constantly checking his iPhone for any tweets that might have the scores of some of the other games that were played that night. East had done what it needed to do to have a chance for a playoff berth. Now, the Thunderbolts needed some help from other teams to improve their playoff chances. But Centore didn't have the results of the other games by the time the two buses pulled up behind the Cranston East school building.

With the players using both the front door and the back emergency exit, within a few minutes both buses were empty, and the locker room was filled with teenage boys still bursting with the excitement over their big victory. By the time the players had changed out of their uniforms and started heading out of the locker room, it was after 11 p.m. The few players who had cars headed to the parking lot, and a few others immediately started walking home. But some of the players just stood in front of the high school talking.

A few days earlier, Tom Centore had said to me that for some of his players, the football field was the "only place they see any reward for their work. The only place they feel good about themselves." It had been a month since they'd experienced a feeling like this after a game—a night when they did something people, beyond their own coaches, would think the Thunderbolts had achieved something significant.

Even though their job was done, some of the players didn't want to end that feeling of accomplishment. So, they stood around the front of the school. Some were waiting for their ride home to arrive, probably hoping it didn't arrive too soon. Somebody mentioned getting something to eat at one of the restaurants on nearby Reservoir Ave., but for many Thunderbolts, the extra cash needed for a late-night snack at one of those restaurants wasn't in their budget.

"I think some of our kids go to the Burger King over the Providence line because it is cheaper," Ken Simone had told me one day at a practice when we were discussing where the players went after a game. "Our kids are in a lot of different economic situations. The only time everything is the same is when they are here together on the field."

Life Isn't Always Fair

You can recite all the mathematical reasoning and all the adult justifications, but the reality is that most high school football players will not understand how two other Division I teams who won fewer League games than Cranston East would be in the playoffs and East would not be. Or how a team that East had defeated in a head-to-head matchup only two days earlier would be practicing for a playoff game Monday afternoon, and the Thunderbolts would be sitting in a classroom having their coach explain why they are not in the playoffs.

But that was the situation Tom Centore was facing as he walked into a Monday afternoon team meeting. It all had to do with how the League had set up the two Division I sub-division alignments. Even before the season started, Tom Centore had been saying there wasn't parity between the two sub-divisions. When the regular season ended Friday night, it was evident Centore knew what he was talking about.

The way the playoff qualifying schedule was set up, each team in a subdivision would play the other six teams in its sub-division, plus one cross-over game against a team from the other sub-division. At the end of the regular season, all seven teams in Cranston East's Division I-A sub-division had won their one cross-over game against the DI-B teams. It was obvious DI-A was a tougher place to play than Division I-B, and six of Cranston East's seven games that counted in the playoff calculation were played against DI-A teams.

The results were at the end of the regular season, three DI-A teams—Cranston East, Cumberland, and Shea—had finished in a three-way tie for the final two playoff berths. When teams finish tied for the final playoff berth in a sub-division, they don't play a tie-breaking game. They use a complicated tie-breaking formula, and this time the formula was working against Cranston East despite the fact that East had a better League record than two of the teams in Division I-B who did earn a playoff berth.

By Saturday morning, Tom Centore had done all the calculations and knew the Thunderbolts were going to be the odd-team out in the tie-breaker. But the League wasn't going to make an official announcement until Monday afternoon. So, when some players were texting him Saturday, Centore told them nothing would be official until Monday, and there would be a team meeting immediately after the final period of the day on Monday.

Of course, that didn't stop the chatter on social media. Some kid from Cumberland tweeted they had heard they were playing Moses Brown in the playoffs. Shea players were writing how excited they were about being in the playoffs in their first year of Division I competition. There may not have been anything official from the League, but most of the Cranston East players had come to the realization that they would not be in the playoffs by the time they walked into the meeting Monday afternoon in the classroom across the hall from the locker room.

Centore had sent a team-wide text telling everybody to immediately report to the meeting room after the final period of the school day, and the coach made sure he was already waiting in the classroom when the players began arriving for the meeting.

Quinn Lanigan came rolling up the hall with his left leg in a cast that was kneeling on a medical-type scooter, which allowed Lanigan to rest his injured leg on the scooter while he propelled himself down the hall with his other leg. He had spent five hours in a busy hospital emergency room Friday night being x-rayed, then being treated for a broken leg. But he was in school Monday morning, and now he was trying to squeeze into one of the classroom desks while still resting his leg on his scooter.

Apparently Robenson Antoine had not heeded Tom Centore's message to come immediately to the meeting after the final class of the day because, as Antoine walked into the classroom while he was unwrapping a sandwich, it was obvious Antoine had managed to make a quick trip after the final period to one of the many fast-food restaurants down the street from Cranston East. After having spent ten weeks watching Antoine playfully interacting with his teammates, but also getting upset when he thought somebody was not giving his "all" in practice, I knew Antoine was hurting as much as any other player on the team about the Thunderbolts not making the playoffs. Nobody had put more effort into producing big plays this season than Antoine, but Robenson was the guy who always tried not to show his emotions; he tried not to let the opponent think he could be rattled. He's the kid who wants people to think nothing upsets him. So, he sat in a desk eating a sandwich, trying to look detached, but actually in emotional turmoil as he waited for Centore to start talking.

Meanwhile, on the other side of the room, the amiable smile that usually consumed Hector Duran's face was missing. There was no hiding the fact that Duran was hurting.

Before long, all the desks were filled, so some players started standing along the wall at the back of the room. Even though most of the players had heard the news that the Thunderbolts were not in the playoffs, they still attended the meeting. It was as if the bad news wouldn't be official until they heard it from Coach Centore.

Centore knew his players were hurting. This would be only the second time since 2011 that Cranston East would not be in the playoffs. For many of the players, the football field was the only place they felt distinctive—the only place they had felt success. Now, some of them felt that feeling was being stolen from them by some convoluted tie-breaking system devised by adults they didn't even know. Centore, however, wasn't going to allow any pity-party. Sure, the excuses could be found. But Centore wasn't going to allow his team an opportunity to blame somebody else for this season's failures.

Yes, the Thunderbolts had a difficult assignment, maybe even unfair. But, even with the odds stacked against them, even with all the freaky injuries, Centore felt it could have been doable. As Centore had been telling his team all season—as he has been telling Thunderbolts teams for sixteen years—"Don't look anyplace else; look inside yourself."

Centore waited until the last player walked through the classroom door before he started speaking. Finally, the coach made it official.

"I know some of you heard, but in case you didn't, the League issued its playoff schedule today, and we are the team that lost-out in the tie-breaker," Centore said in a disappointed tone.

He tried to explain how the playoff tie-breaker was determined: how a Cumberland victory over East Providence in the middle of the season had given Cumberland more quality points than Shea and East in the three-way tie for the third and fourth playoff berths from their sub-division. That meant Cumberland would earn the No. 3 seed, and when it came down to Shea and East for the fourth spot, Shea won on the strength of its head-to-head victory in the first game of the regular season.

Some of the players listened intently as Centore explained, but other just stared out the window. Centore was right: some of them, probably most, knew before they came into the room, but they needed to hear it from Centore. Once that happened, a lot of them didn't really want to be in that room any longer, but they respectfully sat there and listened to their coach. Somebody asked if there was any appeal. Centore told them there wasn't. The unthinkable had happened—Cranston East would not be in the playoffs.

Centore stood at the front of the room looking at a room full of disappointed faces. He understood their pain more than most of the players realized. For Centore, the weekend had been filled with doubts. Had he failed his father? At the beginning of the season, he knew the way his father's health had dramatically declined over the summer that this could be the last season he would share the quest of trying to take a team to the playoffs with his father. Even though the season wasn't completed when Tony Centore died in September, if the team had made the playoffs, Tom could have felt, in a sense, that he and his father had successfully completed their final quest together. There didn't need to be another championship—just making the playoffs would have made it a successful quest. That would have been a major accomplishment for this team, with its plethora of inexperienced players at key positions. But it didn't happen, and now a son worried he had failed honoring his father's memory.

"If you are not disappointed, there is something wrong with you," Centore proclaimed. "Our expectations are always high. I wish I could fix it. I wish I could tell you there was something different, but I can't. We have to move forward."

The calendar was still a few days from flipping over to November, and now there would be no meaningful games to play until the non-League Thanksgiving Day intra-city rivalry game with Cranston West. But there was still some work to be done as a football team. In a move to appease people who were upset that the new playoff format meant the regular season was finishing earlier compared to past years, the League was arranging one meaningless "consolation" game for teams not involved in the playoffs. That game would be played in the second week of November, but nobody was disillusioned that the game, in itself, had any significance. But it was a reason to be together as a team for a couple more weeks of practice; two more weeks of Centore's asking his football family to ponder what football means to them.

"You can be disappointed like we all are," said Centore. "But we still have work to do. I hope you are committed to everything we do. If you love football, you will be. We have to figure what we are going to do. I really hope you guys are going to finish the right way. It may not sound good to you now, but I just hope you are willing to put in that effort. I hope the underclassmen will use this time to get better."

The meeting finished, and most of the players started leaving the room, but Robenson Antoine stayed sitting at his desk eating his fast-food meal, trying to act nonchalant about not making the playoffs.

Hector Duran made no effort to hide the sick feeling in his stomach. Duran immediately rose out of his seat when Centore finished speaking and walked out of the room without saying a word to anybody. Duran had done it all the right way. Everything he did was for the team. He was the heart and soul at practice and in every game. He was the leader. He was the kid who thought about the team before himself every day; the guy who declared, "I can still block" to a coach at the East Providence game, after the trainer told him he was finished for the night because of an injury. He wasn't the star, but he was every bit as important as any member of the team, including the offensive stars like Rayven and Robenson. Hector was the kid with the "can do" spirit. He possessed that American moral fiber some people say was missing in today's young people. But it was never missing in Hector's daily life.

At home he was the "man of the house." That was real life, and Duran was proud of what he does to help his mother, his grandmother, and his younger siblings. But this team was his other family, and now he felt he had failed his football family.

As he was walking out of the room, there was a good chance Duran was asking himself, "Was there something else I could have done?" Over time, Duran will realize there was nothing more he could have done; he had given "over and above" what any coach could have asked. But at this moment, the Thunderbolts' "Man of the House" was a dejected young man.

CHAPTER XXVIII

A FOOTBALL TEST

At the Monday meeting, Tom Centore had given the team a day off from practice Tuesday (Oct. 30), but he said he expected everybody to be at practice Wednesday afternoon. Centore knew that because of the Thunderbolts' convoluted practice regiment, he was asking a lot from his players. Now, it would be dark by the time players were bussed back to their locker room at the high school after practice. That meant most of the players would be walking home in the dark, or ever tougher, some of them would be walking to their part-time jobs in the dark.

"This will be a real test of how much football, how much this team, means to these guys," Centore had said to some of the assistant coaches after the Monday meeting.

So, two days later, Centore was pleased when there was a big turnout for the Wednesday practice session, and there were even more players at practice on Thursday (Nov. 1). Following Thursday's practice, Centore had given everybody the weekend off, but again on Monday there was another good turnout at practice.

That's Just the Way It Is

Tuesday (Nov. 6) was Election Day, and on the ballot were several Cranston city bond issues. If approved, one of the bonds would provide funds for a new football field, with lights, right next to Cranston West High. That would mean the Cranston West football team, and some other West teams, would no longer be sharing Cranston Stadium with teams from Cranston East.

"I can think of a lot of other things this city needs more than a new football field at Cranston West," Isaiah McDaniel had said one day at practice when the issue of a new Cranston West football field was mentioned.

But McDaniel wasn't worrying about trying to "Fight City Hall."

"What are you going to do? That's just the way it is in this city," declared McDaniel, implying that most new educational infrastructure in Cranston seemed to end up on the western side of the city.

Maybe McDaniel wasn't too concerned about the idea of a new field at Cranston West because as he had declared to me a few months earlier, "I'm right where I want to be," in reference to his status as a member of the East education staff along with being the assistant football coach and head boys' basketball coach at his high school alma mater. McDaniel is proud of how he has helped Tom Centore build the Cranston East football program over the past sixteen years. There's no way McDaniel, even if offered, would leave East for a position at Cranston West just because West has better facilities. But McDaniel, like some other people around the city, can't help noticing the obvious athletic infrastructure inequality at East and West.

West student-athletes have practice facilities a short walk from their high school locker rooms; East athletes need to drive around the city to get to their various practice facilities. West track athletes have a comparatively new composite running track a few hundred yards from the high school. East runners don't have a track, not even at Cranston Stadium. But McDaniel isn't going to let the infrastructure inequalities discourage him. Rather than bemoan a possible new facility on the Cranston West campus, McDaniel looks for a bright spot.

"Oh well. If they get the new field, at least we should be able to use the stadium for more practices," McDaniel philosophized.

Election Day also meant there was no school or any regular school bus service. Once again, East players would be facing logistical problems getting to a holiday practice, so I wasn't expecting to see a big turnout for the Tuesday morning practice. But by the time practice started at 10 a.m., at least 90 percent of the varsity players were there, along with some freshmen who Centore had told to start practicing with the varsity after the freshman season had ended last week.

"Every day is one less day we are together on the field," Centore had told the players after the Monday practice, and apparently being together on the field meant something to these players, even if there was no possibility of a championship or even a meaningful game for three weeks.

"I'm shocked there are so many kids here with there being no school or bus to get to practice," said Jarrod Clowery, as he stood in the middle of the practice field with his arm in a sling. "I was a little worried when we first got to the field. It was just Coach Centore, Coach Isaiah, Omar, and me. But all of a sudden, the guys started coming," Clowery continued. "They either got rides or walked to the field."

Maybe standing on the sidelines at practice with his arm in a sling for two months had given Clowery an added perspective on what being part of this team means beyond just the chance to celebrate victories.

"Some of these kids don't yet realize what this is doing for their lives beyond now, but they will someday," Clowery offered about his teammates. "Right now, they just like playing football. But I know if it wasn't for football, there would be several kids on this team who would be failing several courses, maybe even dropping out of school," Clowery added. "They're not worrying about school; they're worrying about not being able to play football. Football keeps them worrying about school, and that will affect their futures. I failed one course my freshman year. I know, if I wasn't worried about being able to play football, I would have failed more."

It may not be text-book reasoning why a teenage boy should be concerned about his schoolwork, but the reality is that for some teenagers, any way you can get them engaged in the pursuit of education is valuable. The football team makes him part of a group with a purpose. Once a teenager is part of the team, the game of football provides an assortment of ways he can experience a feeling of accomplishment, a sense of worth.

"Since I started playing on the offensive line, I'm aways thinking about what I need to do to perform a block," said Clowery. "Nobody but the coaches are going to notice, but I want to work at perfecting my job."

Like a lot of young kids who started playing football simply because it was fun and their friends were doing it, Clowery has come to learn football isn't always about the image.

"That's the thing about this game," Clowery offered. "When I was young, I just liked playing defense because I liked to hit people. People notice big hits. Nobody notices a block, but, regardless, you take pride in doing it right; even if nobody notices it."

Surprisingly, after only ninety minutes of practice, Centore declared, "That's it," and told everybody to "Pull it in."

"I want to thank you for being here this morning," Centore said, as his head panned the circle of players standing in front of him.

"Not everybody is here, but you are here," Centore declared. "I know what some of you are giving up to be here. That's loyalty; that shows character. That's the way you want to live your life. I know a lot of that comes from your families. That's the way I was brought up. That's the way you will want to raise your family."

It was November, and I had now been an honorary member of the Thunderbolts for almost three months. If there was one unquestionable certainty I had learned over those months, it was that for Tom Centore, character should be the core of human existence. It doesn't matter if a teenager comes from a two-parent, blue-collar family living in a three-bedroom Cape in the middle of the city; if home is a water-front home in Edgewood; or if he lives in a rented apartment with three generations of an immigrant family near the Providence city line. When that player shows loyalty to his team, he is demonstrating character.

Character may be free, but it comes with a price tag

Not Much Consolation

The Thunderbolts went through another ten days of practice before playing that basically meaningless consolation game against Barrington on an early Thursday evening in the second week of November. An exhibition game in the second week of November against a team East had beaten two months earlier didn't make much sense, and it was definitely a challenge for Centore to make the practices interesting. With a slew of injured players, which now included Quinn Lanigan, it wasn't surprising the Thunderbolts lost the game by 7 points when they failed to convert on a fourth down and short yardage deep in Barrington territory late in the game.

Holiday Tradition

For about twenty years, it has been a tradition that the Tuesday before Thanksgiving, the players from both the Cranston East and Cranston West football teams would distribute Thanksgiving dinner packages to a few hundred residents at the eight senior housing buildings in the city of Cranston. The dinners, which are prepared by the city's Senior Services Department, are packaged in colorful shopping bags, and the players bring the dinners to every apartment that has indicated it would like to receive a dinner.

The program has a two-fold objective. It brings holiday cheer to senior citizens, some of whom might not be getting a holiday meal. It is also a chance to bring the players from the two teams together when they are not trying to knock each other down on the football field. It's another effort by city officials to create intra-city camaraderie.

So, before they go to practice Tuesday afternoon, the players from both teams, along with their coaches, assemble at a conference room in a combined library/senior center and pick up hundreds of dinner bags. The players then drive around the city delivering the bags to the senior buildings in each team's respective section of the city. It's a wonderful tradition that brings smiles to the faces of hundreds of senior citizens and also gives some teenage football players a chance to understand how a lot of older people live lonely lives.

But if there ever was a time to see the significant difference between the city's two high school football teams, it's at that distribution ceremony. All of the fifteen to twenty Cranston West players came driving up to the library in cars. More than enough West players drive their own cars to school to transport their teammates on the distribution runs. But only a few East players have a car at their disposal after school, so the vast majority of the East players are driven to the library in a school bus—the same school bus that takes them to practice on school-day afternoons.

The composite picture of the two teams standing together as they listened to city officials speaking at a short, pre-distribution ceremony shows an even more striking contrast between two teams from the same city. Only a few of the scarlet red Cranston West game shirts are worn by faces of color, while about 60 percent of the emerald green Cranston East game shirts are worn by players with faces of color.

The Cranston school superintendent, Jeannie Nota-Masse, who is an outstanding education administrator and a dedicated cheerleader for all of the city's high school athletic teams, spoke to the gathering. She talked about how East had played hard this season and how school officials were proud of them. Then she said how West had exceeded all expectations, making it to the divisional Super Bowl. It was a pronouncement that might have been a little tough for some Cranston East players to stomach. The superintendent didn't understand that the difference between Cranston West being the No. 1 seed among the four teams earning playoff berths in the Division I-B sub-division, and Cranston East being one of the four teams that qualified, was only one game.

Cranston West's regular season Division I record was 4–3; Cranston East's final DI slate was 3–4. The superintendent didn't understand the lack of parity between the two Division I sub-divisions. She didn't know that in the regular season cross-over games between the seven teams in East's D1-A, and the seven teams in West's D1-B, was 7–0 in favor of the D1-A teams. She didn't understand that Interscholastic League officials hadn't followed the alignment format for setting up the sub-divisions that a League committee had devised.

The schedule might have played a role in the Thunderbolts not being in the playoffs, but it wasn't an excuse Tom Centore would let his players ponder. In Centore's mind even, with the unequal schedule, East was capable of making the playoffs. If they had played the way they played in the regular season final game against Cumberland; if they had played all season the way they played that night in Portsmouth, when they beat the best quarterback in the state, they wouldn't have needed to sweat out a playoff tie-breaker with two other teams. It could have been another Cranston East vs. Cranston West quarterfinal playoff match, as it had been in 2017 when East won. The basis of Tom Centore's coaching creed is you take responsibility for your own work. You don't look for excuses when thing don't go your way—you look in the mirror.

So, West got a chance to keep its season going in the play-offs, and the Falcons took advantage of the opportunity while East players were watching from the stands. Tom Centore's words in mid-October were probably echoing through the minds of some East players as they stood listening to the mayor and superintendent.

"If we make the playoffs, nobody is going to stop this team," Centore had declared more than once after late season practices. After the victory over Cumberland, a team that had beaten Cranston West in a regular season cross-over game, some East players probably couldn't help but think Centore's evaluation was right.

A Coach Never Stops Teaching

Dayshaun White had other things to worry about as he stood listening to the city officials speaking. White was on Isaiah McDaniel's shit-list, and it had nothing to do with a missed block or a blown tackle.

Although the vast majority of the East players traveled to the library in a school bus, a few seniors piled into one of the players' car for the three-mile drive from the school to the library. McDaniel may be in his late thirties, but he still knows fast-food is seductive to teenage boys, and there were three or four fast-food restaurants between Cranston East high school and the library. So, before the car full of senior players left the school, McDaniel gave explicit instructions: "Go right to the library. That's your first responsibility," McDaniel told the players. "Don't make any stops on the way."

But when White departed the car in the library parking lot and started walking into the building, he was eating a burrito. A female library staff member met White in the hallway and told him he couldn't bring food into the library. White didn't question the woman and immediately headed back outside, but the woman's refusal to allow White to dine in the library wasn't White's biggest problem.

McDaniel had seen the exchange between White and the woman, and he immediately followed Dayshaun outside. For a good five minutes while players from both teams walked past them, McDaniel stood off to the side of the entrance talking to White with a disturbed look on his face. It was obvious McDaniel wasn't pleased with the big lineman. McDaniel's days of teaching White the proper execution of blocking techniques was finished, but he's not done trying to convince Dayshaun that his daily focus should be about carrying out his life responsibilities.

For many football coaches, being a teacher to their players about meeting challenges doesn't end with the final game of a player's season—or even his high school career. White will probably not receive any individual accolades for his play during the 2018 season. He wouldn't be among the long list of Cranston East football players who have earned All-State honors through the decades. But White is one of the great success stories of Cranston East football because of how he used his involvement with the Thunderbolts to turn his life in a positive direction.

Nobody knows what the importance of life lessons learned on the football field can mean in a young man's life better than McDaniel. So, McDaniel is upset that a senior is not putting those lessons of responsibility and accountability learned on the football field to life off the field. It didn't seem to have anything to do directly with a block or a blitz, but, in a sense it does. It was what McDaniel felt had been missing all season on the field by a lot of players. That constant focus on doing things the right way. White had come so far in both his football techniques and his life-coping skills. But now, right up to the final day, his coach was telling him why it was important to do things the right way—on and off the field.

"It wasn't even that he was bringing food into the library. He was told to come right to the library. That was his responsibility as a member of this team," said McDaniel. "Instead, he stopped at Taco Bell. He was thinking of himself first."

Another Disappointment

Maybe the quirky way the season had played out for Cranston East, it wasn't all that surprising that the scheduled 45th annual Thanksgiving Day intra-city game between Cranston East and Cranston West would end up not being played on Thanksgiving Day in 2018.

By the weekend before Thanksgiving, local weather forecasters had begun predicting the holiday weather would be a day of chilly, monsoon-like rain. So as early as Monday, Cranston school department officials began discussing the possibility of postponing the game from Thursday morning to the Saturday afternoon following Thanksgiving. Players and coaches on both teams tried to play down the talk of postponement.

The difference of playing on Thanksgiving morning and playing on the following Saturday afternoon—or any other day besides Thanksgiving—is more than just forty-eight hours. Thanksgiving morning football games are a tradition in southern New England. They have been playing high school games on Thanksgiving morning in Rhode Island for almost a century, and some Massachusetts schools have met on Thanksgiving morning for more than a century. The teams from Boston Latin and Boston English high schools had been playing on Thanksgiving Day for 131 years, going into the 2018 game. In 2018, that Latin-English game was scheduled to be played at tradition-rich, 115-year-old Harvard Stadium.

Thanksgiving morning is the perfect time for a high school football game. Recent high school graduates, who are home from college, go to the game to see former classmates; high school alumni who now live out-of-state travel back home with their families to visit Grandma and Grandpa and go to the game to see their former classmates. Entire families, of two and three generations, go to the game in the morning, then head home for their Thanksgiving dinner. For decades, the Thanksgiving morning games have produced the biggest crows of the season for every Rhode Island high school football team.

These days, with all the distractions of life in the 21st century at most high schools, the Thanksgiving Day game is the only game where players will see any substantial gathering of fans. At a time when tradition seems lost in most parts of the country, a high school football game is still the biggest show in Rhode Island for those three hours on Thanksgiving morning.

But that all changes if the game is postponed from Thanksgiving morning because of poor weather. By Saturday afternoon, or even the Friday night after Thanksgiving, the intrusions of 21st century every-day life takes over again. Early Christmas shopping starts on Black Friday, (the day after Thanksgiving). People who grew up in Rhode Island and now live out-of-state with their families, but were home for the holiday, have already started heading back to their current homes.

For decades, the Cranston East-Cranston West intra-city rivalry game on Thanksgiving morning has drawn the largest crowds of any Rhode Island holiday game. If it is a sunny Thanksgiving morning, even if the temperatures are in the low thirties, there will be close to 5,000 fans at Cranston Stadium. But even if it is a beautiful sunny day, with unseasonably warm temperatures the following Saturday, there would probably only be 400 or 500 fans in the stands. That's why the East and West players and coaches didn't want to hear about a postponement.

But Rhode Island has a funny thing about playing football in the rain. For generations, Rhode Island was one of the few states that regularly postponed football games because of rain. That had changed a little over the past decade, with about half of the forty-two Interscholastic League football teams playing their home games on artificial turf surfaces; but even with so many artificial surfaces in the state, if it's a rainy September or October Friday night in Rhode Island, there's a good chance a majority of the high school football games scheduled for that night will be postponed.

Rhode Islanders just don't like sitting in the rain, watching high school football games. Plus, the forecast for Thursday was not just rain but heavy rain, possibly freezing rain. So even though on the Tuesday morning before Thanksgiving, the sun was shining with temperatures in the mid-thirties, Cranston officials announced that the Thanksgiving Day game had been postponed until Saturday afternoon at 1 p.m.

The Thunderbolts senior players won't finish their high school careers in front of a big crowd—one more disappointment in a season of frustration.

An American Tapestry

Even though there would not be a game Thursday morning, Cranston East still held its annual Thanksgiving prep rally on Wednesday afternoon. During the last period of the day, the entire 1,400-member Cranston East student body packs into the gymnasium for a demonstration of school spirit. At East, a program like this is a tapestry of 21st century American teenage life.

A student Latin dance group opens the program. The school marching band, which has developed a New England regional reputation for how it incorporates classic American showtunes into its football halftime shows, gives a performance. The cheerleaders, the likes of which have been performing on the sideline of American high school football games for generations, delivers a series of cheers. Finally, Tom Centore introduces all of the football players individually. Players who had accounted for a lot of touchdowns this season, like Rayven and Robenson, understandably receive large ovations. However, the largest ovation, especially from the section of the bleachers filled with seniors, was for Hector Duran. Apparently, it wasn't just the payers who understood Hector's importance to the team. The whole student body rose to their feet in a show of affection for the Thunderbolts' "Heart and Soul."

The prep rally ended; the students are dismissed to begin their four-day Thanksgiving break, and the football players started heading to the locker room to change into helmets and shoulder pads for run-throughs in the gym, having been forced inside because of the rain that had already started to fall.

I waked with Hector Duran as he headed toward the locker room.

"Do you think the football team represents what this school is?" I asked Duran.

"Absolutely," Duran declared. "Look at our team, and look at the people who were here today. The students go to football games, they have fun and see themselves on the field. They see how we work together and how successful our team is. That's what makes this season so disappointing. We let the school down."

Then Duran stopped in the middle of his thought—perhaps realizing that football often exposes one of life's cruel realities. The reality that life isn't always fair, but the insight learned from the way the game plays out can be a great life teacher.

"It hurt when we didn't make the playoffs, and we had the same record as two teams in Division I that did make the playoffs," said Duran. "But when I think about it, maybe we didn't deserve to be in a playoff game. A little more work, more focus at practice, maybe we would have been in the playoffs. Hopefully the younger guys on the team noticed that and won't make the same mistakes next year."

CHAPTER XXIX

LAST GAME DAY

"It will be a close game, it always is," Quinn Lanigan offered about the annual Cranston East-Cranston West football game as he stood on the sideline at Cranston Stadium, bracing himself on a pair of crutches.

As expected, because the game had been rescheduled from Thanksgiving morning to the Saturday afternoon following Thanksgiving, there were only a few hundred fans in the stands.

"Even though we have a lot of injuries, and they have had a great season, it will be a good game as long as we don't have any more injuries This is such a big rivalry," Lanigan continued.

Nobody understands the East-West Thanksgiving rivalry game better than Lanigan. He has lived his entire life in a home less than 100 yards from Cranston Stadium. So, he started going to the East-West game before he was even in kindergarten—a little kid dreaming of the day when he would be playing in this classic game. Unfortunately, it's a dream that never became reality.

"I never got to actually play in a Thanksgiving game here at the stadium," declared Lanigan, a melancholy look flashing across his face. "My freshman year, I was on the sidelines watching with the other freshmen. My sophomore year, I was one of the backup quarterbacks, but there also was a senior backup, and Coach wanted him to get into the game. So, I didn't get on the field. Last year I was a starter in the secondary, but I was injured in a playoff game so I couldn't play on Thanksgiving. I was looking forward to finally playing in a Thanksgiving Day Game this year, then this happens," Lanigan said, motioning toward his broken leg. "Maybe I will not feel as bad standing here watching because the game is not being played on Thanksgiving."

Early Morning Phone Call

Even before the Thunderbolts boarded the bus for the short trip from the high school to the stadium, Tom Centore's depleted roster took another hit. While the team was in the school dressing for the game, Centore received a call from Mack Hanley.

"Coach, I'm in the emergency room at the hospital," Hanley announced.

Apparently during the night, Hanley had felt sick, so his parents took him to the emergency room. Preliminary examination showed it wasn't any of the serious ailments that might bring on sudden illness, and eventually the doctors concluded Hanley had suffered a negative reaction to a peanut allergy that he didn't even know he had. But he had spent most of the night in the emergency room. Even as he was listening to Hanley explain his plight, Centore's mind was already thinking of how he was going to fill Hanley's spot as a starting tight end, and now, since his performance in the Cumberland game, also a linebacker.

Apparently bad luck was Hanley's constant companion this season. First, the likeable and insightful senior missed the first month of the season with his arm injury; then, just as he was starting to make a major contribution to the team's play on the field, he was going to miss the final game of his career.

But before Centore could even start making a mental lineup change, Hanley shocked his coach with a declaration,

"I'll still be there, Coach," Hanley proclaimed. "I have been cleared. I'm just waiting to be discharged. I should be there by halftime."

It seemed that even as Hanley was heading to the emergency room late last night, he was thinking about how much being a member of this team meant to him. So, he had his parents being his uniform and all his equipment to the hospital, just in case he was discharged in time to make the game—or at least some of the game.

Mack Hanley had become the paradigm of what being a member of a high school football team can mean to a teenager. He's the smart kid who didn't need football to pave the way for acceptance at a good college. He never played organized football before he entered high school, and since that first day he joined the East football team as a freshman, he has known he would never play organized football beyond high school.

He was a multi-sport high school varsity athlete and, talent-wise, football wasn't his best sport—basketball was. He could have attended one of the state's private parochial schools, like his father did. But he wanted to attend East because this was his school, in his city—the city where he had spent his entire life. Living in the moderately up-scale, middle class Edgewood community a few miles from the Providence city line, he had a slight understanding of diversity growing up. But when he enrolled at Cranston East, he was immersed into the most diverse high school in Rhode Island, and he loved it. His maturity and intellect allowed him to realize this team was teaching him important life lessons in human relationships. The type of lessons that set the basis for living a fulfilling adult life.

He started playing football because he thought it would be fun, and it has been. But the game had taught him so much more than he expected. He found himself in the unique role of being a minority white kid on a public high school football team, but living in a city where he is a member of the city's majority race. He has learned so much from the experience.

He didn't see any meaningful playing time until his junior season last fall, and even then, it was a backup role. With his intelligence and leadership qualities, he would have made a great captain this season. But when other players with more playing experience were named captains, Haney never questioned Tom Centore's selections.

When he broke his wrist in the first week of practice, requiring a month in a cast, some people said he should just forget football and get ready for the basketball season. After all, basketball was his best sport. But in Hanley's mind, he was a member of the football team, so he came to practice every day; he stood on the sidelines, talking to his teammates; he listened to the coaches and looked for some way he might be able to help his team. That big contribution finally came that night in Cumberland, when he made the game-winning fumble recovery.

But now, another dilemma had struck. Some young men in Hanley's position might have headed home from the hospital. After all, he had spent a better part of the night in the emergency room; he wasn't a star of the team; this wasn't any kind of a championship game; plus, the stands would be virtually empty because the game wasn't being played on Thanksgiving.

Why not head home, get some rest, and get ready for the start of basketball practice in two days? He'd had his one shining moment in the football spotlight that night in Cumberland, so why bother going out of his way to get to a game, the outcome of which might already be decided by the time he arrived at the field?

"I didn't want to miss it just because I was in the hospital," Hanley would tell me later in the day, after he had arrived at the game just before halftime. "My parents taught me you should never quit if you can possibly do something. Even if the game didn't mean much to most people. I didn't want to miss out. I wanted to show I was committed for all four years. I didn't want to end with my not being on the field."

People who have never played high school football often ask why being part of a high school football team is so special.

Mack Hanley is part of the answer.

Injury Bug Still Biting

Quinn Lanigan was right—the game was close. That is, until the injury bug that had been stinging the Thunderbolts all season struck in droves.

With West holding a slim lead late in the second quarter, Rayven Deoliveira rolled-out to the right and picked up good yardage, until he was stopped by a hard hit. Rayven was usually quick to get up after being hit, but this time he just lay there. Trainor Kate Chaffee rushed onto the field and began treating Deoliveira, but it was obvious he had sustained a substantial injury. It took about five minutes, but eventually Rayven was helped off the field by a couple of teammates. It wasn't a career-ending injury—probably at any other time during the season he would be back for the next game. But he was done for this day, which meant his high school football career was finished.

With Lanigan also out of action, it forced Tom Centore to move Robenson Antoine from pass receiver to quarterback, a position he hadn't played since he was twelve years old. Using both his speed and athleticism, Antoine ran-off a few big plays, including a touchdown pass. But the Bolts' defensive secondary was now seriously depleted. To make matters worse, Antoine was also shaken up in the fourth quarter and was out for the rest of the game. By the end of the game, West had rolled to a 53–21 victory.

I Wish I Could Have Made It Better

The game ended; the teams exchanged their usual midfield handshakes, then both teams knelt at midfield as mayor Allan Fung presented the mayor's trophy to a jubilant Cranston West team. Outstanding Offensive and Defensive Players of the Game were presented to players from both teams. Robenson Antoine was named East's offensive player, and Jamari Mason was the Thunderbolts' top defensive player. For Mason, finally there was a bright moment in a season that had held so much promise, but became an autumn of frustration.

As soon as the ceremonies ended, Centore led the Thunderbolts about 20 yards down the field toward the north end zone and had all the players take a knee for the final time of the season. There was still one final football life lesson to be taught.

"I appreciate the effort you guys gave today," Centore declared. "We haven't played in a long time, and the effort you gave today was outstanding. I know it wasn't what you wanted this year, but you learned from it and got better."

Then Centore started looking around the circle of players as he directed his remarks to the approximately fifteen seniors on the team. This would be the final time they met as a football family. Sure, they would head back to the school and change out of their uniforms in the locker room one more time; in the days and months to come, some will see each other in the hallways during the school day. But those will be individual acts. This would be the last time they met as the 2018 football family.

"To the seniors—thank you," Centore said, with a solemn expression as he stared at the faces of guys like Robenson Antoine, Hector Duran, Mack Hanley, Jamari Mason, Rayven Deoliveira, Dayshaun White, and Quinn Langton. "You were part of a Super Bowl championship team last year. We had only lost two league games in two years before this season. That's quite a class," Centore pronounced.

"I wish I could have made things better; it has been long year for all of us," Centore declared. "But we are going to build on it. We have been here before. We know what it will take to get back. Seniors, this is your day—thank you for what have you have done for this program."

From all around the circle of players came unprompted shouts of "Thank You, Coach."

Last Time

After the team broke from its final huddle, the players spent some time milling around the field, talking to the few family members who had come down to the field. All around them were West players and fans taking celebration photos. With both teams needing to board buses for the trip back to their respective schools, and only a few hundred fans in the stands, it wasn't long before the stadium field was void of players, coaches, and spectators, and the parking lot was virtually empty.

I watched the East team bus heading out of the parking lot, then I started walking toward my car, watching a few remaining cars pull out of the parking lot. By the time I reached my car, only one other car was still in the parking lot. I was about to get into my car when I realized the driver of that other car was Quinn Lanigan. I watched as Lanigan slowly put the crutches into the back seat of his car, all the time looking back toward the now empty stadium playing field. For a few minutes, he just stood outside the driver's side door. I could tell he wasn't in a rush to drive away, so I started walking toward Lanigan's car.

"Tough to leave for the last time as a player," I yelled from about ten yards away, as I continued walking toward his car.

My question startled him. He had been so engrossed in his thoughts, he didn't even realize there was another car still in the parking lot. Lanigan looked at me as I headed toward him, and he didn't vacillate with his answer.

"Yes," Lanigan admitted

"You know I walked by this place every day on my way to elementary school when I was a little kid. I would look over at the stadium and dream that someday I was going to play on his field in front of fans in those stands, and I did it. It was great."

Then Lanigan hesitated for a moment.

"I can't believe the four years have gone by so quickly. I'll come back and watch games here at the stadium, but it will never be the same as being on the field with my teammates," Lanigan offered, with a reflective look toward the field.

"Was it worth it with all your injuries?" I asked

"Of course," Lanigan declared. "If injuries are what you are worried about, believe me the whole experience is worth some bumps and bruises. It sucked this year when I got hurt and couldn't finish the season, but everything leading up to that was well worth it."

That may be the American high school football player's gospel.

EPILOGUE

In the fall of 2019, I was no longer an "honorary" member of the Cranston East football team, but I still spent considerable time watching the Thunderbolts playing out their 2019 season while I put the finishing touches on this book. It wasn't long after the start of the 2019 season that Tom Centore came to realize how talented the 2018 team was.

"I didn't realize how much we were going to miss some of the guys from 2018," Centore said to me in the fall of 2019 as Cranston East continued to lose games. The Thunderbolts eventually lose all nine games on their 2019 schedule. It was the first time in his seventeen-year head coaching career that a Centore-coached team had not won a game.

The one bright spot in the season was that, despite East not winning a game, at the end of the season, Omar Reyes was named to the *Providence Journal* First-Team All-State team. That award signified Reyes was one of the best twenty-five players in the state of Rhode Island. The guy Tom Centore singled-out as the example of how to do things the right way back when Reyes was a junior during the 2018 season had developed into one of the top players in the state and was looking forward to playing college football.

Tom Centore certainly didn't like coaching a team through a winless season, but when he and I talked after the season-ending 2019 Thanksgiving Day game, he was still excited about the challenge of rebuilding the Cranston East football program again. Ken Simoni had retired from coaching, but Isaiah McDaniel was still there ready to help Centore rebuilt the program, along with some of the other devoted, veteran members of the coaching staff.

Unfortunately, within a few months, life would change for Cranston East football players—as well as virtually every other Rhode Island high school student.

On March 1, 2020, two students at St. Raphael Academy in Pawtucket, who had been on a school trip to Italy, became the first confirmed cases of Covid-19 in Rhode Island. A week later, R. I. Gov. Gina Raimondo declared a state of emergency because of Covid. On March 16, the state public schools were closed for in-person learning, and a week later, students began distance learning. Omar Reyes, and his fellow members of the Class of 2020, never attended another in-person class at Cranston East.

The spring of 2020 was a catastrophe for Rhode Island public high school students. Throughout the state, teachers—who had only limited experience with remote learning—now found it their primary education vehicle. In addition to all student academic work being conducted remotely, all R.I. Interscholastic League spring sports were cancelled; throughout the state, proms and other end-of-the-school-year traditional social events were cancelled, and most high schools—if they managed any type of graduation—did it remotely.

As soon as the governor initiated remote learning, Tom Centore suspected it might create problems for some of his football players. Centore knew many of his players, especially those who had recently moved to Cranston after receiving their early schooling in Providence, learned better face-to-face. Throughout 2020, national media reports were revealing that Centore's players were not the only students having problems with remote learning. One national study claimed 50 percent of students weren't paying attention to the remote learning sessions or were not turning in their assignments on time.

Because of the pandemic, Rhode Island high school football—as well as Rhode Island education in general—was facing a lot of uncertainty going into the summer of 2020. Yet despite the uncertainty of whether there would even be a high school football season in the fall of 2020, Centore and his coaching staff conducted pre-season workout sessions for East players in July and early August. Even though the players were missing most of their normal summertime activities, forty-some players showed up for the twice-a-week workouts at the stadium. Unfortunately, in late August, the R.I. Interscholastic League—similar to most northeastern states' high school organizations—announced there would no high school football competition in the fall of 2020.

The cancellation of the 2020 fall schedule meant the rebuilding of the Cranston East football program was being put on hold. For the first time in eighteen years, Cranston East football players would not be spending autumn school-day afternoons together under Tom Centore's watchful eye. They would not be hearing Centore's daily life-lesson tutorials mixed with a football game plan. "The Coach" would not be there motivating them, at a time in their lives when they needed motivation on issues in their lives well beyond the football field.

The fall of 2020 was also an education debacle for many Rhode Island public high school students, especially some Cranston East students. The governor had declared that there would in-person learning for all public schools, but each school system was allowed to determine how that in-person instruction would be enacted. Some districts, including Cranston, enacted a hybrid model that included in-person instruction on certain days of the week and remote learning on other days. Students were also allowed the option of not attending in-person instruction at all and registering as a totally remote student. With the Covid numbers on the rise, many parents were fearful of their children attending in-person learning, even though the students were required to wear masks. Plus, it didn't take long after the start of the school year for those students who did venture into school for in-person instruction to realize it was a different high school experience from what they had been accustomed to.

The students were required to wear masks at all times, which reduces aspects of non-verbal communication like laughing and smiling. There was no socializing in the school corridors between classes. As one veteran high school teacher quipped to me in the fall of 2020, "The students are like zombies. There's no socialization."

Teachers could not personally meet with students in their classroom to answer any questions about the day's lesson. Tom Centore is a guidance counselor, yet he couldn't meet his students in-person. All meetings, even when both Centore and the student were in the same school building, had to be remote sessions. At East, as the school year progressed, fewer and fewer students were coming to school for in-person instruction.

In October of 2020, a Rhode Island media report claimed only 25 percent of R.I. students were actually in school. Centore knew the in-person percentage was even lower at Cranston East. In addition to alleviating the fear of contracting the virus in the school building, selecting the remote option plan also gave students a chance to spend more time working at their part-time jobs. This, at a time when many families needed help because of the financial hardships created by Covid. Given the ingenuity of today's young people, it's not surprising some students figured out how to both fulfill their requirements for remote learning and also earn money working. Teachers were noticing how some students would sign-in that they were on remote learning, but rather than the students being in their bedrooms at home, the teachers could tell the students were working in a warehouse and or in a store because the ceilings were higher than their bedroom ceilings.

Many of Centore's players also lacked an adequate space where the student could work during his remote classes or adequate WIFI communication in their home. Also, for some of Centore's players, the physical shortcomings were not their only problem. One of Centore's constant challengers over the previous few years with some of his players, especially the players who recently moved to Cranston from the Providence school system, was to get the players to understand the importance of turning in their academic assignments. Reminding the players of the importance of turning in assignments was almost a daily segment of Centore's end-of-practice speech. A missed assignment might not mean as much in a classroom when teachers are having daily, in-person interactions with students. But in "Online Learning," for many teachers, turning in an assignment was a key indicator of engagement, so missed assignments also counted against a student's class participation grade.

During the fall of 2018, while spending the season with the East football team, I came to understand that the key to Tom Centore's coaching success was personal communication with his players—both on and off the field. As Ken Simone had said about the East players on that first day of practice back in August of 2018, "When they believe you care about them as more than football players, you have them for life."

Now that personal contact was gone.

Centore knew some of his players were struggling and felt isolated without their football family. Which is why Centore was worrying about more than just his players missing three months of football drills during the fall of 2020. Like educators from around the country, Centore knew the pandemic had left the American public education in crisis. Some students were not only falling far behind academically; they were also floundering emotionally. Centore knew that without their football family, some of his players were feeling depressed, anxious, and scared about their futures.

When school resumed after the 2020 holiday season, Centore was starting to feel that the pandemic might have foiled any hopes of his being the architect of another rebuilding program for Cranston East football. That trust Ken Simone talked about between Centore and his players wasn't built overnight; it was built over time. Now, Centore had missed an entire school-year of young men learning the value of being a Cranston East football player.

In January 2021, Cranston East students—some of whom had not actually been in school for almost a year—were taking tests that would be part of their mid-term grades. For student-athletes, the results of those tests would determine their eligibility for the spring-time third marking period. Tom Centore wasn't surprised when those mid-term grades revealed a plethora of academically ineligible football players.

The R.I. Interscholastic League did play an abbreviated season of spring football in 2021. Basically, it was a "make-up" for the missed 2020 fall season. Tom Centore coached

Cranston East during that 2021 spring season, but forty-five of the Cranston East players, who had planned on playing if there had been a 2020 fall season, were ineligible because of the mid-term marks they received in January 2021.

Cranston East lost all three of the games it played in that 2021 spring season. Two other scheduled games were cancelled because of Covid concerns.

By that time, Centore was fifty-two years old. He had been a high school football coach for thirty years—nonstop. He loved his players; he loved what Cranston East football stood for—on and off the field. He had proved what could be done, but a pandemic the likes of which American education had never seen, meant it would take time to rebuild the Cranston East football program. Centore started asking himself if it was time for another coach to lead the new rebuilding program.

In June of 2021, Centore announced his resignation as the Cranston East football coach. About a month later, Isaiah McDaniel, the man who had helped Centore begin the rebirth of Cranston East football in 2004 while he was still a Cranston East student, was named the new head coach.

Tom Centore might have relinquished the title of head football coach, but he wasn't completely ready leave Cranston East football players. He was remaining at Cranston East as a guidance counselor, and in that role, his door would always be open to East players looking for counsel—whether it was a question about their academic course selections or issues in their lives outside the walls of Cranston East high school.

During that "pre-Covid" 2018 high school football season, I discovered how a dedicated coach—who is a person of character and whose basic creed is rooted in concern for the complete well-being of his players—used the game of high school football to give a racially, ethnically, and economically diverse group of young men a gratifying future. That is the story I have tried telling in this book.

Ironically, going into the 2022 fall season, the senior members of that 2018 team have been the last Cranston East football players who have not had some portion of their high school experience affected by Covid.

The two-year Covid pandemic has taken a devastating toll on American public education. It will take time—and a lot of work from dedicated educators—but I am optimistic the American public high school experience will rebound from the devestating effects of Covid. After fifty years of writing stories about high school student-athletes, I believe high school athletics—especially high school football—will play a major role in that recovery.